DUE

D0883139

Advances
in Economic Theory

Advances
in Economic Theory

Edited by Mauro Baranzini

St. Martin's Press · New York

WITHDRAWN

ITHACA COLLEGE LIBRARY

© Mauro Baranzini 1982

All rights reserved. For information write:
St. Martin's Press Inc., 175 Fifth Avenue, New York,
NY 10010
Printed in Great Britain
First published in the United States in 1982

ISBN   0-312-00636-5

Library of Congress Catalog Card No. 82-42613

Contents

PART FOUR: MONETARY THEORY AND MONETARY POLICY

PART FIVE: GROWTH AND INCOME DISTRIBUTION

PART SIX: ECONOMETRICS AND MATHEMATICAL ECONOMICS

Preface

This volume contains a selection of the papers presented at the economic theory and econometrics seminar held at The Queen's College, Oxford, between Michaelmas term 1978 and Trinity term 1981. The contributors are scholars from many different countries, the majority of whom have been or are presently associated with this university; and the topics analysed by them cover a wide spectrum, ranging from classical, marginalist and Keynesian economics to the problems of general equilibrium and quantitative methods.

The institution at which the seminars took place is no casual choice. Since 1969 Queen's College has sponsored the Florey European Studentship Scheme, originally planned by Lord Howard Florey, provost of the college and Nobel laureate for the therapeutical discovery of penicillin. Lord Florey's aim was two-fold: to invigorate the college and Oxford by bringing to them the best research students of continental European universities, and to strengthen the ties of international co-operation in most fields of academic research.

Thanks to the initiative of some present and former recipients of the Florey Scheme in the field of economics, Queen's College has in the past few years become a place of meeting and discussion for a number of British and continental research students and academic visitors of the sub-faculty of economics.

The Queen's College, Oxford   MAURO BARANZINI

Acknowledgements

I want to express my gratitude to all those institutions and persons who contributed to the realization of this book. Thanks are first of all due to The Queen's College, Oxford, for providing seminar and research facilities. I would also like to thank the Centre for Research in Economic Analysis (CRANEC) of the Catholic University of Milan for assistance and hospitality during an important phase of the realization of the volume. Financial support from the Italian Consiglio Nazionale delle Ricerche (CNR) and Swiss National Science Foundation is also gratefully acknowledged.

The debts accumulated in the preparation of this book are numerous. Several contributors have offered comments and criticism on other chapters, and the editor is indebted to them for this. Similarly several colleagues, students and anonymous reviewers have provided detailed advice and criticism with regard to content, style and presentation. Responsibility for all remaining errors remains entirely and unreservedly with the authors and editor.

Finally my gratitude to my wife Evelina, for her encouragement and support, knows no bounds.

MAURO BARANZINI

List of Contributors

Pietro Balestra, professor of econometrics, University of Geneva (Switzerland) and University of Dijon (France)

Mauro Baranzini, lecturer in economics, The Queen's College, University of Oxford

Mario Biagioli, research fellow, University of Modena (Italy) and Linacre College, University of Oxford

Christopher J. Bliss, reader in international economics and fellow of Nuffield College, University of Oxford

Heinrich Bortis, associate professor of economics, University of Fribourg (Switzerland)

Carlo Casarosa, professor of economics and director of the Institute of Economics, University of Pisa (Italy)

Alvaro Cencini, research fellow of the Swiss National Science Foundation, London School of Economics

Alberto Chilosi, professor of economics, University of Pisa (Italy)

Roberto F. Cippà, research fellow of the Swiss National Science Foundation, The Queen's College, University of Oxford

Meghnad Desai, reader in economics, London School of Economics

Nicholas H. Dimsdale, fellow and praelector in economics, The Queen's College, University of Oxford

Vinicio Guidi, lecturer in economics, University of Florence (Italy) and Linacre College, University of Oxford

Roy McCloughry, visiting lecturer, Centre for Banking and International Finance, City University, London, and London School of Economics

Giuseppe Mazzarino, research officer, Institute of Economics and Statistics, University of Oxford

Luigi L. Pasinetti, professor of economics and chairman of the Faculty of Economics, Catholic University of Milan (Italy); formerly reader in economics, University of Cambridge

Roberto Scazzieri, lecturer in economics, University of Bologna (Italy) and Linacre College, University of Oxford

Augusto Schianchi, associate professor of economics, University of Parma (Italy) and Linacre College, University of Oxford

Bernard Schmitt, professor of economics, University of Dijon (France) and University of Fribourg (Switzerland)

Introduction

MAURO BARANZINI

I

In the last 20 years, most of the discussions among economists have focused upon issues that are controversial, often because they are rooted in different ways of looking at the 'scope and method' of economic science; the Cambridge controversies in the theory of capital, profit determination and income distribution are an eloquent example of this turn of events.

At least partly because of such debates, but also as a result of the publication of *Production of Commodities by Means of Commodities* by P. Sraffa, there has been a revival of interest in the objects and methods of economics such as has not been seen since the publication of *The Nature and Significance of Economic Science* by Lionel Robbins in 1935 and of *The Political Element in the Development of Economic Theory* by Gunnar Myrdal in 1953.

What has slowly emerged is a new way of looking at the evolution of economic ideas, of which the most authoritative statements are those by J. Hicks and L. L. Pasinetti, who have both pointed out that it is no longer possible to consider the development of economic theory as a linear evolutionary process, starting from Adam Smith. A number of alternative 'paradigms' characterize the past and present situation of our science, and both Hicks and Pasinetti seem to agree on a fundamental distinction between the theories centred on the analysis of production phenomena and those centred on the analysis of exchange. Hicks, in order to emphasize the distinction, labels as 'political economy' the first group of theories (following a definition already used by the classical economists) and as 'catallactics' the second group (in accordance with a terminology already used by Edgeworth and von Mises).

Talking about the study of the 'flow of wealth which the classics called *political economy*', Hicks argues that:

> There is of course no question that the flow of wealth is pro-
> duction; things are produced, and it is in these products that the
> flow of wealth consists. But the things that are produced are
> heterogenous; it is not obvious that we can take them together
> and reduce them to a common 'stuff'. What is implied in the
> classical approach is that for essential purposes we can take
> them together. We can represent them by a flow of wealth,
> which is so far homogenous that it can be greater or less. (1976,
> p. 210)

A bit further on, discussing the 'marginalists' revolution', he writes:

> The essential novelty in the work of these economists was that,
> instead of basing their economics on production and distribu-
> tion, they based it on exchange. I therefore propose to make
> use of a term which was sometimes used, at the time in question,
> to mean the theory of exchange; it was called catallactics. So I
> shall re-name the so-called marginalists as catallactists. (1976,
> p. 212)

Pasinetti also draws a distinct line between the two approaches by pointing out that the concept of production (or industry, as he defines it) is mainly *dynamic*, while that of trade is essentially *static* (1981, ch. I, pp. 1–25). Moreover, for Pasinetti,

> Industry is a process of augmenting wealth through a material
> increase in the quantity and number of products, to be achieved
> by the practical application of the advances of science, division
> and specialisation of labour, better organisation, invention and
> utilisation of new sources of energy and new materials. Unlike
> trade, industry requires changes in the organisational structure
> of society. (1981, pp. 2–3)

Trade, on the other hand, concerns the problem of how to reach the best allocation of resources in a situation where a plurality of indi-viduals (at the micro-level) or of economic systems (at the macro-level) have an externally given amount of resources or goods and try to gain advantage through exchange. In this case economists do deal with a rationality problem, which is usually expressed by one or more mathematical functions to be maximized under a certain number of constraints.

Hence the *process of learning*, which is crucial for the theory of production, is replaced by the problem of rationality, which characterizes the theory of exchange. These two frameworks can also be considered in a time perspective; while the latter deals mainly with short-term issues, the former refers mainly to long-term structural problems. These differences have important implications not only with respect to the outcomes of economic analysis, but especially in connection with the choice of the basic assumptions of the models considered. For too long this aspect of economic theory has been overlooked.

In the analysis that follows, it may be worth retaining and analysing the implications of this important dichotomy relative to the 'scope and method' of economic analysis, so as to clarify the assessment of the framework in which the various authors develop their analyses.

II

This book is divided into six Parts, as follows:

Part One   Production Analysis
Part Two   Microfoundations of Macroeconomics
Part Three   Macrofoundations of Macroeconomics
Part Four   Monetary Theory and Monetary Policy
Part Five   Growth and Income Distribution
Part Six   Econometrics and Mathematical Economics

As the reader may easily find, no attempt has been made to conceal, implicitly or explicitly, scientific disagreements between the various papers. The reason is that, in most cases, differences of opinion can be reduced to, and can help to clarify, the above-mentioned distinction between economics as primarily a theory of exchange and economics as primarily a theory of productive processes.

If one considers the whole area of problems dealt with by theories that belong, respectively, to one or the other approach, it will appear that each approach (even if it originally referred to a special set of problems) has successively been extended so as to cover the whole area of economic analysis.[1] This process of extension has often involved deep transformations of the objects being studied. For instance, the scale-efficiency relationships studied by the marginalist economists are not quite the same phenomena that were considered by the classical economists; the 'macroeconomy' considered in the framework of the general equilibrium approach involves an entirely different picture from the 'macroeconomy' considered as a system that cannot be reduced to the sum of its parts; and the phenomena of long-run income distribution and capital accumulation appear to be governed by alternative laws.

It is our opinion that the existence of different approaches in economic analysis cannot be considered simply as a temporary anomaly, to be eventually eliminated with the disappearance of all the conflicting views except one. The reason is that the whole complex of economic problems seems to justify the emergence of two different approaches, each originated by the consideration of a special set of phenomena, but with a tendency to offer explanations for an increasingly wider class of phenomena.

If one accepts this view as to the evolution of economic analysis, it follows that many issues that have divided, and still divide, economists are to be explained by the adoption of alternative views as to the object of economics. The past evolution of our science seems to suggest that the co-existence of different points of view is not a mere accident, but results from the structure of economics and from its special position 'on the edge of the sciences' (Hicks, 1979, p. 2). This implies that it would be inappropriate, at least for the time being, to reject one approach in favour of the other, and also to attempt a conciliation between the two. We believe that a more positive attitude towards the disagreements among economists is required, and that an explicit recognition is by now due of the fact that scientific advance in our science has often consisted of the almost contemporaneous development of separate lines of inquiry.

The present collection of essays is meant to offer a contribution to the understanding of the different approaches. We also hope that in this way economics will appear as a more interesting science than when it is seen as the application of one approach only, to the partial or complete exclusion of the other.

III

Part One of the volume deals with the analysis of production, and the paper by Scazzieri (chapter 1) offers the opportunity to reconsider the foundations of production theory as it is nowadays accepted by most economists. The study of the relationships of output scale to productive efficiency is deeply rooted in the history of economics. However, there would be few economists who would declare themselves satisfied with the current state of the arts in relation to this topic. The reason is that economic theory does not seem to provide (or to seek) explanations for the category of phenomena denoted by expressions such as 'increasing and diminishing returns', 'economies and diseconomies of scale', and so on. On the other hand, scale-efficiency relationships seem to provide a fertile arena where endless combats are fought, often starting with differences in basic definitions, and turning upon the logical consequences of alternative assumptions.

A well-known discussion concerning the character of scale-efficiency relationships took place (mainly in the *Economic Journal*) among Clapham, Pigou, Robertson, Sraffa and others during the 1920s. Another seminal debate took place among Chamberlin, Hahn and McLeod in the *Quarterly Journal of Economics* during the late 1940s. One of the main questions arising from the former debate was the difficulty of filling the 'empty boxes' of diminishing, constant and increasing returns industries. The latter debate was concerned with the issue of input divisibility in relation to increasing returns to scale, and turned upon the most appropriate way of defining factors' 'natural' units. Both debates were founded on definitional issues, and reflected the fact that, from a certain moment onwards, the study of variable returns had become a field for the discovery of *a priori* logical relations, necessarily true once certain basic assumptions are accepted.

In the specific case of scale economies, the contemporary situation has recently been described in the following terms:

> Theoretical contributions had clarified the conditions under which scale increases could be integrated into, and even reinforce, systematic static economic theory. But the combination of restrictions involved in defining scale leaves unclear the sources of potential economies and even the relevance of this concept to any substantial sector of industry. On the other hand, the observationally oriented approaches had obviously demonstrated persuasive insights into the factors associated with improving the competitiveness of larger production units without, however, clarifying the role of scale among the various other contributions to such superior performance. (Gold, 1981, p. 10)

A similar argument, we believe, would also apply to the cases where scale increases are associated with decreasing productive efficiency.

The core of Scazzieri's contribution is to be found in the idea that scale–efficiency relationships are treated in a distinctly different way depending on whether we consider the classical or the 'post-classical' theory of production. The most important difference is that decreasing and increasing efficiency were considered in the classical approach as the outcome of producers' choice among technical alternatives, when the choice takes place under constraints expressing the limited availability of certain inputs (such as land) or the indivisibility of certain production processes. A completely different view is characteristic of modern treatments, where scale–efficiency relationships are no longer explained by variations of scale affecting producers' choice, and decreasing and increasing efficiency are instead regarded as the direct outcome of natural or technological laws. This might appear like a paradox in the evolution of production theory, for the view of scale–efficiency phenomena accepted by neoclassical economists severs the link between such phenomena and technical choice; and such an outcome seems to contrast with the pervasive role of choice in the neoclassical view of the world. However, the contrast is perhaps only an apparent one, and further research might show that such a characteristic of neoclassical economics is yet another aspect of the general tendency of such an approach to shift emphasis from production to exchange phenomena.

Scazzieri, after presenting an analytical reconstruction of the two basic approaches to the study of scale–efficiency phenomena in production, discusses in detail the logical prerequisites of the classical model, particularly for what concerns the condition of scale-invariance of the efficiency ranking of production techniques. In the final part of his paper the author discusses the general 'philosophy' of the two approaches and concludes that the classical approach can provide a useful starting point for the formulation of an *economic* theory of scale–efficiency phenomena.

IV

Part Two offers contributions in the field of the microfoundations of macroeconomics, which has attracted a good deal of interest in the recent economic literature. Two of the papers (those of Bliss and Cippà and Cippà and Guidi) deal with the temporary equilibrium theory.

In the belief that the distinction between microeconomics and macroeconomics is highly artificial, most of the recent economics literature has been concerned with the construction of models that incorporate Keynesian features inside a general equilibrium framework. For this task the extreme assumptions of the Walrasian models make them an inadequate tool. In particular, the complete information that characterizes the general equilibrium analysis is obviously in contrast with the idea, underlying Keynes' theory, that economic units have imperfect knowledge of their future environment. This explains the revival of temporary equilibrium analysis, first enunciated by Lindhal in *Studies in the Theory of Money and Capital* (1939) and then developed by Hicks in *Value and Capital* (1939). Temporary equilibrium models can be conceived either in postulating price flexibility or, as developed by the French School, following the fix-price method and assuming that adjustments are made by quantity rationing. Neither approach is complete or pretends to give an exhaustive explanation of the real world. In both cases, however, steps have been made towards reality, and interesting conclusions have been suggested.

Bliss and Cippà's competitive temporary equilibrium model (chapter 2) examines the consequences of economic agents having different and inconsistent price expectations. The authors suggest that the capital market in an uncertain world ought to be seen as imposing quantity constraints on agents' actions, even if all prices are flexible and all markets are perfectly efficient. This particular rationing scheme allows the authors to deal with the problem of consistency of future plans and to define a new notion of temporary equilibrium with rationing: the *consistent temporary equilibrium*, i.e., a situation in which all existing markets 'clear' and where every virtual demand equals the corresponding supply.

Cippà and Guidi's paper (chapter 5) starts with a discussion of the general equilibrium model, in which they critically analyse the main assumptions that limit the possibility of studying important economic realities. From this point of view they consider the extensions of the original model of Arrow and Debreu; in particular, they concentrate on the temporary equilibrium models with quantity rationing as developed by Drèze and Benassy.

The other two papers of this Part are by Casarosa (chapter 3) and Chilosi (chapter 4). In his paper on Keynes, Casarosa maintains that the conventional presentation of Keynes' aggregate analysis is seriously flawed, since it considers the aggregate expected demand as a function that reflects the entrepreneurs' expectations about aggregate

expenditure. Casarosa's aim is to show that this view has no microeconomic foundations in an atomistic framework and that Keynes'
aggregate expected demand and supply analysis is simply an extension of the analysis of the firm to the whole economy. In this
context, contrary to Patinkin's view, Keynes' statement, that at
every point of effective demand entrepreneurs' expectations of
profits are maximized, is proved to be correct.

Of somewhat more historical nature is the contribution by Chilosi
(who had Kalecki among his teachers at the Warsaw School of Planning and Statistics). His essay illuminates the intellectual path that
led to the formulation of Kalecki's theory of increasing risk. This
path can be traced back through Breit (who was a close associate of
Kalecki in Warsaw) to Hicks' work in the early 1930s. The paper also
highlights some interesting aspects of Breit's *Beitrag* of 1935, such as
the introduction into the theory of investment of (1) imperfect competition elements, (2) the 'double counting of risk' (to be found also
in Keynes' *General Theory*), (3) the explanation, on the basis of risk,
of the fluctuations in interest rates during the business cycle, and
(4) the relationship between long- and short-run interest rates in the
slump. Breit's 'Keynesian' attitudes towards economic policies in the
Depression are also discussed.

V

Part Three of the volume contains three contributions of what has
been defined as 'L'Ecole de Dijon et Fribourg', a stream of economic
thought which has emerged particularly in France since the middle
1960s.[2]

Linked with the analysis of Ricardo and Keynes, Schmitt's theory
is, nevertheless, far from being a simple reinterpretation of their
works. On the contrary, starting from a new analysis of money,
Schmitt sets himself to solve the main problem with which Ricardo
was confronted: the determination of an invariable measure of value.
The central point of this approach is represented by a concept of
production and income that is radically different from the neoclassical one. Income is no longer conceived as a flow of expenditures
through time, but as a result of a constantly renewed process of
creation. The traditional idea of income as a continuous or discontinuous function of time is rejected and substituted by what the
author calls a 'quantum theory of production'.

According to Schmitt, income is therefore the instantaneous
measure of a production that is necessarily related to a finite period

of time. Every time that a new production takes place, its measure is given instantaneously through the monetary payment of its cost. This payment is a kind of emission where money and production are one and the same reality, i.e. income. Thus, according to Schmitt, another difficulty is overcome, namely the dichotomy between real and monetary phenomena (which is solved, following Keynes, by measuring income in wage-units). According to this interpretation, rent, profit and interest represent a variable part of labour's income; and they are not, as is generally said, an irreducible component of national income.

After arguing that labour is the sole factor of production, Schmitt develops his theory according to the two main concepts already present in Keynes' works: the concepts of creation and destruction. Hence, the Keynesian identities between income and the money cost of production on one side, and between income and its final expenditure on the other side, are integrated into a theory of 'emissions', where production is a positive emission of income ('creation') and final purchase a negative emission ('destruction'). In other words, the payment of wages creates a completely new income which is totally destroyed by its expenditure, the two operations being logically instantaneous since any expenditure is effective only at the very instant it takes place.

Within this theory, Keynes' identities are firmly established, and it becomes impossible to explain inflation in terms of disequilibrium, either between saving and investment or between total demand and total supply. A new solution is presented, and the main cause of inflation is identified in the working of the banking system, whose operation does not conform to the logical definition of money.

The papers by Schmitt (chapter 6), Cencini (chapter 7) and by Schmitt and Cencini (chapter 8) should give a first, though necessarily concise, idea of this approach. In chapter 6 the importance of a new analysis of time in economics is stressed; chapter 7 is a critique of the neoclassical determination of relative prices; in chapter 8 the two emissions corresponding respectively to the 'creation' and 'destruction' of income are related to the problem of its division between wages and profits.

VI

Part Four presents four essays on monetary economics, the first two in the field of monetary theory and the last two in the field of monetary policy.

The paper by Desai (chapter 9) has been written to show that grafting the monetary component into a general equilibrium model is, just as the Hayek–Sraffa debate indicated, a very arduous task. Taking that debate as a starting point (not to mention the historical reasons) seems to be the right thing to do, since over the last few years there has been a revival of attempts to re-examine the foundations of monetary theory and in particular to define a monetary economy in a general equilibrium context. As Desai points out, many of the conclusions to be found in the Hayek–Sraffa debate are relevant in assessing the validity of more recent contributions; in this framework, the links between the early debate and the more recent one is of utmost interest and relevance. At the end of his work Desai writes that 'A fully-fledged Walrasian economy where prices are flexible does not need money in any essential way. In this sense Sraffa was correct in locating the importance of money in Hayek's model to the institutional appendage of the banking system – an appendage since it had not been worked into a Walrasian model'. This does not mean, of course, that the distinction between a barter and a monetary economy may not be 'challenging'; the integration of the monetary factors in the analysis of real models is one of the most promising areas of our science.

Desai's contribution is followed by McCloughry's paper (chapter 10), in which Hayek's concept of monetary neutrality is compared with Koopmans' concept of monetary equilibrium. The analysis shows that, while Koopmans was trying to widen out the concept, Hayek was placing additional restrictions on his concept of neutrality, so abandoning it as an operational target of monetary policy. Neutral money becomes synonymous with the implicit conditions under which one can conduct real analysis, rather than with the policy criteria for preventing disequilibrium in a monetary economy. Following McCloughry, Sraffa went too far when, in his rejoinder, he characterized Hayek's position as maintaining that the money rate of interest should be equal to all the own rates of interest in a barter economy, a position that would indeed be 'curious', as Desai claims. Part of the confusion in the Hayek–Sraffa debate arises because Hayek is thinking in terms of intertemporal equilibrium, and not in the traditional long-period framework, as is Sraffa.

The paper by Dimsdale (chapter 11) contains a discussion of some of the principal issues that have arisen during the current debate on monetary policy in the UK. The emphasis on monetary policy in Britain has increased since the acceptance of targets for government borrowing and the money supply by the Labour Government in

December 1976 on the recommendation of the IMF. It has been reinforced by the Conservative Government's 'medium-term financial strategy', which sees monetary policy as the principal means of checking the rate of inflation. The monetary measures of the Conservative Government of Mrs Thatcher have been critically reviewed by the bipartisan Treasury and Civil Service Committee. The discussions of the Committee have developed into the widest evaluation of monetary policy in Britain since the Report of the Radcliffe Committee in 1959. The views of academic and official economists have been sought on a broad range of issues. These include the aims of economic policy, the instruments and effects of monetary policy, and the impact of public sector borrowing and of the exchange rate.

Commenting on the outcome of the Committee's activities to date, Dimsdale maintains that the variety of views expressed by witnesses on a range of monetary issues are of greater interest than the policy recommendations contained in the Committee's report. These are relatively weak and may well not be influential.

The paper by Dimsdale is followed by a contribution in the field of applied monetary economics by Biagioli (chapter 12). It may be worth recalling the general framework of this paper. In the last 20 years a monetarist 'counter-revolution' – as Friedman has called the main stream of attack to previously dominating Keynesian views – has spread out in several fields of applied and theoretical economics. As to the theory of international adjustment mechanisms, the monetarist view tries to extend the quantity theory of money (which assumes that inflation is 'neutral', in the sense that it does not affect either real variables or relative prices) to an international setting, and claims that exchange rate movements are also 'neutral'. This monetarist view is summarized by the proposition that all persistent balance-of-payments imbalances are due to increases of the money supply exceeding the pace at which real output is growing. A corollary of this proposition is that neither fiscal policy nor exchange rate variations can be relied upon as instruments apt to achieve the external balance (contrary to what is usually stated by Keynesian authors).

The paper by Biagioli aims at assessing the validity of such an hypothesis by considering Italian quarterly data covering the period from 1973 to 1978: the econometric test performed yields results partly inconsistent with such an hypothesis. This indicates that the main reason why a model embodying the basic monetarist propositions does not fit the Italian experience is that arbitrage between Italian and foreign commodities and assets has not been as large as it

is assumed by monetarist authors. In other words, the floating of the
lira has been incapable of eliminating the balance of payments constraint, contrary to what was assumed by most of the literature on
flexible exchange rates before 1972.

                                    VII

Part Five deals with several aspects of economic growth, income
distribution and capital accumulation in the framework of both
classical and neo-Keynesian theories. These issues have attracted a
great deal of attention in the economic literature of this last quarter
of a century.

In his paper on Ricardo (chapter 13), Casarosa presents a model of
the Ricardian theory of distribution and economic growth which is
in line with the interpretation recently put forward by a number of
economists (including Hicks, Hollander and Casarosa himself), which,
contrary to the traditional (i.e. Sraffa–Pasinetti) interpretation, gives
emphasis to the forces of supply and demand for the determination
of the wage rate. Within the framework of the model, different
aspects are discussed, and the notion of dynamic equilibrium path is
used to describe the movements of the system over time. The main
feature of such a dynamic path is that the wage rate is, in general,
above its natural level and coincides with it only in the stationary
state. Casarosa argues that the 'new view' allows for an elucidation
of all Ricardo's propositions concerning the tendencies of the wage
rate and of the rate of profits during the process of growth. More
precisely, Casarosa shows that, although the Ricardian economy
cannot move along a steady growth path because of decreasing
returns, the notion of dynamic equilibrium turns out to be quite
useful to restrict the possible trajectories that the economic system
might follow during the process of growth. Moreover, if the marginal
product of labour decreases slowly enough, the actual path of the
economic system is likely to remain most of the time in a very close
neighbourhood of the dynamic equilibrium path, so that one should
be able to describe the motion of the system as if it followed the
dynamic equilibrium path. As the author points out, the role played
by the dynamic equilibrium path in this case is exactly the same as
that played by the natural equilibrium path in Pasinetti's model.

Next comes a reply by Pasinetti (chapter 14), which challenges some of the propositions put forward by Casarosa in the preceding chapter. More precisely, for Pasinetti the interpretation of the Ricardian system followed by Casarosa simply belongs to a stream of economic thought (which goes back to Marshall) that tries to incorporate the basic propositions of Ricardo into the analytical framework based on the working of supply and demand. Thus, following Pasinetti, a formalization of Ricardo's analysis that emphasizes his hints at the forces of supply and demand is not new at all, since the pre-Sraffa economic literature includes several attempts that have been written with the purpose of reconciling Ricardo with marginal economic theory.

Chapter 15 reconsiders an aspect of the Cambridge controversies in the theory of capital, profit determination and income distribution. During the debates that characterized these controversies, several neoclassical economists (including Meade, Samuelson and Modigliani) suggested that the introduction of the life-cycle hypothesis into the traditional two-class growth model (with fixed propensities to save) of Kaldor and Pasinetti would prevent the Cambridge equation ($P/K = n/s_c$) from applying; in this way the distribution of income between profits and wages would no longer be determined as in the neo-Keynesian model. The paper explores the implications of the introduction of the life-cycle hypothesis into the above-mentioned two-class growth model, and shows that the determination of the equilibrium rate of interest is basically similar to that obtained in the traditional Kaldor–Pasinetti model. More precisely, the rate of interest in this case turns out to be (a) independent of the form of the production function, (b) determined by the behavioural parameters of the capitalists' class only, and (c) higher than the natural rate of growth. The historical importance of the intergenerational bequest of the classes (as opposed to their life-cycle savings) is also focused upon.

In chapter 16, Bortis critically analyses the way in which the equilibrium of individual firms and that of the economy as a whole are linked together in Wood's model of distribution and growth. The author's conclusion is that either the distribution of income is determined in a macroeconomic way according to the neo-Keynesian theory of income distribution, or Wood's microeconomic formulation must be in accordance with such a theory. In the latter case, however, a chronic tendency to unemployment may occur as the equilibrium (warranted) rate of growth of the economy may fall short of the natural rate of growth.

VIII

Part Six offers two contributions in the field of econometrics and one in mathematical economics.

The paper by Balestra (chapter 17) examines the use of qualitative variables in a regression context. As the author points out, while in classical regression the use of qualitative variables is well known, its extension to multiple qualitative variables and to generalized regression has not been analysed in the recent literature. The increasing role of qualitative factors in applied research widely justifies a systematic look at the problem of specifying and estimating a regression equation whose explanatory variables are both quantitative and qualitative. This analysis provides some original results which require very simply computational procedures, so extending the number of tools available to the applied scientist. More importantly, these results reassess the role played by multiple qualitative explanatory variables in regression analysis.

Chapter 18, by Mazzarino, starts from the evidence that economic time-series quite often show an underlying trend, at least over a fairly long period of time. Moreover, trends are, by definition, smooth and can then be thought of (in a somewhat artificial way) as polynomials or exponential functions. Additionally, for particular time-series, a polynomial of higher order may be required, which from sample theory turns out to have unstable coefficients. More importantly, the fitting by least-squares has to be carried out at any time when additional terms are added to the series. Instead of fitting a polynomial to the whole series, Mazzarino provides a function that can be fitted to n terms of the polynomial by the technique of moving averages. In this way, for any given function, a fixed set of weights can be obtained, which is then applied to smooth the series.

The final paper by Schianchi (chapter 19) has been written with the aim of tackling a basic problem of the theory of natural resources exploration, namely the optimum policy for exploration activity or reserves assessment. A boost to this field of research has come, since the early 1970s, from the rapid increase in the price of most raw materials and of energy in particular; however, this particular problem has not received much attention in the recent literature, apart from an article by Pindyck in the *Journal of Political Economy* (1978) in which the reserve base is treated as the basis for production and exploratory activity as the means of increasing or maintaining reserves. For Pindyck, 'potential reserves' are unlimited, but as depletion ensues, given amounts of exploratory activity result in even smaller discoveries. Within this framework resource producers must determine, at the same time, the optimal rates of exploratory activity and production; Pindyck shows that, if the initial reserve endowment is small, at first production will increase as reserves are developed, while later production will decline as both exploratory activity and the discovery rate fall.

The original aspect of Schianchi's approach is to be found in the application, in the stochastic context, of portfolio choice theories to this kind of problem. His main conclusions can be summarized as follows. In the deterministic case, i.e. when exploration continues with certainty, conventional marginal results are confirmed. In the stochastic case, i.e. when energy consumption is stochastic and exploration does not necessarily lead to new reserves, deterministic results must be adjusted to incorporate an uncertainty parameter, and different 'risk attitudes' may lead to an alternative optimum exploration policy, as in the case of portfolio analysis. This outcome is not totally intuitive, since one should expect the various activities to be univocal, even if implemented with a different degree of intensity.

NOTES

1 A more thorough discussion of these issues is to be found in the editors' introduction to the two volumes by Quadrio Curzio and Scazzieri (1977), which I reviewed in the *Economic Journal* (Baranzini, 1979, pp. 480-2). According to Quadrio Curzio and Scazzieri (p. 11, our translation): 'if it is true that the fundamental ideas initially relate to different areas of study, it is also true that the theories constructed on these subjects were subsequently extended to almost the entire field of economic analysis. For example, the English classical economists, starting with the fundamental idea of production, applied themselves to international trade no less than the mercantilists, and to exchange no less than the marginalists. The same can be said about the marginalists and the problem of production.'
2 For an appraisal of the main features of this School see, for instance, Devillebichot (1969).

REFERENCES

Baranzini, M. (1979) Review of Quadrio Curzio and Scazzieri (1977), in *Economic Journal*, p. 480-2.
Devillebichot, G. (1969) 'Note sur les travaux de Bernard Schmitt', *Revue d'économie politique*, pp. 693-702.

Gold, Bela (1981) 'On Size, Scale, and Returns: A Survey', *Journal of Economic Literature*, March, pp. 5-33.

Hicks, J. (1976) '"Revolutions" in Economics', in *Method and Appraisal in Economics*, ed. S. J. Latsis, Cambridge University Press, pp. 207-18.

Hicks, J. (1979) *Causality in Economics*, Basil Blackwell, Oxford.

Pasinetti, L. L. (1981) *Structural Change and Economic Growth: A Theoretical Essay on the Dynamics of the Wealth of Nations*. Cambridge University Press.

Quadrio Curzio, A. and Scazzieri, R. (eds) (1977) *Protagonisti del pensiero economico*, 2 vols, Il Mulino, Bologna. Vol. I: *Nascita e affermazione del marginalismo (1871-1890)*; Vol. II: *Tradizione e rivoluzione in economia politica (1890-1936)*.

Part One

Production Analysis

1

Scale and Efficiency in Models of Production

ROBERTO SCAZZIERI*

I INTRODUCTION

The economists' approach to production phenomena is often characterized by a special interest in the relation between the scale and the efficiency of production activity. Indeed, we may say that the phenomena of decreasing and increasing efficiency, seen as a consequence of an expanding output, were among the most important factors that attracted the economists' attention to a detailed consideration of production processes. Production theory, as emerged from the work of the classical economists, was based on the two building blocks, represented by the Smithian theory of increasing efficiency and by the Malthusian and Ricardian theory of decreasing efficiency.

Statements about scale–efficiency phenomena are also common in the theories of production that emerged from the marginalist revolution of the 1870s.

The analysis of scale–efficiency relationships is central in the synthesis of the classical and marginalist theories attempted by Alfred Marshall in his *Principles.*

Finally, a number of results of modern economics depend on special assumptions about scale–efficiency relationships. Instances can be found in the convexity of production possibility sets that is assumed in most works on general equilibrium, and in the constant returns to scale that are assumed in the proofs of the 'non-substitution' theorem.

---

* Research support from the Italian Consiglio Nazionale delle Ricerche (CNR) is gratefully acknowledged.

In spite of the recognized importance of scale–efficiency relation-ships, their study has seldom been a central topic of research for modern economic theorists. On the other hand, the topic has received much greater attention by applied economists, as is shown by the large amount of empirical literature relating to the subject. An out-come of this situation is that the propositions about scale–efficiency relationships that one finds in the economic literature are often statements that describe an empirical law or an *ad hoc* assumption, whereas it is relatively uncommon to find theoretical statements about the kinds of scale–efficiency relationships that are to be expected under various conditions.

The aim of this paper is to show that such a situation is the conse-quence of the substitution of the scale–efficiency model character-istic of the classical economists for an altogether different model. The latter, even if foreshadowed by Turgot in the eighteenth century, played no part in the development of classical production theory. As we shall argue below, the new model made it unnecessary to have an economic theory of scale–efficiency relationships, since such relationships came to be considered as the result of natural or tech-nological laws.

In section II we shall discuss the two basic models of scale-efficiency phenomena. Section III deals with the problem of existence of an efficiency ranking of production techniques which is invariant with respect to changes in the output level. Our interest in this problem derives from the importance in the classical model of assuming a scale-invariant ranking of techniques, and from the role played by the criticism of such an assumption in shifting attention away from the classical approach to scale–efficiency phenomena. As a conclusion of this section, we shall argue that, while not all the rankings can satisfy scale-invariance, such a requisite has to be met by any *efficiency* ranking of production techniques.

In section IV we shall consider the alternative analytical represen-tations of production technology which are associated respectively with the classical and the post-classical models of scale-efficiency phenomena.

In section V we shall compare the two approaches and find that the classical theories can provide a useful starting point in the formu-lation of an economic theory of scale–efficiency phenomena.

II ALTERNATIVE MODELS OF SCALE-EFFICIENCY PHENOMENA

In order to describe the classical model, one has to consider the two different theories dealing with decreasing and increasing efficiency respectively.

The classical theory of decreasing efficiency stems from Sir James Steuart's analysis of how an increase in population would generally require the introduction of 'a more operose species of agriculture, the produce of which may be *absolutely* greater, though *relatively* less' (Steuart, 1767, vol. I, p. 129).

The subsequent formulations made it clear that such an association was the consequence of introducing less efficient methods of production. Sir Edward West, in his *Essay on the Application of Capital to Land,* pointed out that:

Each equal additional quantity of work bestowed on agriculture yields an actually diminished return, and of course, if each equal additional quantity of work yields an actually diminished return, the whole of the work bestowed on agriculture in the progress of improvement yields an actually diminished proportional return. Whereas it is obvious that an equal quantity of work will always fabricate the same quantity of manufactures. (West, 1815, p. 6)

In West's opinion, this happens because:

The additional work bestowed upon land must be expended either in bringing fresh land into cultivation, or in cultivating more highly that already in tillage. In every country the gradations between the richest land and the poorest must be innumerable. The richest land, or that most conveniently situated for a market, or, in a word, that which, on account of its situation and quality combined, produces the largest return to the expense bestowed on it, will of course be cultivated first, and when in the progress of improvement new land is brought into cultivation, recourse is necessarily had to poor land, or to that, at least, which is second in quality to what is already cultivated. It is clear that the additional work bestowed in this case will bring a less return than the work bestowed before. And the very fact that in the progress of society new land is brought into cultivation proves that additional work cannot be bestowed with the same advantage as before on the old land. For 100 acres of the rich land will, of course, yield a larger return to the work of 10 men than 100 acres of inferior land will do, and if this same rich land would continue to yield the same proportionate return to the work of 20 and 30 and 100 as it did to

that of 10 labourers, the inferior land would never be cultivated
at all. (West, 1815, pp. 9–10)

Other important qualifications of the principle of decreasing
efficiency are to be found in Malthus' pamphlet on the *Nature and
Progress of Rent*:

> The machines which produce corn and raw materials . . . are the
> gifts of nature, not the works of men; and we find, by experi-
> ence, that these gifts have very different qualities and powers.
> The most fertile lands of a country, those which, like the best
> machinery in manufactures, yield the greatest products with
> the least labour and capital, are never found sufficient to supply
> the effective demand of an increasing population. The price of
> raw produce, therefore, naturally rises till it becomes sufficiently
> high to pay the cost of raising it with inferior machines and by
> a more expensive process; and as there cannot be two prices for
> corn of the same quality, all the other machines, the working of
> which requires less capital compared with the produce, must
> yield rents in proportion of their goodness. Every extensive
> country may thus be considered as possessing a gradation of
> machines for the production of corn and raw materials, including
> in this gradation not only all the various qualities of poor land,
> of which every large territory has generally abundance, but the
> inferior machinery which may be said to be employed when
> good land is further and further forced for additional produce.
> As the price of raw produce continues to rise, these inferior
> machines are successively called into action; and as the price of
> raw produce continues to fall, they are successively thrown out
> of action. (Malthus, 1815, pp. 38–9)[1]

The accounts of decreasing productive efficiency by the English
classical economists, of which we have given two examples, share a
common logical structure, whose elements are set forth below.

(1) It is assumed that there is a set S of production techniques,
    exogenously given, each technique being defined as a particular
    set of input–output coefficients.
(2) An efficiency ranking on S is introduced.
(3) A given output level q is considered.
(4) A subset S^* of S is determined, whose elements are production
    techniques that (a) can produce q, (b) satisfy a set of exogenously

given constraints expressing the limited availability of certain inputs.

(5) Producers choose the best element of S^*.

In the classical approach, decreasing efficiency is presented as an instance of scale-induced technical change, brought about by the need to use less efficient production techniques when at least one element of the output vector is produced by a process that is the only consumer of a non-producible input, and the output target for such a commodity is above a certain lower bound.

Agriculture, which is implicitly defined as the set of all land-using production processes, satisfies such a condition. The same is true of mining activities, if we consider each such activity as the exclusive consumer of the mines from which a given mineral is extracted. On the other hand, the above condition is not met in the case of any single land-using process, as well as in the case of processes whose inputs can all be produced.

The stress by the classical economists on decreasing efficiency considered as a tendency characteristic of special branches of production, such as agriculture and mining, is thus to be seen as a result of their own special approach to scale–efficiency phenomena.

We shall now consider the classical theory of scale-induced increasing efficiency. Such a theory is partly based on two well-known propositions by Adam Smith:

(1) The productivity of labour depends on the extent of the division of labour.
(2) The extent of the division of labour depends on the extent of the market.

The relationship between the division of labour and its 'productive powers' is explained by Smith in the following way:

This great increase of the quantity of work, which, in consequence of the division of labour, the same number of people are capable of performing, is owing to three different circumstances; first, to the increase of dexterity in every particular workman; secondly to the saving of the time which is commonly lost in passing from one species of work to another; and lastly, to the invention of a great number of machines which facilitate and abridge labour, and enable one man to do the work of many. (Smith, 1976, p. 17)

The operation of the first cause is described as follows:

> The division of labour, by reducing every man's business to some one simple operation, and by making this operation the employment of his life, necessarily increases very much the dexterity of the workman. A common smith, who, though accustomed to handle the hammer, has never been used to make nails, if upon some particular occasion he is obliged to attempt it, will scarce, I am assured, be able to make above two or three hundred a day, and those, too, very bad ones. A smith who has been accustomed to make nails, but whose sole or principal business has not been that of a nailer, can seldom with his utmost diligence make more than eight hundred or thousand nails in a day. I have seen several boys under twenty years of age who had never exercised any other trade but that of making nails, and who, when they exerted themselves, could make, each of them, upwards of two thousand three hundred nails in a day. (Smith, 1976, p. 18)

As to the second cause, Smith observes that:

> The advantage which is gained by saving the time commonly lost in passing from one sort of work to another, is much greater than we should at first view be apt to imagine it. It is impossible to pass very quickly from one kind of work to another, that is carried on in a different place, and with quite different tools. A country weaver, who cultivates a small farm, must lose a good deal of time in passing from his loom to the field, and from the field to his loom. When the two trades can be carried on in the same workhouse, the loss of time is no doubt much less. It is even in this case, however, very considerable. A man commonly saunters a little in turning his hand from one sort of employment to another . . . Independently, therefore, of his deficiency in point of dexterity, this cause alone must always reduce considerably the quantity of work which he is capable of performing. (Smith, 1976, pp. 18–19)

As to the effect of machinery, Adam Smith, after observing that 'everybody must be sensible how much labour is facilitated and abridged by the application of proper machinery' (1976, p. 19), points out that:

The invention of all those machines by which labour is so much facilitated and abridged, seems to have been originally owing to the division of labour. Men are much more likely to discover easier and readier methods of attaining any object, when the whole attention of their minds is directed towards that single object, than when it is dissipated among a great variety of things. But in consequence of the division of labour, the whole of every man's attention comes naturally to be directed towards some one very simple object. It is naturally to be expected, therefore, that some one or other of those who are employed in each particular branch of labour should soon find out easier and readier methods of performing their own particular work, where-ever the nature of it admits of such improvement . . . (Smith, 1976, p.20)

It is worth distinguishing between two different types of efficiency improvements that can be associated with the division of labour. One is the increase in efficiency that may result from the discovery of new ways of doing things (something like Arrow's 'learning by doing'). The other is the increase in efficiency that is associated with the division of labour simply because producers would probably not specialize if they could not foresee some definite advantage springing directly from the division of labour itself. Contrary to the former type of improvement, the latter phenomenon does not imply a change in the technological horizon (the set of production techniques known to producers) and is instead associated with a change in the degree of utilization of a machine or a plant.

Adam Smith was overlooking the latter type of improvement, by laying more stress on phenomena of the 'learning by doing' kind, and then establishing a direct link between such phenomena and the scale of production activities (his 'extent of the market'). However, the idea that some advantage has to be foreseen in order to introduce the specialization among production activities is already apparent in the following passage from the *Wealth of Nations*:

When the market is very small, no person can have any encourage-ment to dedicate himself entirely to one employment, for want of the power to exchange all that surplus part of the produce of his own labour, which is over and above his own consumption, for such part of the produce of other men's labour as he has occasion for. (Smith, 1976, p. 31)

The type of efficiency improvement that can be seen as a necessary consequence of the division of labour was placed in the foreground by authors such as Melchiorre Gioja (1815–17, vol. I), Charles Babbage (1835) and Karl Marx (1887). In all of their works, the theory of increasing efficiency is based on the consideration of productive factors, such as tools and machines, that do not need to operate continuously in the production process in which they happen to be used.[2] An increase in output scale (generally, in output per unit of time) makes it possible to use such factors in a way that minimizes their degree of idleness.[3]

The discovery that division of labour is rooted in the need for using specialized tools and machines, and not simply in 'a certain propensity in human nature..., the propensity to truck, barter and exchange one thing for another' (Smith, 1976, p. 25), is due to Melchiorre Gioja. Babbage and Marx analysed this phenomenon further.

In his analysis of the reasons that make the division of labour necessary, Gioja noted that 'the mixed practice of all activities would require the introduction and useless waste of enormous capitals. *This waste is avoided by the division of labour*' (Gioja, 1815–17; vol. I, p. 101; our translation and italics). In the chapter on division of labour of his work *On the Economy of Machinery and Manufactures*, Babbage maintained that the three causes of the advantages of the division of labour considered by Adam Smith, although important, do not suffice in accounting for 'the cheapness of manufactured articles, as consequent upon the division of labour' (Babbage, 1835, p. 175). The 'most important and influential cause' is, in Babbage's opinion, that:

> The master manufacturer, by dividing the work to be executed into different processes, each requiring different degrees of skill or of force, can purchase exactly that precise quantity of both which is necessary for each process, whereas, if the whole work were executed by one workman, that person must possess sufficient skill to perform the most difficult and sufficient strength to execute the most laborious, of the operations into which the art is divided. (Babbage, 1835, pp. 175–6)

According to Babbage, the optimal proportions among fund factors are possible only at certain levels of output. This introduces in the production process a special kind of indivisibility:

When the number of processes into which it is most advantageous to divide it [viz., the production of a given commodity], and the number of individuals to be employed in it, are ascertained, then all factories which do not employ a direct multiple of this latter number, will produce the article at a greater cost. (Babbage, 1835, p. 212)

The same phenomenon was noted by Marx:

When once the most fitting proportion has been established for the numbers of the detail labourers in the various groups when producing on a given scale, that scale can be extended only by employing a multiple of each particular group. (Marx, 1887, p. 338)

Such a property was considered by Babbage 'one cause of the great size of manufacturing establishments, which have increased with the progress of civilization' (Babbage, 1835, p. 213).

Of the two different approaches to increasing efficiency that we have considered, the former does not lead to a definite relationship between productive efficiency and output scale.[4] On the other hand, the consideration of fund factor utilization leads to a relationship between output scale and productive efficiency such that, whenever changes of the latter are observed, changes in output scale have to be assumed. The attention given to the latter class of efficiency improvements led to a theory whose logical structure is similar to that of the classical theory of decreasing efficiency. The elements of such a theory are set forth below:

(1) There is a set S of production techniques, exogenously given.[5]
(2) There is an efficiency ranking on S.
(3) A given output level q is considered.
(4) A subset S^* of S is determined, whose elements are production techniques that (a) can produce q, (b) can satisfy constraints expressing the existence of lower bounds on activity scale.
(5) The best element of S^* is chosen.

A common feature of the classical theories of scale–efficiency phenomena is the idea that changes in output scale determine changes in the set of production techniques available to producers. Sequences of decreasing and increasing efficiency are then explained by the hypothesis that, at any output scale, producers will normally make the required commodity bundle by using, among the available techniques, that particular technique or technical mix that will permit them to obtain the 'best' structure of production, given the efficiency ranking of techniques.

It is an essential assumption, in the classical treatment of scale-efficiency phenomena, that the ranking over technical alternatives is invariant with respect to changes in the scale of production. The reason is that, given scale invariance, changes in the techniques being used at any given output level can be explained by the existence of constraints that eliminate different subsets of production techniques at different output levels. Without scale invariance, there will be no change in technical choice that could be explained by the latter mechanism, since, assuming choice to be governed by the place of each technique in the efficiency ranking, technical choices might change not only because the changes in the output level may eliminate subsets of production techniques, but also because they may induce changes in the efficiency ranking itself.

Scale–efficiency phenomena were thus originally explained by changes in the output scale, via a mechanism centred on producers' choice from among technical alternatives.

The treatment of scale–efficiency phenomena that became dominant since the second half of the nineteenth century is characterized instead by the fact that such relationships were no longer *explained* by variations of scale affecting producers' choice, and came to be regarded as the direct outcome of natural or technological laws.

This change is already apparent in John Stuart Mill's *Principles*. There we read that:

> After a certain, and not very advanced, stage in the progress of agriculture, it is the law of production from the land, that in any given state of agricultural skill and knowledge, by increasing the labour, the produce is not increased in an equal degree; doubling the labour does not double the produce; or, to express the same thing in other words, every increase of produce is obtained by a more than proportional increase in the application of labour to land. (Mill, 1965, vol. I, p. 174)

The above passage is important because its first part contains a new formulation of the theory of decreasing efficiency, whereas its second part (from 'to express the same thing in other words' to the end) presents the classical formulation as a special case of the former.

Having shifted the emphasis on to a continuous, non-proportional relation between labour inputs and the quantity produced, which applies more immediately to the case of intensive cultivation, Mill reduces to such a formulation the extensive case too:

> When, for the purpose of raising an increase of produce, recourse is had to inferior land, it is evident that, so far, the produce does not increase in the same proportion with the labour. The very meaning of inferior land, is land which with equal labour returns a smaller amount of produce. (Mill, 1965, vol. I, p. 174)

The main consequence of the change of emphasis is that attention is no longer focused on the discontinuity associated with the cultivation of a new type of land (extensive case) or with the transition from one technique to another on the same land (intensive case). The law of diminishing returns is formulated in general terms, and is taken to describe a functional relation between the units of a variable input and the associated output increments, held to be characteristic of all the cases of 'excessive application of resources or of energy in any given direction' (Marshall, 1961, vol. I, p. 356).

The law of diminishing returns became a special case of the general law governing the productive result associated with changes in input proportions. Such changes were taken to be hypothetical, and the whole issue became a matter of conceptual experiments to determine the elasticity of output when the quantity of a limited number of inputs was changed and all the remaining inputs were kept constant.

Important changes also affected the treatment of increasing efficiency. On the one hand, the classical idea that efficiency improvements are associated with a greater division of labour, and that changes in output scale affect productive efficiency simply by making increased specialization possible, was gradually superseded by the idea that large-scale production is the main cause of increasing efficiency, rather than a simple prerequisite for it (cf., for instance, Mill, 1965, vol. I, p. 131). The careful analysis of production processes that characterized the classical approach was not developed further, and the idea of a functional relation between cost of production per unit of output and output per unit of time was explicitly introduced into economic theory, becoming the basis of the transformation of the classical theory into a theory of the economies of large-scale production. On the other hand, the emphasis on input co-ordination, characteristic of the post-classical treatment of decreasing efficiency, attracted the economists' attention to a way of analysing the scale–efficiency phenomena, which had passed unnoticed ever since its original formulation by Turgot.[6]

A. R. J. Turgot, in a comment on a prize essay, had written that:

> Seed thrown on a soil naturally fertile but totally unprepared would be an advance almost entirely lost. If it were once tilled the produce will be greater; tilling it a second, a third time, might not merely double and triple, but quadruple or decuple the produce, which will thus augment in a much larger proportion than the advances increase, and that up to a certain point, at which the produce will be as great as possible compared with the advances. (Turgot, 1808, p. 317, transl. in Cannan, 1929, p. 75)

Turgot was then arguing that 'Past this point, if the advances be still increased, the produce will still increase but less and less until, the fecundity of the earth being exhausted, and art unable to add anything further, an addition to the advances will add nothing whatever to the produce' (p. 318; Cannan, 1929, p. 75).

Increasing and decreasing efficiency are thus considered as consequences of a general law of input co-ordination (the 'Law of Variable Proportions') and appear to be related with each other, in the sense that both are seen as a result of the operation of the same cause (a sequence of changes in one input, keeping the other inputs constant).

Of the two different approaches to increasing efficiency that are to be found in the post-classical writers, the former is often grounded on a mere description of the efficiency improvements that may follow an enlargement of the scale of production. The latter approach is instead the expression of a developed theoretical framework, and was sometimes considered as the 'true' law of increasing efficiency, even in the case of economies of large-scale production *à la* Marshall.[7] We may therefore say that, from the point of view of economic theory, the laws of increasing and decreasing returns based on the Law of Variable Proportions represent the purest expression of the post-classical approach to scale–efficiency phenomena.

The essential elements of the scale–efficiency model based on variable proportions are:

(1) The consideration of an input–output space X^{m+1}: the first m elements of any vector of this space are input quantities, the last element is quantity of output.

(2) The consideration of the production techniques generated by variations in x_i ($i : 1, \ldots, m$), under the condition x_j = constant

for all $j \neq i$ ($j : 1, \ldots, m$): this step defines a set S', of production techniques, which replaces the set S considered in the classical models of decreasing and increasing efficiency (see above).

(3) An hypothesis about the way in which the output level q varies as one goes through the sequence of techniques so generated.

(4) The consideration of an efficiency ranking on S', based on the different 'returns' associated with each element of S'.

III THE SCALE INVARIANCE OF EFFICIENCY RANKINGS: A DISCUSSION

We have already seen that the classical models of scale–efficiency phenomena are subject to a stringent condition on the exogenously given ranking over technical alternatives; for such a ranking needs to be scale-invariant if scale–efficiency phenomena are to be explained by the classical theories.

The shift from the classical to the post-classical approach resulted from the influence of various factors, among which the criticism pointing to the difficulty of determining a scale-invariant ranking of lands was of considerable importance. This can be seen from the following passage by Marshall:

There is no absolute measure of the richness or fertility of land. Even if there be no change in the arts of production, a mere increase in the demand for produce may invert the order in which two adjacent pieces of land rank as regards fertility. The one which gives the smaller produce, when both are uncultivated, or when the cultivation of both is equally slight, may rise above the other and justly rank as more fertile when both are cultivated with equal thoroughness. (Marshall, 1961, vol. I, p. 157)

The discovery that, under certain conditions, scale-induced reversals in the fertility ranking of lands are possible seemed to undermine the classical theory of decreasing efficiency in its extensive formulation, making it impossible to explain decreasing efficiency in terms of producers' choice. This led not only to the substitution of the intensive for the extensive case in most treatments of decreasing efficiency, but also to the introduction of a completely different model of scale–efficiency phenomena (see above).

One of the clearest formulations of the view that the classical approach is vitiated by the possibility of efficiency reversals is to be found in a paper by the mathematician Karl Menger (1954). There one finds a careful analysis of the conditions under which efficiency reversals are possible. It is worth considering this author's view in some detail.

In Menger's opinion, an essential feature of the classical theory is that 'if the entire demand for agricultural products can be met by using only the most fertile pieces of land, then only the most fertile pieces of land are actually used, and the rest is left idle' (Menger, 1954, p. 455). Menger then discusses a case in which two types of land are available; '(1) fertile land, on x units of which a cost outlay of y units yields $E_1(x, y)$ units of product; (2) less fertile land, on x units of which a cost outlay of y units yields $E_2(x, y)$ units of product' (Menger, 1954, p. 456). The assumed ranking can be expressed by the inequality: $E_2(x, y) < E_1(x, y)$ (cf. Menger, 1954, p.456).

Let b denote the demand for agricultural output, and $\bar{x}_1$ the quantity of fertile land that is available. It is assumed that b can be met by production on the fertile land only, so that there will be some x_1 and y_1 such that: $x_1 = \bar{x}_1$ and $E_1(x_1, y_1) = b$.

According to Menger, from the assumption that (1) the fertility ranking is as above and (2) it is always better to produce a given output with a smaller cost outlay than with a larger one, it follows that 'even if it is possible to produce b on x_1 units of second-grade land, it is preferable to produce b on x_1 units of first-grade land' (Menger, 1954, p. 456). The classical economists, however, would also maintain that 'it is advisable to meet the entire demand by using first-grade land only and leaving the rest idle' (p. 456). In Menger's opinion, the classical result does not follow from the assumptions stated above:

> If enough second-grade land is available, it is quite possible that much (or even all) of the production on first-grade land can be replaced by more economical production with smaller cost outlays on large areas of second-grade land. As an extreme example, suppose that $E_1(\bar{x}_1, y_1) = b$, that there are 16 $\bar{x}_1$ units of second-grade land available and that b can be produced on these 16 $\bar{x}_1$ units with a cost outlay of $y_1/2$. Then, clearly, the entire demand b will be met by using second-grade land only and leaving the fertile land idle, rather than by using fertile land only and leaving the second-grade land idle. (Menger, 1954, pp. 456–7)

In order to discuss Menger's argument we shall assume, for the sake of simplicity, that only labour inputs are used, together with land, in agricultural production.

Let q denote the output level. When $\bar{y}_1$ labour units are used on a plot of first-grade land, and the same quantity of labour is used on a plot of second-grade land, the average labour productivity will respectively be $q/\bar{y}_1$ and $q'/\bar{y}_1$, with $q > q'$, provided the two plots are of equal extension. Menger's argument implies that, by increasing the area of second-grade land which is cultivated, the average labour productivity on land of this kind will increase, thus making cultivation cheaper than on first-grade land. This case can be studied by considering the effect on output of changes in the quantity of labour employed on a given plot (see figure 1.1). The doses of labour used on the given plot are represented on the axis Ox. The average and marginal outputs corresponding to each number of doses are represented on the axis Oy, thus obtaining the average productivity curve OPD and the marginal productivity curve OAB. M is the point of maximum average labour productivity.

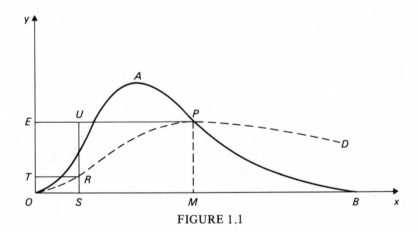

FIGURE 1.1

The curves in figure 1.1 represent a situation in which, when the quantity of labour is increased while keeping all the other inputs constant, one has first a region of increasing output increments and then a region of diminishing output increments.

The shape of the curves in figure 1.1 is that which can be derived from the law of variable proportions. The use of such a law was criticized by Piero Sraffa, whose remarks are worth quoting:

If we assume that a given plot is homogeneous over the all of its surface, we can obtain, for each fraction of that surface, a pair of curves analogous to those of fig. 1 [This is figure 1.1 of our paper] . . . Therefore, for each fraction of the given plot, the maximum productivity will be equal to *MP*. Consider now again fig. 1: a consequence of our assumptions is that on neither of the two curves can a point whose abscissa is less than *OM* be an equilibrium point: if a cultivator decides to employ a quantity of capital and labour (for example *OS*) less than that needed in order to cultivate all the plot under conditions of maximum productivity, it is advantageous for him to cultivate not the entire plot, thus obtaining the quantity of output *OTRS*, but only that fraction of the plot which, with the same quantity of capital and labour, attains the point of maximum productivity and gives the output *OEUS* (the ratio of such a fraction to the area of the entire plot is given by the ratio of *OS* to *OM*). When we increase the quantity of capital and labour employed in cultivation, the productivity curve will be a straight line such as *EP* up to the point of maximum productivity. Only beyond this point will the curve start to decrease. All in all, productivity can be constant or decreasing, but never increasing. (Sraffa, 1925, pp. 284–5, our translation)

Menger's argument is based on the assumption that, by increasing the area of second-grade land under cultivation, there will be an increase in the average productivity of the other inputs (in our example, an increase in the average productivity of labour). However, the considerations outlined by Sraffa suggest that such an increase is possible only if: (1) before the extension of cultivation on second-grade land too many workers were employed on too little land, so that the average productivity of labour was below its maximum; or (2) second-grade land is not homogeneous, so that, when additional land is brought under cultivation, a new pair of productivity curves ought to be considered. In case (1), the increase of the area of second-grade land under cultivation can be seen, from the point of view of factor proportions, as the equivalent of a decrease in the number of workers employed on the area that was previously cultivated. The productivity increase is thus to be explained by a movement towards the point of maximum labour productivity, a result analogous to what one could obtain by reducing the number of workers in the interval $]M, B]$ on the labour axis of figure 1.1. In case (2), extended cultivation could bring about an increase in the productivity of labour even if the cultivation was previously carried out at the point of maximum labour productivity.

Case (1) would be inconsistent with the assumption of rational producers' behaviour. The reason for this is that, if no indivisibility assumption is introduced, each producer should be considered to be free to decide about the extension of land under cultivation, so that it should be possible to have the most efficient input proportions at any output scale.

Case (2), on the other hand, makes it impossible to consider Menger's second-grade land as land of a uniform quality. Such a case is therefore irrelevant to his argument, which is based on the possibility of a reversal in the fertility ranking of 'only two grades of land' (Menger, 1954, p. 456).

We may conclude that the possibility of reversals in the fertility ranking of lands, as a result of changes in the scale of production, seems to depend on the consideration of an efficiency ranking that is bound to lead to such reversals.[8] Once the land qualities are correctly identified, the scale-invariance of the fertility ranking depends on choosing a proper criterion on which lands should be compared.

The latter condition might seem a rather stringent one. However, it is possible to show that using an efficiency criterion which leads to scale-invariance is an essential prerequisite for a logically consistent employment of efficiency rankings.

In order to understand that, it is important to distinguish between the efficiency rankings and the 'natural' rankings on which the former are based. A natural ranking is a relation based on some scale property of the objects being ranked, having no connection with any expression of preference. An efficiency ranking is a relation based upon: (1) a natural ranking over objects; (2) an expression of preference founded on the position of each object on the natural ranking.[9]

The scale-induced reversals of an efficiency ranking (such as the fertility ranking of lands) are the consequence of reversals in the natural ranking which is based on the actual characteristics of the objects being considered. On the other hand, the possibility of reversals in the natural ranking brings about the possibility of reversals in the efficiency ranking which is based on the former.

It seems possible to argue that a natural ranking subject to reversals cannot be the basis of a properly formulated efficiency ranking. The reason is that no preference ranking may assign a given object to more than one position at the same time, whereas this would be the consequence of basing the efficiency ranking on a natural ranking subject to reversals. This implies that, whenever an efficiency ranking is used, one must assume that such a ranking is based on a natural ranking immune from reversals. Under such conditions, an efficiency ranking among techniques of production will be invariant with respect to changes in the output scale (an instance is given by the efficiency ranking of lands based on the maximum average labour productivity on each plot).

IV SCALE-EFFICIENCY PHENOMENA AND THE ANALYTICAL REPRESENTATION OF PRODUCTION TECHNOLOGY

In this section we shall argue that the difference between the classical and the post-classical models of scale-efficiency phenomena is associated with a difference between the analytical representations of production technology which characterize the two approaches.

Before discussing this point, it may be worth commenting briefly on what we mean by 'analytical representation' in the present context.

Any kind of production theory needs assumptions on the nature of production relationships. Such assumptions are not necessarily realistic, since their purpose is not to mirror reality but to give a factual basis to the statements of the theory. In other words, the actual description of production phenomena is one thing; the 'descriptive assumptions' on which the theory is based is another.

By analytical representation of production technology is meant the set of assumptions about production relationships that represent the starting point in building a theory of production phenomena.

We have already seen (cf. section II above) that the classical theories of scale-efficiency phenomena are characterized by the consideration of a set S of production techniques, which are exogenously given. Each such technique is associated with a given set of input-output coefficients. Any change in the input-output coefficients relative to the production of a certain commodity is considered as a change in the technique used in producing such a commodity.

This is not so in the case of the post-classical model, which starts from the consideration of an input-output space X^{m+1}. In any vector of this space the first m elements are input quantities and the last element is a quantity of output. The set of production techniques, S', is generated by variations in the input quantity x_i, for $i = 1, \ldots, m$, under the condition x_j = constant for all $j \neq i$ ($j : 1, \ldots, m$). What is essential to the latter approach is a special hypothesis about the way in which the output level varies as one goes through the sequence of techniques so generated. It is assumed that there will be first a region of increasing output increments and then a region of diminishing output increments. The post-classical model of scale-efficiency phenomena includes, in the analytical representation of production technology, a 'law' which generates changes in input–output coefficients.[10] It is impossible to determine the set S' of production techniques without knowing first the rule that generates such techniques from the input–output space X^{m+1}.

In the post-classical model of scale–efficiency phenomena, production techniques are generated by the law of variable proportions, so that a scale–efficiency relationship enters the analytical representation of production technology.

The assumption of a nonlinear relation between input requirements and the output scale is thus characteristic of the post-classical production theory. No such assumption is to be found in the analytical representation of production technology accepted by the classical economists.

As a consequence, if we base on the analytical representation of technology the curve of input requirements for a given factor of production we shall end up with a straight line in the case of the classical theory and with a proper curve in the case of the post-classical theory. Given the technique of production, only proportional changes in input requirements, as output varies, are consistent with the assumptions of the classical theory.

In the case of the post-classical theory, we face a rather different problem, since the input requirements curve can no longer be based on an exogenously given technique. One has to consider a vector such as $(x_1, x_2, \ldots, x_m, y)$, and then to compute the quantity of input x_i which is needed in order to obtain an increasing level of output (denoted by y). Provided we take all the other inputs as constant, input requirements can be derived from the law of variable proportions, and will increase first at a decreasing, and then at an increasing, rate.

It is worth stressing that, even if the analytical representation of production technology implies, both in the classical and in the post-classical theories, a special view of input–output relationships, this does not mean that the associated theory will be unable to account for input–output relationships of a different kind. In particular, the analytical representation based on linear input–output relationships is compatible with a theory of nonlinear input–output relationships, as in the case of the classical theories of decreasing and increasing efficiency.

Scale–efficiency phenomena lead, when considered in the framework of the classical theories, to piece-wise linear input requirement functions, such as the one represented in figure 1.2. A consequence

Roberto Scazzieri

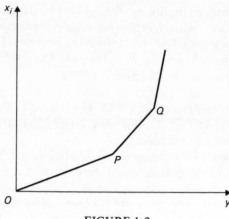

FIGURE 1.2

of assuming linear input–output relationships in the analytical representation of production technology is that changes in input requirements are taken to be proportional to changes in the output scale over substantial ranges of output variation. Changes in the slope of the input requirement line, such as those occurring at points P and Q in figure 1.2, are compatible with the linearity assumed in the analytical representation. However, such a representation does not offer any reason for the changing slope. Nonlinear input–output relationships can be represented by a broken-line function (as in figure 1.2) but have to be explained by a theory of scale–efficiency phenomena.

This is not so in the case of the post-classical theory of production, where the assumption of nonlinearity enters the analytical representation of production technology. This makes it more difficult to use economic theory in explaining nonlinear input–output relationships. The reason is that we would find ourselves in the position of considering such relationships partly as phenomena to be explained by economic theory and partly as relationships that have already been described in the analytical representation. In the latter case, an economic explanation of the nonlinearity is impossible (we would have to explain a given relationship in terms of theory having the same relationship among its basic assumptions).

The consideration of the classical and post-classical approaches permits us to draw a line between two essentially different methods which can be used by economists in dealing with the scale–efficiency phenomena in production. The respective merits of each will be discussed in the following section.

V CONCLUDING REMARKS

So far we have been comparing the different approaches to scale–efficiency phenomena in terms of the logical structure of the various theories. We shall now compare such theories in terms of their respective generality.

The classical approach is compatible with the consideration of any state of the production system, provided it is possible to find an unambiguous efficiency ranking of such states.[11] In particular, the classical approach makes it possible to consider any kind of qualitative change that may take place in the inputs as the output scale is varied.

On the other hand, the efficiency ranking used by the classical economists, which is the expression of a special criterion on which to base technical choice, the criterion of cost minimization, does restrict the methods of production that can be compared. The reason is that the use of cost minimization as a criterion of technical choice makes it difficult to consider rankings of methods based on characteristics different from those on which the cost-minimizing choices are based.

In short, the classical approach is completely general, in terms of its descriptive assumptions, if we refer to the number of states of the production system over which a natural ranking is possible. Such an approach is, instead, less general if we consider the special efficiency ranking introduced by the classical economists over states of the production system.[12]

The post-classical theories of decreasing and increasing efficiency are based on the consideration of the output increments associated with different amounts of a given variable input, all the other inputs being fixed. This implies that it is possible to rank only a limited number of states of the production system, viz. those states having the given variable input and the given set of fixed inputs. No ranking can exist over states that differ among themselves with respect to the identity of the variable and/or fixed inputs.

The descriptive assumptions underlying the post-classical approach are therefore rather restrictive. The main consequence is that qualitative changes in the inputs being used are ruled out, when a sequence of decreasing or increasing efficiency is described by such relations. On the other hand, the same relations do not depend on technical choice. Indeed, the theories that incorporate such relations take the scale–efficiency phenomena as natural *data,* on which technical choice is based. This means that the restrictive assumptions on technical choice that characterize the classical approach have no place in the theory of variable proportions. The latter is indeed compatible, at least in principle, with any criterion of choice.

The classical and the post-classical approaches to scale–efficiency phenomena can be seen as the expressions of a fundamental dichotomy. The classical approach is based on the idea that such phenomena can be explained by economic theory considering the interactions between producers' choice and physical or technological constraints. The post-classical writers adopted instead a radically different view, since scale–efficiency phenomena were left unexplained by economic theory, and referred to the working of certain 'natural' laws.

The former method is surely more straightforward if one wants to formulate an economic theory of this type of relation. On the other hand, such an approach leads to the linearity assumption in the analytical representation of production technology, so that the possibility of a purely physical or biological explanation of certain scale–efficiency relations is ruled out *a priori*.

On the contrary, the point of view chosen by the post-classical writers implies that only an extra-economic explanation is possible.

However, such an outcome is not a necessary consequence of admitting that scale–efficiency phenomena can partly be explained by laws independent of producers' choices. The reason is that, at least in principle, it is possible to have an economic theory of such phenomena and also to allow natural or technological laws to play a part in their determination. If one accepts the latter point of view, the analytical representation of production technology can no longer be based on the linearity assumption, unless *ad hoc* qualifications are introduced. Additionally, it will be possible to deal with the cases in which scale–efficiency phenomena arising from producers' choices appear in conjunction with nonlinearities based on natural or technological laws.

NOTES

1 We may note that two different types of decreasing efficiency are considered in Malthus' passage. One is associated with the cultivation of less and less fertile lands (*extensive* decreasing efficiency); the other is associated with the use of less and less efficient methods of production on a given plot of land (*intensive* decreasing efficiency).

2 The term 'fund factor' has been used in order to denote inputs of this kind (cf. Georgescu Roegen, 1970). Their main characteristic is that they enter the production process as inputs and leave the same process as outputs of a

special kind. The fund factors may remain idle, after doing a certain productive task, if they are not immediately employed in another task. For such factors, apart from the case of scrapping, are normally available as means of production even after they have been used in a specific task.

3 A modern analysis of this phenomenon is to be found in Georgescu Roegen (1970).

4 The reason is that changes in the technological horizon are not necessarily the consequence of a greater division of labour. It follows that phenomena of 'learning by doing' cannot be the basis of a theory of scale-induced technical change.

5 Each technique is defined as a particular set of input–output coefficients.

6 Edwin Cannan, in his *Review of Economic Theory*, writes: 'I do not know that these observations of Turgot were published at all till they appeared in Du Pont's collection of Turgot's works, 1808-11, and I doubt if any notice was taken of them till I quoted them in *Production and Distribution,* 1893, whence Marshall introduced them into the third edition of his *Principles* (pp. 49-50)' (Cannan, 1929, pp. 75-6).

7 Edgeworth, for instance, maintained that the law of variable proportions might explain not only the cases of increasing returns *à la* Turgot, but also those originating from 'the general principle that size is favourable to multiplication of parts, and so to cooperation' (Edgeworth, 1911, p. 553), as well as from 'the classical trio of advantages attributed by Adam Smith to Division of Labour' (p. 554).

8 In the case considered by Menger, the natural ranking of lands is based on the inequality $E_2(x,y) < E_1(x,y)$, where x are the units of land, y is the 'cost outlay', $E_1(x,y)$ and $E_2(x,y)$ are, respectively, the units of product obtained on lands 1 and 2. Such an inequality may clearly be reversed, at a greater scale of production, if land 2 is initially under-cultivated.

9 Our distinction between natural ranking and efficiency ranking is based on the idea that any grading situation requires to place the relevant objects on an ordered scale, which depends only on the qualities of the objects and is independent of any expression of preference. Such an ordered scale is the natural ranking on which an efficiency ranking can be based. For a discussion of this problem, cf. Urmson (1950) and Harré and Secord (1972).

10 Each vector of the space X^{m+1} is of course associated with a vector of input–output coefficients.

11 Each state is characterized by a different technique or technical mix.

12 On the distinction between natural rankings and efficiency rankings, cf. section III above.

REFERENCES

Babbage, C. (1835) *On the Economy of Machinery and Manufactures,* 4th edn, Charles Knight, London.

Cannan, E. (1929) *A Review of Economic Theory,* P. S. King & Son, London.

Roberto Scazzieri

Edgeworth, F. Y. (1911) 'Contributions to the Theory of Railway Rates', *Economic Journal*, XXI, 346-70 and 551-71.

Georgescu Roegen, N. (1970) 'The Economics of Production', *American Economic Review*, LX, 1-9.

Gioja, M. (1815-17) *Nuovo Prospetto delle Scienze Economiche*, G. Pirotta, Milan.

Harré, R., and Secord, P. F. (1972) *The Explanation of Social Behaviour*, Basil Blackwell, Oxford.

Malthus, T. R. (1815) *An Inquiry into the Nature and Progress of Rent*, John Murray, London.

Marshall, A. (1961) *Principles of Economics* (1st edn 1890), ed. C. W. Guillebaud, Macmillan, London.

Marx, C. (1887) *Capital: a Critical Analysis of Capitalist Production*, translated from 3rd German edn by Samuel Moore and Edward Aveling, and ed. by Frederick Engels. Swan, Sonnenschein, Lowrey & Co., London.

Menger, K. (1954) 'The Logic of the Laws of Return. A Study in Metaeconomics', pp. 419-81, in *Economic Activity Analysis*, ed. O. Morgenstern, John Wiley, New York; Chapman and Hall, London.

Mill, J. S. (1965) *Principles of Political Economy* (1st edn 1848), ed. J. M. Robson, with an introduction by R. F. McRae, University of Toronto Press.

Scazzieri, R. (1981) *Efficienza produttiva e livelli di attività*, Il Mulino, Bologna.

Smith, A. (1976) *An Inquiry into the Nature and Causes of the Wealth of Nations*, (1st edn 1776), ed. R. H. Campbell, A. S. Skinner and W. B. Todd, Clarendon Press, Oxford.

Sraffa, P. (1925) 'Sulle relazioni fra costo e quantità prodotta', *Annali di Economia*, II, 277-328.

Steuart, Sir J. (1767) *An Inquiry into the Principles of Political Oeconomy*, A. Miller and T. Cadell, London.

Turgot, A. R. J. (1808) *Observations sur le mémoire de M. de Saint-Péravy en faveur de l'impôt indirect*, vol. 4, pp. 312-43 in *Oeuvres de Turgot*, Imprimerie De Delance, Paris. (first written in 1768).

Urmson, J. O. (1950) 'On Grading', *Mind*, LIX, 145-69.

West, Sir E. (1815) *Essay on the Application of Capital to Land*, T. Underwood, London.

Part Two

Micro-Foundations of Macroeconomics

2

Temporary Equilibrium with Rationed Borrowing and Consistent Plans

CHRISTOPHER J. BLISS and ROBERTO F. CIPPÀ*

I INTRODUCTION

This paper is concerned with the temporary equilibrium approach to economic theory, with some of the possibilities of extending that approach and with some of the problems that the approach gives rise to. 'Temporary equilibrium' is a term coined by Hicks (1939), but it could be extended to cover a number of models that are not as complete and formal as his Walrasian type of model but which nevertheless are situated in the short run. We here include most attempts to give a formal expression in terms of a closed model to Keynes' theory.

Broadly speaking, two types of approach have been adopted: the fix-price and the flexi-price approaches. In the former case, which reaches its peak of achievement in the writings of the French economists such as Malinvaud (1977), Benassy (1975, 1976) and Grandmont (1977), it is assumed that prices do not vary in the short run and that the equilibrium of the economy, which must then include some rationing of agents, is described. In the latter case, most prices are assumed to be flexible. This is the original path taken by Keynes in the General Theory, and by Hicks (1937) in setting up his *IS/LM* model. In each of these cases an exception was made for money wages, the rate of which was taken as given. Hence, strictly, Keynes' theory, or the *IS/LM* model, should be classified as partly flexi-price but with a little fix-price added. It was this feature, and not the demand for money specification, that gave rise to the non-classical result of unemployment as part of the solution in certain cases.

* R. Cippà's research has been supported by the Swiss Science Foundation.

If some prices are not to be assumed given and invariant, then the only way to get to results different from the familiar results of Walrasian general equilibrium theory, in which there can be no involuntary unemployment, is to assume the absence of certain markets. The most popular candidates for deletion from the list of possible markets have been the forward or the contingency markets of Arrow–Debreu equilibrium theory. Hence it is assumed, for example, that there are no markets in which claims for many goods for delivery in future periods can be transacted. Where uncertainty is taken into account there is the further possibility of assuming the lack of certain contingency markets, in which promises to deliver specified goods in certain states of the world are transacted (as for example, but only one example, insurance contracts). We shall not consider uncertainty in this paper and henceforth we shall neglect this potentially important topic.

Since Hicks first introduced it, the temporary equilibrium approach has proved to be enormously fruitful (see the survey by Grandmont, 1977). The present paper represents an extension of the approach along new lines. Before describing our own approach we note one feature that stands out strongly from previous research.

While the proofs have sometimes required ingenuity, it has generally proved possible to prove the existence of temporary equilibrium. This is the case whether current prices have been assumed rigid or flexible, although of course where prices have been assumed rigid the equilibria that are shown to exist have been rationed equilibria. Hence one could say, adopting a controversial definition of 'Keynesian', that the conclusions have been anti-Keynesian in the sense that involuntary unemployment – viz. failure of the labour market to clear – seems to depend upon price rigidity – indeed, upon the rigidity of the wage rate relative to some other value, which might be money.

Another general remark is worth recording. Both the main assumptions that delineate temporary equilibrium theory from other kinds of equilibrium theory can be criticized as being somewhat arbitrary and lacking a form of justification in the behaviour and constraints of agents. In each case one is assuming that some kind of equilibrium is attained in which it would in principle be possible for agents to make mutually gainful trades, which opportunities are not exploited. This is obvious in the case of price rigidity. Suppose that the price of a certain good, which without loss of generality we can call 'hatpins', is set at such a level that there is an excess demand from would-be buyers, who are then rationed. This implies that some buyers would willingly pay more for their hatpins to have their allocation increased, and the sellers would then benefit by receiving a higher price. Why does this change not come about? This is a question on which fix-price theorists have been notably silent, but it is one that demands an answer for an economic theory that will carry conviction.

The same type of point applies, perhaps with less obvious force but nevertheless with some force, to the assumption that forward markets are absent. If A would like to buy hatpins forward, were a market to exist for forward purchase and sale of that commodity, and B would like to sell them forward, what stops them entering into a private arrangement to affect this transaction, hence partially creating the market? One can think of a number of handicaps to setting up these private trades, but they should ideally be in the model. Without them the assumption that no forward trading takes place is rather *ad hoc*.

Another assumption that needs to be questioned is that of fixed-price expectations. This has been common and its convenience is obvious, but it gives rise to some quite profound difficulties because one should explain something of how agents arrive at their expectations and how they are constrained in equilibrium.

What we want is clear in outline: price expectations should be reasonable. The argument that will follow throws light on what properties price expectations would have to have to be reasonable in an equilibrium situation. The upshot is to throw doubt on the traditional approach to temporary equilibrium in which agents are allowed to have different price expectations in equilibrium (even though we are concerned only with temporary equilibrium). Indeed, as is often the case, the only convincing specification turns out to be rational expectations of some kind.

Before explaining these ideas in more detail we shall survey the general equilibrium of Arrow, Debreu and others and its development in the direction of temporary equilibrium.

One of the most important results of economic theory in the last 25 years has been the formulation of the Arrow–Debreu model of general equilibrium. This model must be considered at a very abstract level and is not concerned with actual description at all. Rather, it is concerned with the purely logical task of showing that the independent behaviour of all economic agents connected only by a price system can be consistent. Such a high abstraction and generality is at the same time its strength and its weakness, and it is not at all surprising that the debate about whether it could constitute the appropriate logical framework within which to develop more descriptive and normative theories still divides economists.

The basic assumptions underlying general equilibrium models is that the price system gives full information to the agents, that all forward markets are open, so that decisions are taken once and for all at the beginning of all periods, and that inconsistency in plans can be eliminated instantaneously and without costs by price adjustments. It is not our task to discuss the validity of the latter assumption: perfect and instantaneous price flexibility can easily be assumed, since we are interested in equilibrium positions rather than in real economic dynamics. However, even inside this 'static' framework, general equilibrium analysis can be criticized for how it deals with the problem of time. In this paper we shall analyse the implications of rejecting the essentially timeless structure of the competitive Arrow–Debreu model on the existence of equilibrium and on the relative consistency of agents' plans.

If we drop the assumption that for all commodities at all period of time the corresponding market is open, so that agents, in formulating their plans, take into account in addition to the existing prices their own expectations on future prices, the identity between market-clearing positions and consistency in plans no longer holds. Furthermore, we could argue that if it is assumed, as in most temporary equilibrium models, that the market for trading claims on the present against claims on the future is perfect, this relationship can in general not even be defined. However, as has already been shown (Bliss, 1976), the *a priori* assumption of a perfect capital market in an uncertain world is illogical. One way of obtaining this important property is that the market imposes quantity constraints on agents' actions, even if all prices are flexible and all the existing markets are perfectly efficient. This can be done by introducing a set of reference prices constraining borrowers, which should reflect the market opinion about the future. By deriving a perfect capital market by means of the reference prices, we also open up the possibility of studying the relationship between market-clearing positions and consistency in individuals' plans at a disaggregated level; and therefore a new concept of equilibrium can be defined: the consistent temporary equilibrium, where all the existing markets are cleared and all the excess planned demands are equal to zero for all goods. This equilibrium displays rationing, as well as market efficiency by means of price flexibility; thus it corresponds neither to a full Arrow–Debreu intertemporal equilibrium nor to the notions of temporary equilibrium with quantity rationing as proposed by the recent literature inside a fix-price method of analysis.

The aim of this paper is to give a simple exposition of the notion of consistent temporary equilibrium, and in order to fulfil our purpose as clearly as possible we choose to describe the model step by step as it developed during the research. Having this in mind, the reader must not be surprised if the following pages look much more like a sequence of propositions, discoveries of illogicalities, new propositions and so on, rather than a conclusive model. Indeed, we must say that the proof of the existence of a consistent temporary equilibrium in its final version is not given here, as it would enormously increase the degree of difficulty of the paper because of the mathematical tools involved. Nevertheless, we think that the basic ideas can be understood even from this voluntarily limited exposition.

II TIME AND GENERAL EQUILIBRIUM

The simplest procedure to interpret general equilibrium theory in the context of time is to regard commodities at different dates as different commodities. In doing this it is not necessary to alter the general framework of the atemporal model. As a pure logical construction, it is in fact perfectly possible to suppose the existence of a market for each good, in which agents are all faced by the same price. In the case of future goods, transaction has to be seen as a delivery at a future date, and the price must be interpreted as the present quotation for future delivery. Formally, the difference between this intertemporal interpretation and the atemporal model is simply that the number of markets has been multiplied by the finite number of periods involved. Since all markets are open, there exists a complete set of prices which enable the agents to receive the perfect information they need for the formulation of their plans of action. In this sense, the introduction of time does not alter the world of complete certainty that characterizes the atemporal model of general equilibrium. Optimal consumption and production decisions are therefore chosen in the first period, and there is no necessity to revise them in the subsequent periods. The analogy between the atemporal and the intertemporal model is evident, and the existence of an equilibrium for the economy can be proved in a similar way. The equilibrium is defined as a situation in which all excess demands on all markets are less than or equal to zero, and since agents' plans depend only on the set of existing prices, it is clear that no inconsistency of plans is possible if those prices are equilibrium prices. An intertemporal equilibrium is always consistent, but of course in this context equilibrium and consistency are only two different definitions for the same situation.

However, one could argue that general equilibrium models do not capture an essential characteristic of time. In the real world time implies uncertainty, at least for the system as a whole, in the sense that most markets for future goods do not exist. Since consumption and production decisions are intertemporally defined, agents must replace the non-existing prices for future commodities by expectations, certain or probabilistic, and in general expected prices differ. Thus, agents' plans do no longer depend on the same set of prices, and even if the existing markets clear, consistency of future plans can only be a fluke.

III TEMPORARY EQUILIBRIUM

Temporary equilibrium analysis is an attempt to deal with more realistic assumptions and to confront directly the problems of short-run equilibrium in a world in which the future is uncertain. The dynamic process of an economic system where the available information is changing over time is reduced into a sequence of periods in which passing time does not influence economic decisions. Inside each single period the set of the open markets is not complete, in the Arrow–Debreu sense, so that part of the information about scarcity required by the agents is subjectively defined. Open markets are supposed to be perfectly efficient and prices adjust simultaneously. In the short run expectations, or their formation rules, are given and can be revised only with respect to the sequence of periods. At the beginning of each period agents form consumption and production plans involving current and future goods, on the basis of the existing and expected prices. A temporary or short-run equilibrium is defined as a situation where all the existing markets clear, even if the non-existent forward markets could display inconsistency in demands and supplies if those were to be realized. The link between the present and the future is supplied by a complete set of forward markets at least for one good, but their efficiency can guarantee only that in equilibrium the present value of the aggregate planned demand for future goods is equal to the present value of the aggregate planned supply. As the individuals' expectations about prices are arbitrarily given, nothing can be said about the planned excess demand for each good.

Before proceeding to details, we shall briefly analyse the relationship between equilibrium and consistency of plans with respect to an alternative definition of equilibrium: the equilibrium over time also due to Hicks (1965). An economy is said to be in equilibrium over time if in all periods all the existing markets are cleared and all expected future prices will be realized equilibrium prices in the subsequent periods, so that plans can continue to be executed without any revision. Such a definition of equilibrium implies of course consistency for all plans in all periods, but it also implies that expected prices are equal for all agents. This common belief can only be the result of an adjustment and cannot be explained inside a single period, since the basic characteristic of short-run analysis is indeed the absence of markets where these processes could take place. The adjustments in expectations could be adaptively linked to the simultaneous adjustment in current prices, but assuming this for all goods would not help us very much since an equilibrium situation would always present identity between current and future prices for the same good and all agents, preventing us from dealing with an equilibrium theory associated with the more realistic assumption of different beliefs about the future.

For the sake of simplicity we shall assume that the time horizon is divided into only two periods, the present denoted by the subscript 0, and the future by the subscript 1. Furthermore, we shall assume that there are no initial debts. This saves us from facing the problems in proving the existence of an equilibrium caused by speculation and bankruptcy. In a three- or more-period model it is in fact conceivable that agents act on the money market as speculators, if they expect the term structure of interest rates to vary. They can buy money only in the hope of selling it later and thereby gaining. As a consequence, the money excess demand function might not necessarily be continuous and bounded. Discontinuities may also arise from the fact that the initial distribution, if supposed to be the distribution of the debt of the previous period, can be inappropriate if the expectations from which it has been derived have been falsified, and therefore a temporary equilibrium might not exist without bankruptcy. These two phenomena are indeed very realistic aspects of a capitalistic economy, and their implications should be worth analysing. However, they are not concerns of this paper.

Suppose there are N goods, denoted by n ($n = 1, \ldots, N$), and T agents, denoted by i if they are households and by j if they are producers. In the present all current markets and a restricted set of forward markets are open; thus the ruling price vector in terms of a unit of account is $(\mathbf{p}_0)$. For simplicity of exposition we shall assume that only one element belongs to the set of forward markets, and one might think of the corresponding good as money. The choice of the good money can be arbitrary and does not depend on its intrinsic characteristics. This good comes to play a very important economic role. It becomes, in fact, the only possible link between the present and the future. By acting in this particular market, agents can transfer purchasing power from one period to the other by lending or borrowing, as an indirect way possibly for them to realize their future plans. In this section the money market is supposed to be perfect and the present price for future money is denoted by p_M. We shall criticize and relax this assumption in the following sections. In period 0 households and firms form consumption and production plans depending on the existing prices and on their beliefs of what future prices will be. They all face the price vector

$$(\mathbf{p}_0, p_M) \tag{1}$$

but taking into account also their expectations, denoted by

$$\mathbf{p}_1^{ij} \tag{2}$$

the relevant price vector for their choices becomes

$$(\mathbf{p}_0, p_M \mathbf{p}_1^{ij}) \tag{3}$$

Households' optimal plans (x_0^i, x_1^i) maximize their intertemporal utilities subject to the budget constraints, whereas firms' choices (y_0^j, y_1^j) maximize the present value of profits inside their production possibilities. By assuming strict convexity in preference and production sets and expression (2) as uniquely defined or a continuous function of $\mathbf{p}_0$, we can deduce that agents' optimal plans are single-valued and continuous functions of the current prices, including p_M. From these plan vectors only the first elements, i.e. x_0^i and y_0^j, represent realized market transactions, x_1^i and y_1^j being purely conjectural. Excess future demands and supplies for goods cannot be relevant economic signals except as aggregates through the money market, the only market in which agents show future intentions.

We can now generate demand functions on lines similar to those of static competitive general equilibrium theory. The only complication concerns the distribution of profits by firms – obviously, since the amount of profit a particular firm will make is a matter for conjecture. For simplicity we assume that firms distribute profits to their owners in period 1, the future. However, households conjecture what those distributions will be. If a firm makes a profit in the present in excess of its investment requirements, then it lends this surplus on the money market for later distribution. This way of treating profits, which is not essential to the argument, has the advantage that there is no profit distribution in the present. If a household expects to receive dividends in the future, it can borrow money in anticipation to finance present expenditure should it so choose. The assumption of course implies that households have a disincentive to save because they see firms as saving for them; on the other hand, firms are less inclined to borrow because they are re-investing profits in real assets or in bonds. This is not an unrealistic way of viewing the matter.

The agent's conjectural net transfer in period 1 is also a continuous and bounded function of the existing prices, and let us denote it by

$$D^{ij}(\mathbf{p}_0, p_M).\tag{4}$$

Solving the following maximization problems,

$$\max U^i(\mathbf{x}_0^i, \mathbf{x}_1^i)\tag{5}$$

subject to

$$\mathbf{p}_0\mathbf{x}_0^i + p_M\,\mathbf{p}_1^i\mathbf{x}_1^i \leqslant p_M D^i(\mathbf{p}_0, p_M)\tag{5a}$$

and

$$\max (\mathbf{p}_0\mathbf{y}_0^j + p_M\mathbf{p}_1^j\mathbf{y}_1^j)\tag{6}$$

subject to

$$(\mathbf{y}_0^j, \mathbf{y}_1^j) \in Y^j\tag{6a}$$

where Y^j represents the production possibility set, we can derive the optimal excess demands and supplies for current goods and money. The ith household transacts $\mathbf{x}_0^i$ in the current markets and its excess of future net expenditure over expected anticipated future profits on the money market; i.e.,

$$M^i = \mathbf{p}_1^i\mathbf{x}_1^i - D^i(\mathbf{p}_0, p_M).\tag{7}$$

If M^i is positive, the household is saving; if it is negative the household is borrowing. Its realized optimal plan is therefore (x_0^i, M^i), which is continuous on (p_0, p_M) and satisfies

$$p_0 x_0^i + p_M M^i = 0 \tag{8}$$

as it will not waste an opportunity to consume. Similarly, the producer, who is demanding or supplying future money if its present profits are either less or greater than its investment requirements, is characterized by an excess supply vector (y_0^i, M^j) continuous on (p_0, p_M) and satisfying

$$p_0 y_0^i - p_M M^j = 0. \tag{9}$$

The global excess demands in the existing markets are simply derived by aggregating with respect to the agents. Their sum in terms of unit of account will be zero, satisfying Walras' Law, i.e.

$$p_0 \left(\sum_i x_0^i - \sum_j y_0^j \right) + p_M \cdot \sum_i \sum_j M^{ij} = 0. \tag{10}$$

The correspondence between prices and global excess demands is obviously bounded and continuous, so that proving the existence of a temporary equilibrium for the economy becomes an easy task. Using a fixed-point theorem it can be shown that there always exists at least one non-negative price vector for which all global excess demands are less than or equal to zero.

However, it should be worth noting once more that consistency of future plans is neither a condition nor an implication of the existence proof. As long as they are only indirectly linked through the money market, the relationship between temporary equilibrium and consistency of plans cannot be explicitly defined.

IV CONSTRAINED TEMPORARY EQUILIBRIUM

In the previous section we supposed that the capital (money) market was perfect. In such a market, bonds issued by different firms and households were assumed to be perfect substitutes for each other and the amount of transactions depended on nothing but prices. However, although this can be a reasonable assumption for general equilibrium models, where agents have full information, in a short-run analysis, where uncertainty about the future can not be eliminated, the commitments of different agents are not homogeneous. Bonds can not be assumed to be undifferentiated goods, since the subjective riskiness that agents attach to them depends on their own information, and therefore may not be uniform. Dividing bonds into risk classes and assuming that for each class the corresponding market is perfect does not eliminate the illogicality, since such division can not be defined objectively. We are entitled to deal with a perfect capital market only if we can justify why agents having different information, and therefore different expectations about future prices, transact in it anonymously. In other words, we must explain why, for each transaction, the subjective belief about riskiness or any other characteristic is the same for all agents. An obvious step in the direction of easing this problem is to constrain agents somewhat. We propose here to put a constraint in the capital market which has to be conceived as a filter in realizing borrowing willingness. For the borrowers to be entitled to supply bonds, they must conform to a rule of financial prudence, which convinces lenders that the repayment will be guaranteed. Assuming this kind of constraint on borrowers' behaviour may not be very realistic, but it is not illogical. On the other hand, a perfect capital market in an uncertain world is no longer an assumption, but becomes a consequence. This approach has been developed in Bliss (1976). For the sake of simplicity we shall assume that each realized transaction in the capital market is seen as perfectly safe, but of course this is not a necessity for the method proposed to be valid. Furthermore, we shall notice that the guarantee of repayment may not be effective, since all we need is lenders' conviction that this will be the case.

As long as our analysis is confined inside one period of time and does not concern the sequence of periods, the possibility of failure in real repayment does not cause any problem. In this paper we suppose that loan applications are accepted, and therefore that lenders believe they are perfectly safe, if they are compatible with a set of reference prices, denoted by $\bar{p}_1$, which reflects the market opinion about what the future will be. Financial actions are accepted or refused according to whether the plans of borrowers evaluated at $\bar{p}_1$ are feasible or not. One should think of the market opinion as a kind of average of agents' beliefs, and therefore the value of the reference price vector should depend on all expected prices and current prices. It could be argued that the appropriate value to assign to $\bar{p}_1$ cannot be derived inside one single period, but should more realistically reflect agents' beliefs and price changes over time. In this context we should also take into account the fact that individuals' expectations might react according to the constraints they perceive in realizing their plans. So far we have not developed these possible extensions of the model. The main concern of our analysis is more essential, and does not depend on the specific values of p_1^{ij} and $\bar{p}_1$, so that we shall continue to consider them as arbitrarily given. We shall however come back to this problem later.

Introducing the above solvency requirement, consumers' and producers' optimal excess demands and supplies for current goods and future money are given by the solution of the following maximization problems: for the consumers (x_0^i, x_1^i) must satisfy

$$\max U^i(x_0^i, x_1^i) \tag{11}$$

subject to

$$p_0 x_0^i + p_M p_1^i x_1^i \leqslant p_M D^i(p_0, p_M) \tag{11a}$$

which is the usual constraint, and additionally subject to

$$p_0 x_0^i + p_M \{\bar{p}_1 x_1^i - D(\bar{p}_1)\} \leqslant 0, \qquad \forall i \tag{11b}$$

which is the market constraint, where $D(\bar{p}_1)$ is an estimate of their dividend incomes based on the reference prices. Putting constraints (11a) and (11b) together, the choice made by the consumer concerning his excess demand for future money must satisfy

$$\bar{p}_1 x_1^i \leqslant p_1^i x_1^i - D^i(p_0, p_M) + D(\bar{p}_1) = M^i + D(\bar{p}_1). \tag{11c}$$

Furthermore, we must assume that every consumer can always satisfy the market constraint; i.e., there always exists for each $\bar{p}_1$ at least one feasible plan for which the consumer does not need money for the future, so that the constraint (11c) is binding only in the case where the consumer is borrowing. If this will not be the case, his choice will be limited only by equation (11a).

The producers will choose (y_0^j, y_1^j) in order to

$$\max (p_0 y_0^j + p_M p_1^j y_1^j) \tag{12}$$

subject to

$$(y_0^j, y_1^j) \in Y^j \tag{12a}$$

and subject to

$$\bar{p}_1 y_1^j \geqslant - M^j, \qquad \forall j.\tag{12b}$$

The constraint given by (12b) means that the production plans must be perceived as feasible by the market; i.e., all the future profits evaluated according to the market opinion about future prices must be sufficient to guarantee the repayment of the commitments undertaken on the money market. Since complete inactivity or inactivity in the future are elements of the individuals' production sets, no further assumption is required in order to guarantee that the intersection between the sets of agents' and the market-feasible plans is not empty. In other words, there always exists at least one production plan that satisfies the market constraint.

We are now able to prove the existence of a constrained temporary equilibrium for the economy in a way similar to that followed for proving the existence of an unconstrained temporary equilibrium. In fact, the set of actions perceived as feasible by the market is convex, and if we also assume its uniqueness, its intersections (which always exist) with the agents' consumption and production sets are also convex. Thus, even if agents' choices are confined to these sets, the resulting realized demands and supplies for current goods and future money still maintain their properties of continuity with respect to the existing prices, and their aggregate sum in terms of value satisfies Walras' Law. Therefore the conditions for the existence of a fixed-point in the price correspondence are once more fulfilled.

Since the constraint imposed on the capital market through the reference prices concerns only the sets of feasible actions, it is clear that, as long as we assume market efficiency, all realized excess demands in equilibrium are less than or equal to zero, i.e., all the existing markets clear; and that from the equilibrium prices we cannot derive any information about the possible disequilibrium or inconsistency in future plans. However, in contrast to unconstrained temporary equilibrium, in this model prices are no longer the unique distributors of information, since it is reasonable to assume that in filtering borrowers' plans the market will acquire knowledge of their future intentions.

V A NECESSARY EXTENSION

Given the assumption of an increase in the available information, we can deal again with the problems concerning consistency in individuals' plans; and as an implication of the introduction of the reference prices we shall be able to reduce further the set of the possible constrained temporary equilibria by imposing some consistency requirements as well. Indeed, we shall say that such a development of the analysis becomes a logical necessity with respect to the assumptions that guarantee the capital market to be perfect. In fact, following the analysis proposed, and assuming that future expected prices might be different from agent to agent, we cannot retain all possible values of the reference price vector. The starting point of our analysis was that the capital market cannot be assumed to be perfect in a temporary equilibrium context. If we want to retain this property, it must be derived from other assumptions which do not contain illogicalities in themselves. We proposed the method of constraining borrowers' actions through reference prices, and we proved the existence of a constrained temporary equilibrium. However, in our simple two-period model, with market efficiency and given tastes and production possibilities, $\bar{p}_1$ can logically be assumed by the market to be future-ruling prices only if its estimation of future demands and supplies leads to consistency of plans. Therefore only in the case where future plans are expected by the market to be equilibrium future-realized supplies or demands can we continue to justify our derivation of a perfect capital market. In fact, if this were not the case, how could we affirm that all lenders perceive as perfectly safe bonds accepted by the market on the basis of $\bar{p}_1$ that will never be realized future prices? Thus it is necessary to develop the model, the constrained temporary equilibrium being based on a property of the capital market that we cannot prove in absence of consistency requirements.

VI CONSISTENT TEMPORARY EQUILIBRIUM

We have shown that, by constraining the capital market by means of reference prices, we do not upset the possibility that a market-clearing equilibrium will exist, and that in vetting the borrowers' plans the market receives the necessary information permitting it to become aware of the potential disequilibrium that will occur if these plans were to be realized. One should notice that the market does not obtain any information concerning the projected plans of lenders, since it would be absurd to suppose that they have to submit themselves to a test. In the following development it will be assumed that all borrowers are firms (and all firms borrowers), and all lenders are households, and in fact that all households are identical: in other words, we are thinking of a representative household. We also showed that, even if from a mathematical point of view $\bar{p}_1$ can be arbitrarily chosen, the internal coherence of the analysis requires that we can retain as equilibrium prices, besides those resulting from the market competition, only the reference price vectors that, if eventually the markets for future goods were open and, other things being equal, one of those vectors were effectively to provide the ruling prices, the resulting excess demands are less than or equal to zero in all markets. A situation characterized by a market-clearing vector (p_0, p_M) and $\bar{p}_1$ satisfying the above condition is defined as a consistent temporary equilibrium.

One should notice that the definition of consistent temporary equilibrium does not imply that, if in the present all agents were allowed to realize their plans, these would be necessarily consistent, since lenders' plans in no way depend on $\bar{p}_1$. Since they are not constrained by the market, their expected dividend payments may differ from the amount the market thinks they will receive, so that their future plans may be different from what the market thinks they will be able to realize. The consistency requirement must therefore be seen as the equality between what the borrowers will realize and what the market thinks the lenders will be able to realize. More precisely, the consistent temporary equilibrium analysis can be summarized as follows.

Assuming that the market vets borrowers' plans, for each value of the current prices it is possible to define what the firms' planned excess net supplies will be, i.e. what the values of

$$\sum_j y_1^j(\bar{p}_1) \tag{13}$$

are for each good.

On the other hand, if we expect for certain that the reference prices $\bar{p}_1$ will in effect be the future-realized prices, and if we assume that the tastes of the representative households are known and do not change, we can also calculate the future excess demands of households. In fact, since we already know what lenders have saved on the basis of their own expectations, and from the firms' plans we can derive what their dividend payments will be, we also know what amount of money the household will dispose of in the future. Let us denote these future excess demands by

$$\sum_i x_1^{im}(\bar{p}_1) \tag{14}$$

where the superscript m indicates that the values of (14) are market evaluations and do not necessarily correspond to what households have planned. As previously shown, since the market cannot expect $\bar{p}_1$ to be the equilibrium ruling prices in the future if

$$\sum_i x_1^{im}(\bar{p}_1) \lessgtr \sum_j y_1^j(\bar{p}_1) \tag{15}$$

the only rationing schemes we can logically use in the capital market are those characterized by $\bar{p}_1^*$ for which

$$\sum_i x_1^{im}(\bar{p}_1^*) = \sum_j y_1^j(\bar{p}_1^*). \tag{16}$$

In other words, the correct answer to the illogicalities of the *a priori* assumption of a perfect capital market can only be the consistent temporary equilibrium analysis.

It is easy to show that under the usual assumptions a consistent temporary equilibrium always exists. In fact, excess demands for present goods, future money and calculated excess demands for future goods all depend continuously on $(p_0, p_M \bar{p}_1)$, and since the households' dividends are evaluated by the market as if $\bar{p}_1$ will be realized prices in the future, they satisfy the following budget constraint:

$$p_0 \left(\sum_i x_0^i - \sum_j y_0^j \right) + p_M \bar{p}_1 \left\{ \sum_i x_1^{im}(\bar{p}_1) - \sum_j y_1^j(\bar{p}_1) \right\}$$
$$+ p_M \sum_{ij} M^{ij} = 0. \tag{17}$$

Under these conditions we can easily derive a price correspondence which has always at least one fixed point.

The analysis so far presented does not differ, in its technical aspects, from the usual general equilibrium models. This analogy holds also in what concerns the stability of such an equilibrium. In fact, let us suppose that p_0, p_M and $\bar{p}_1$ react to whether the corresponding excess demand is different from zero. Even if for future plans no market is open, we can suppose that a sort of efficiency characterizes the vetting of plans, in a way as if future plans were to be realized. It should be noted that we assume this kind of adjustment as instantaneous, so that no real time is involved and therefore there is no change in the available information. Furthermore, we assume that prices are expressed with respect to a *numéraire* (with positive price) and that the economy has the diagonal dominance property for all goods, except for the *numéraire*. This means that there is some units' vector in which to measure goods such that the diagonal terms of the matrix of the partials dominate (i.e. are greater in absolute terms) the off-diagonal terms. Let us denote this vector by **r** and suppose it to be strictly positive and independent of prices. If the economy has the diagonal dominance property, the Jacobian of the partials evaluated at the equilibrium prices has the Gale property. Since the *numéraire* price is positive we can deduce that the equilibrium is unique. As a consequence, if the dynamic rule is stable, the equilibrium for the economy is globally stable.

We suppose that the price adjustment rule is the following:

$$\frac{d}{dt} \cdot \begin{bmatrix} p_0 \\ p_M \\ \bar{p}_1 \end{bmatrix}_h = \dot{p}_h^* = 0 \quad \text{if } p_h^* \leq 0 \quad \text{and} \quad z_h(\mathbf{p}^*) < 0 \tag{18}$$

$$\dot{p}_h^* = \phi_h\{z_h(\mathbf{p}^*)\} = p_h^* z_h(\mathbf{p}^*) \qquad \text{otherwise}$$

where

$$z_h(\mathbf{p}^*) = \begin{bmatrix} \sum_i x_0^i - \sum_j y_0^j \\ \sum_{ij} M^{ij} \\ \sum_i x_1^{im}(\bar{\mathbf{p}}_1) - \sum_j y_1^j(\bar{\mathbf{p}}_1) \end{bmatrix}_h \tag{19}$$

and the subscript h denotes the good (including future goods), and ϕ_h is a sign preserving function with $\phi_h(0) = 0$, $\phi_h' > 0$. We are entitled to treat all prices and excess demands in the same manner because they all display the same properties of boundness, continuity and uniqueness, so that the same properties hold for $z(\mathbf{p}^*)$ with respect to $\mathbf{p}^*$. Therefore, since the similarity with general equilibrium models having the same characteristics is evident, it is not surprising if no specific interesting results will be obtained (cf. Arrow and Hahn, 1971). If we assume that the time-path of prices, given an initial positive position, is bounded and uniquely determined by the initial conditions, then there exists necessarily a convergent subsequence of it. The limit to which prices tend as time tends to infinity will therefore be equilibrium prices. Since our model is not a model of a pure exchange economy and production is explicitly taken into account, we must suppose that the *numéraire* is neither a produced good nor an input, and that an increase in the price of good h will decrease the output of good $h' \neq h$ if h' is produced by the economy, or decrease the demand for that good if it is not. Furthermore every good, including the *numéraire*, is demanded in positive amount at every set of prices and its excess demand is positive when the price is zero.

It would be very difficult to prove the stability of our equilibrium by solving the differential equation system (18) to obtain an explicit form of the solution path. Instead, it is possible to show stability from the existence of a continuously decreasing Lyapounov function, which in our case takes the following form:

$$L(\mathbf{p}^*) = \max \frac{p_h^*\{z_h(\mathbf{p}^*)\}}{r_h} \tag{20}$$

where r_h is the hth element of $\mathbf{r}$. Equation (20) is indeed a Lyapounov function. In fact, for all h for which

$$L(\mathbf{p}^*) = \frac{p_h^*\{z_h(\mathbf{p}^*)\}}{r_h} \tag{21}$$

the derivative of excess demands with respect to time (setting $z_{hh'}(\mathbf{p}^*) = dz_h(\mathbf{p}^*)/dp_{h'}^*$) is:

$$\frac{dz_h(\mathbf{p}^*)}{dt} = \sum_{h'} z_{hh'}(\mathbf{p}^*)\, \phi_{h'}\{z_{h'}(\mathbf{p}^*)\} \tag{22}$$

$$= \frac{\sum_{h'} z_{hh'}(\mathbf{p}^*)\, r_{h'}\, \phi_{h'}\{z_{h'}(\mathbf{p}^*)\}}{r_{h'}}$$

$$= z_{hh}(\mathbf{p}^*)\, r_h \,\frac{p_h^*\{z_h(\mathbf{p}^*)\}}{r_h} + \sum_{s>h'\neq h} z_{hh'}(\mathbf{p}^*)\, r_{h'}$$

$$\times \frac{p_h^*\{z_{h'}(\mathbf{p}^*)\}}{r_{h'}}$$

$$= z_{hh}(\mathbf{p}^*)\, r_h\, L(\mathbf{p}^*) + \sum_{s>h'\neq h} z_{hh'}(\mathbf{p}^*)\, r_{h'}\, L(\mathbf{p}^*) \qquad (23)$$

where s denotes the *numéraire*.

If the economy has the diagonal dominance property we have

$$|z_{hh}(\mathbf{p}^*)|\, r_h > \sum_{s>h'\neq h} |z_{hh'}(\mathbf{p}^*)|\, r_{h'} \qquad (24)$$

so that (23) must necessarily be negative at every non-equilibrium level of $(\mathbf{p}^*)$, and $L(\mathbf{p}^*)$ is always declining as long as the economy does not reach an equilibrium. Thus $L(\mathbf{p}^*)$ is a Lyapounov function and, under the assumptions made, the consistent temporary equilibrium is globally stable.

VII ANOTHER EXTENSION

It has been shown that under the usual assumptions a consistent temporary equilibrium always exists. However, in making such assumptions we are once more faced with problems arising from the internal coherence of the model. In fact, if, as a derivation of the increased information available to the agents, it is no longer possible to assume that the individuals' expected prices differ from the reference prices, the aim of our analysis, which is the study of situations where the future is uncertain and where agents hold different expectations, is unrealized. In other words, if the increased information owing to the market rationing forces the agents as a logical necessity to accept a common belief about the future, our analysis will essentially be reduced to a simple Arrow–Debreu model of intertemporal equilibrium. Given the very strict assumptions of the previous exposition, this seems to be the case. In fact, agents know $\bar{\mathbf{p}}_1$, and also know that whatever $\bar{\mathbf{p}}_1$ the market chooses, future plans will be consistent; we have already shown that only consistent temporary equilibrium positions can be retained. Thus, since agents accept efficiency for future markets, they cannot continue to believe that

$\mathbf{p}_1^{ij} \neq \bar{\mathbf{p}}_1$ will be the future realized price vector. In fact, if $\mathbf{p}_1^{ij} \neq \bar{\mathbf{p}}_1$ were to be hypothetical realized prices, they would never be equilibrium prices, because the already known inconsistency in plans associated with the assumed market efficiency would lead to a simultaneous adjustment in future prices when future markets are eventually opened.

At this stage, two possibilities are open. The first one is to reject the whole analysis and look for a different answer to the illogicality concerning the assumption of a perfect capital market. The second one is to retain the method proposed and to relax some assumptions of the original model in order logically to justify the difference between either the individuals' expected price vectors or between these vectors and the reference prices given by the market. We choose to follow the second way. As a conclusion of this paper we shall briefly expose the solution we gave to the above problem, without giving, however, the formal treatment of such an extended model.

VIII CONCLUSIONS

The obvious reason by means of which we can continue to justify the assumption that agents maintain different expectations in the consistent temporary equilibrium framework is that they may not accept as valid all the information the market offers. Suppose, for example, that firms expect households' tastes to change, and the market does not. In light of what has been previously said, their plans will be constrained by $\bar{\mathbf{p}}_1$, such that (16) is true if $\bar{\mathbf{p}}_1$ were to be realized. Firms, however, will think that the information about

$$\sum_i \mathbf{x}_1^{im}(\bar{\mathbf{p}}_1) \tag{25}$$

is wrong, and therefore will not accept $\bar{\mathbf{p}}_1$ as future equilibrium (realized) prices, even if from the market point of view this is perfectly correct. The fact that they are rationed on the basis of what they see as a wrong expectation will very likely change their original beliefs and therefore their plans, but this is not sufficient to guarantee that the final result of this kind of adjustment will lead to a common belief about the future. Such an iterative process can in fact generate a situation where $\bar{\mathbf{p}}_1$ and $\mathbf{p}_1^j$ are different, but the reasons that force them to adjust have disappeared. Of course, if the disequilibrium between virtual plans and realized plans could be helpful in explaining the dynamic of the system over time, its size should be defined only with respect to the final values of $\bar{p}_1$ and p_1'.

One way of introducing changes in consumers' tastes is to consider the model inside a stochastic context, where preferences and agents' endowments are defined as random variables depending on the state of the economic environment. Since the occurrence of a particular state is determined according to a probability law, subjectively defined, it is logical to conceive that the expected prices differ from $\bar{p}_1$, and that at the same time they are seen by the agents as future equilibrium prices. When eventually the economy moves to the next period, the values of the new equilibrium price vector will depend on which specific expectations have been fulfilled.

These considerations stimulate us to generalize the analysis and focus our attention on the conditions for which an equilibrium at one date gives rise to an environment compatible with an equilibrium at the next date. The analysis becomes sequential and more difficult. Pre-existing contracts and spot markets at every date are no longer compatible with the above simple formalization of the model, but at the same time strengthen the reasons for which the method proposed can be justified, reducing considerably the 'quasi-perfect' information about future plans that the market can perceive in the simple two-period model.

REFERENCES

Arrow, K. J. and Hahn, F. H. (1971) *General Competitive Analysis*, North-Holland, Amsterdam/Oxford.

Benassy, J. P. (1975) 'Neokeynesian Disequilibrium Theory in a Monetary Economy', *Review of Economic Studies*, pp. 503-23.

Benassy, J. P. (1976) 'The Disequilibrium Approach to Monopolistic Price Setting and a General Monopolistic Equilibrium', *Review of Economic Studies*, pp. 69-81.

Bliss, C. J. (1975) *Capital Theory and the Distribution of Income*, North-Holland, Amsterdam/Oxford.

Bliss, C. J. (1976) 'Capital Theory in the Short-Run', pp. 187-202 in *Essays in Modern Capital Theory*, ed. M. Brown, K. Sato and P. Zarembka, North-Holland, Amsterdam/Oxford.

Debreu, G. (1959) *Theory of Value*, Cowles Foundations, John Wiley, New York.

Grandmont, J. M. (1977) 'Temporary General Equilibrium Theory', *Econometrica*, pp. 535-72.

Hicks, J. R. (1937) 'Mr Keynes and the Classics', *Econometrica*, pp. 147–59.

Hicks, J. R. (1939) *Value and Capital*, Clarendon Press, Oxford.

Hicks, J. R. (1965) *Capital and Growth*, Clarendon Press, Oxford.

Keynes, J. M. (1936) *The General Theory of Employment, Interest and Money*, Macmillan, London.

Malinvaud, E. (1977) *The Theory of Unemployment Reconsidered*, Basil Blackwell, Oxford.

Radner, R. (1972) 'Existence of Equilibrium Plans, Prices and Price Expectations in a Sequence of Markets', *Econometrica*, pp. 289–303.

3

Aggregate Supply and Expected Demand Analysis in Keynes' General Theory: An Essay on the Micro-Foundations

CARLO CASAROSA*

I INTRODUCTION

The accepted formulation of Keynes' aggregate supply and expected demand analysis can be summarized with the help of figure 3.1, where Z and D are, respectively, the aggregate supply and expenditure functions.

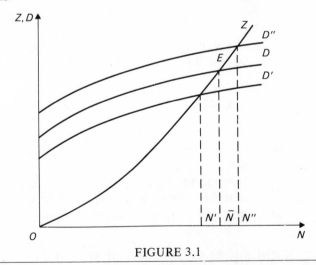

FIGURE 3.1

* I should like to thank Sir John Hicks for very helpful comments on an earlier draft. Needless to say, the customary disclaimer applies. Some of the results obtained in the present paper have been anticipated in a Note which appeared in *The Economic Journal*, March 1981.

Financial support by Consiglio Nazionale delle Ricerche (CNR) and British Council is gratefully acknowledged.

At every moment – so the story goes – the entrepreneurs realize the level of employment that corresponds to the point where the aggregate supply and expected demand functions are equal. The aggregate expected demand function is the entrepreneurs' expectation of the aggregate expenditure function. Therefore, if the expectations are right, the aggregate expected demand function of the entrepreneurs coincides with the aggregate expenditure function[1] and entrepreneurs realize the level of employment $\bar{N}$, which is the short-run equilibrium level of employment. On the other hand, if the expectations are wrong, the expected demand function is represented by curves such as D' and D'' and producers realize levels of employment such as N' and N''. However, the unwanted accumulation or decumulation of stocks that ensues in these cases induces the producers to revise their expectations and therefore their employment decisions. This process goes on until the expected demand function coincides with the expenditure function and employment reaches its short-run equilibrium level.

Working on the basis of the notion that the expected demand function is the entrepreneurs' expectation of the expenditure function, Patinkin has recently maintained that the Keynesian theory of effective demand is incompatible with the principle of profit maximization of marginal analysis. He has even suggested that Keynes' claim, that at the point of intersection of the aggregate supply and demand curves 'the entrepreneurs' expectation of profit will be maximized', should be deleted from the General Theory.

In the present paper it will be argued that:

(1) Keynes' aggregate supply and expected demand analysis is the extension to the system as a whole of the theory of the competitive firm;

(2) at the point of intersection of the aggregate supply and demand functions, the entrepreneurs' expectation of profit is maximized and therefore Patinkin's criticism is groundless;

(3) there is no microeconomic foundation for the idea that in a competitive (or atomistic) market the expected demand function is the entrepreneurs' expectation of the expenditure function.

II THE SHORT-RUN THEORY OF THE FIRM IN
THE GENERAL THEORY

Keynes accepts the Marshallian theory of the competitive firm and confines himself to some qualifications related to the concept of user cost. However, in order to be able to aggregate, he introduces the notions of aggregate supply and expected proceeds (demand) functions for the individual firm.

Keynes does not explicitly restate the theory of the firm in terms of aggregate supply and expected demand functions, but it is very easy to fill the gap. The aggregate supply function of firm i is:[2]

$$z_i = p_i^s y_i(n_i) \qquad i = 1, 2, \ldots, r \tag{1}$$

where: z_i = aggregate supply price, p_i^s = supply price of a unit of output, y_i = amount of output, n_i = level of employment. In the following we assume that the user cost is zero and the production function is 'well behaved' and has a maximum at $n_i = \hat{n}_i$. In perfect competition:

$$p_i^s = w/y_i'(n_i) \quad \text{for } 0 < n_i \leqslant \hat{n}_i \tag{2}$$

$$p_i^s(0) = 0.$$

Therefore, by substituting in (1) we get:

$$z_i = wy_i(n_i)/y_i'(n_i) \quad \text{for } 0 < n_i \leqslant \hat{n}_i \tag{3}$$

$$z_i(0) = 0.$$

From the assumptions about the form of the production function it follows that, in the interval $(0, \hat{n}_i)$, $z_i'(n_i) > 0$ and that, in the neighbourhood of $\hat{n}_i$, $z_i''(n_i) > 0$. Without loss of generality we assume that the aggregate supply curve of the firm is convex from below throughout (see figure 3.2).

As for the aggregate expected demand function, since the short-run expectations of the entrepreneur concern only the price[3] of his product, we have:

$$d_i^e = p_i^e y_i(n_i) \tag{4}$$

where: d_i^e = expected total demand (proceeds), p_i^e = expected price. From the assumptions about the production function, it follows that (4) is concave from below in the interval $(0, \hat{n}_i)$.

We can now formulate the profit maximization condition of the firm in terms of aggregate supply and expected demand functions.

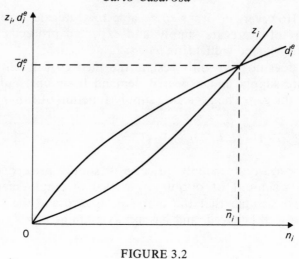

FIGURE 3.2

Expected profits, P_i^e, are given by:

$$P_i^e = p_i^e y_i(n_i) - wn_i.$$

Therefore, if $p_i^e \leqslant w/y_i'(0)$, the equilibrium level of employment is zero, while if $p_i^e > w/y_i'(0)$, it is given by the value of n_i that satisfies the equation:

$$p_i^e y_i'(n_i) - w = 0. \tag{5}$$

Hence, if the entrepreneur finds it convenient to produce at all, his profit-maximizing equilibrium condition can also be written as:

$$p_i^e y_i(n_i) = w y_i(n_i)/y_i'(n_i) \tag{6}$$

or, by substituting from (1) and (4), as:

$$d_i^e(n_i) = z_i(n_i). \tag{6'}$$

We may call the amount of employment that satisfies (6'), say $\bar{n}_i$, the equilibrium level of employment for the 'day'[4] and the value of the aggregate demand function that corresponds to it, $\bar{d}_i^e$, the 'daily' equilibrium level of the aggregate expected demand or 'effective demand' of firm i.

III THE 'DAILY' EQUILIBRIUM OF THE ECONOMIC SYSTEM

Given the price expectations of the firms, the 'daily' equilibrium level of employment for the whole economic system is:

$$\bar{N} = \sum_i \bar{n}_i$$

and the corresponding effective demand:

$$\bar{D}^e = \sum_i \bar{d}_i^e.$$

However, Keynes derives the 'daily' equilibrium value of employment and the corresponding effective demand in terms of aggregate supply and expected demand functions for the whole economy. That is, Keynes extends to the system as a whole the analysis employed to explain the decisions of the individual entrepreneur.[5]

If we assume that there are no production externalities, the aggregate supply function for the whole economy is simply the sum of the aggregate supply functions of the firms:

$$Z = \sum_i z_i = \sum_i \frac{w y_i(n_i)}{y_i'(n_i)} \tag{7}$$

where Z is the aggregate supply price for the whole economy.

In a situation of equilibrium the firms belonging to the same industry either do not find it profitable to produce at all or have the same supply price per unit of output. Therefore, assuming that the economy produces one commodity only, the distribution of total employment among the firms is uniquely determined and total production,

$$Y = \sum_i y_i(n_i),$$

is a differentiable function of N.[6]

By taking the first derivative of Y with respect to N and substituting into (7) we have:

$$Z = wY(N)/Y'(N) \tag{8}$$

and, in wage units:

$$Z_w = Y(N)/Y'(N) \qquad\qquad (8')$$

where $Z_w = Z/w$. Given the assumptions about the form of the individual production functions $Z'_w(N) > 0$ and, at least in the neighbourhood of

$$\hat{N} = \sum_i \hat{n}_i,$$

we have $Z''_w(N) > 0$. Without loss of generality we assume $Z''_w(N) > 0$ throughout (see curve Z in figure 3.3). We may call (8) the equilibrium aggregate supply function for the whole economy. From now on, when we speak of the aggregate supply function for the whole economy we mean the equilibrium supply function.

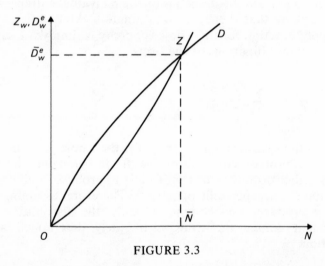

FIGURE 3.3

Let us now consider the demand side. The aggregate expected demand function for the whole economy is obviously the sum of the expected demand functions of the firms:

$$D^e = \sum_i d_i^e = \sum_i p_i^e y_i(n_i) \qquad\qquad (9)$$

and, if we assume that the entrepreneurs have identical price expectations, we have:

$$D^e = p^e \sum_i y_i(n_i) \tag{10}$$

where D^e is the aggregate expected demand price (or proceeds) for the whole economy.

The relation between D^e and N is not a function but a correspondence. However, since the aggregate expected demand function is simply a device to derive the level of employment which the entrepreneurs as a whole find convenient to realize, we assume that the distribution of total employment among the firms, which is implicit in the aggregate supply function, holds on the demand side as well. Consequently, the aggregate expected demand function for the whole economy becomes a differentiable function of total employment:

$$D^e = p^e Y(N) \tag{11}$$

and, in wage units:

$$D^e_w = p^e Y(N)/w \tag{11'}$$

where $D^e_w = D^e/w$. Given the assumption about the technology, it is clear that the first derivative of (11) is positive, while the second is negative (see curve D, in figure 3.3).

From the way we have derived our aggregate supply and expected demand functions for the whole economy, it follows that, if $p^e > w/Y'(0)$, the 'daily' equilibrium condition for the whole system is:

$$D^e(N) = Z(N)$$

and, in wage units:

$$D^e_w(N) = Z_w(N). \tag{12}$$

In fact, since the equilibrium condition for the individual firm is given by (6), for the economy as a whole we have:

$$\sum_i p^e_i y_i(n_i) = \sum_i \frac{wy_i(n_i)}{y'_i(n_i)}$$

ITHACA COLLEGE LIBRARY

which, given the assumptions that the firms have identical price expectations, is identical to (12).

We may call the value of N that satisfies (12) the equilibrium level of employment for the 'day' and the value of the aggregate expected demand function that corresponds to it, the aggregate effective demand for the whole economy.

On the basis of this formulation of Keynes' analysis it is easy to see that, contrary to Patinkin's view (1976, pp. 92–3), Keynes' proposition that at the point of effective demand the 'entrepreneurs' expectation of profit will be maximized' is clearly correct, not only in the sense that each entrepreneur maximizes his expected profits, but also in the sense that profits expected by the entrepreneurs as a whole are maximized. In fact, since profits expected by the entrepreneurs as a whole are given by:

$$P^e = p^e \, Y(N) - wN$$

they are maximized when:

$$p^e \, Y'(N) - w = 0.$$

At the 'daily' equilibrium position this condition is satisfied, for (12) can also be written as:

$$p^e \, Y(N) = w Y(N)/Y'(N) \tag{12'}$$

and therefore profits expected by the entrepreneurs as a whole are maximized.

Notice, however, that while the entrepreneurs' expectations of profit are maximized at every point of effective demand, these expectations are realized only when actual demand is equal to effective demand, as we shall see in the next section.

IV AGGREGATE EXPENDITURE FUNCTION AND SHORT-RUN EQUILIBRIUM

The theory of effective demand explains the 'daily' equilibrium level of employment on the basis of the price expectations of the producers. Now, if the actual market outcomes are as expected, the entrepreneurs have no reason to revise their price expectations and, hence, their employment and output decisions. Therefore the economic system can be said to be in its short-run equilibrium position. If, on the contrary, the actual market outcomes differ from the expected ones, the entrepreneurs revise their price expectations and, hence, their employment and output decisions.

In order to determine the short-run equilibrium position of the system and to show the interplay between the decisions of the producers and the decisions of the buyers, we must introduce the aggregate expenditure function, which describes the behaviour of consumers and investors. The problem here is that the level of income in wage units is a function both of the level of employment and of the price–wage ratio. Therefore, to obtain aggregate expenditures as a function of N only, we must specify, for each level of employment, the price–wage ratio.

It seems natural to choose the price–wage ratio that is implicit in the aggregate supply function. Under this assumption we have the aggregate expenditure function:

$$D_w = C_w(Y_w) + I_w \quad \text{with} \quad Y_w = Z_w(N) \quad \text{and} \quad 0 < C'_w < 1 \quad (13)$$

where: D_w = total expenditures, C_w = consumption expenditures, I_w = investment expenditures, all expressed in wage units. As for the shape of (13), assuming I_w constant, we have: $Z'_w(N) > D'_w(N) > 0$ (see figure 3.4, where D' is the aggregate expenditures function).

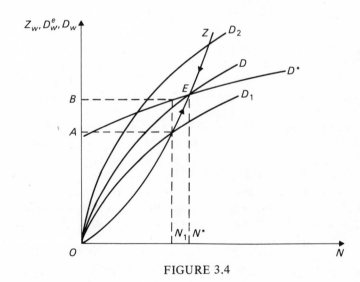

FIGURE 3.4

The condition of short-run equilibrium is clearly:

$$D_w = D_w^e = Z_w. \tag{14}$$

In fact, when (14) is satisfied, the expenditures that consumers and investors intend to make are exactly equal to the revenue expected by the producers. Therefore the latter have no reason to revise their price expectations and, hence, their employment and output decisions.

On the other hand, if $D_w \gtreqless D_w^e = Z_w$, the entrepreneurs' revenue expectations are proved wrong and therefore the entrepreneurs revise their price expectations and, hence, their employment and output decisions.

Given the shape of the aggregate expenditure and supply functions, the short-run equilibrium always exists,[7] even if there is no reason why it should imply full employment of labour.[8]

Is the short-run equilibrium stable? Keynes was not much interested in spelling out in detail how the system would work out of the short-run equilibrium. Therefore, in most of his analysis he assumed that the price expectations were always right, and hence he worked only with the aggregate supply and expenditure functions.

However, the mechanism of adjustment that Keynes had in mind can be briefly described as follows. Let us assume that the initial price expectations of the entrepreneurs are such as to determine the aggregate expected demand function D_1. On this basis the entrepreneurs realize the level of employment N_1 and expect to obtain a revenue OA from the corresponding output. But, at the level of employment N_1, consumers and investors would like to spend $OB > OA$. Consequently, the actual market price turns out to be higher than expected and, since the elasticity of price expectations of the producers can be assumed positive and less than unity, producers' stocks end up smaller than planned.

The 'surprise' registered in the first period brings about an upward revision of price expectations and therefore an upward shift of the expected demand function. At the new level of employment the gap between the expected demand of the producers and the intended demand of consumers and investors will be reduced. Therefore, we can conclude that the 'daily' equilibrium of the economic system converges over time to the short-run equilibrium unless there is a permanent overshooting.

A perfectly symmetrical process of adjustment is at work if the initial price expectations of the entrepreneurs are too optimistic.

V EXPECTED DEMAND FUNCTION AND
EXPENDITURE FUNCTION

From the above analysis it is evident that the aggregate expected demand and expenditure functions have completely different foundations and that they remain distinct even when the entrepreneurs' expectations are right. Yet, as we have recalled in the Introduction, the conventional account of the Keynesian theory views the expected demand function as the entrepreneurs' expectation of the expenditure function, so that, when the expectation is right, the expected demand function coincides with the expenditure function.

This interpretation of the expected demand function has been largely accepted since it has not been realized that its microeconomic implications are completely incompatible with the theory of the firm operating in an atomistic (let alone perfectly competitive) market. In fact, to obtain the expected demand function of the entrepreneurs as a whole, as an estimate of the aggregate expenditure function, we must assume that each producer is trying to guess the impact of his output and employment decisions on the demand function of the commodity he produces and hence on its price. And this implies that each firm has to make a guess on how the output and employment decisions of the other firms are related to its own decisions and on how consumers react to the output and employment decisions of the firms as a whole!

Now, these assumptions would make sense if the production of commodities were concentrated in the hands of only one or few producers, but they are wholly unacceptable for an atomistic market. Yet, something like this must be assumed at the micro-level to justify the conventional interpretation of the expected demand function.

The confusion between the expected demand function and the expenditure function has undoubtedly been favoured by the wording of the General Theory, where Keynes uses the same expression 'aggregate demand function' for both functions. But, whatever Keynes' responsibility, the notion that the expected demand function is the producers' estimate of the expenditure function is clearly a theoretical aberration which has strangely survived.

VI CONCLUSIONS

The main results obtained in our paper may now be summarized.

(1) The Keynesian short-run theory of the firm is a reformulation, in terms of aggregate supply and expected demand functions for the firm, of the Marshallian theory of the competitive firm.
(2) The theory of effective demand extends the analysis under (1) to the system as a whole.
(3) Keynes' claim that at the point of effective demand 'the entrepreneurs' expectation of profit will be maximized' is correct; however, profit expectations are realized only when the economic system is in short-run equilibrium.
(4) The point of effective demand (or 'daily' equilibrium) of the economic system is attracted towards the short-run equilibrium position, which is determined by the aggregate supply and expenditure functions.
(5) The aggregate expected demand function for the economy as a whole is *not* the producers' guess of the expenditure function; the two functions are distinct even when the entrepreneurs' expectations are right.

NOTES

1 See Davidson (1972, pp. 24-5, 116-18, 122-4); Millar (1972, pp. 604-8); Patinkin (1976, pp. 90-2); Weintraub, E. R. (1979, pp. 41-2); Weintraub, S. (1966, pp. 126-7); Wells (1978).
2 On this point Keynes (1936, pp. 44-5) is very clear.
3 See Keynes (1936, pp. 46-7).
4 In the General Theory the 'day' is defined as 'the shortest interval after which the firm is free to revise its decisions as to how much employment to offer. It is, so to speak, the minimum effective unit of economic time' (Keynes, 1936, p. 47, n.1).
5 The idea that Keynes' supply and expected demand analysis is simply an extension of the theory of the competitive firm to the system as a whole was first suggested by Vandenborre (1958, pp. 207-10). However, Vandenborre's derivation of the aggregate supply and expected demand functions was far from satisfactory. This issue has been examined in detail in a recent paper of mine: see Casarosa (1978, pp. 1379-83).
6 If the firms are identical the aggregate production function is clearly differentiable in the interval $(0, \hat{N})$, where

$$\hat{N} = \sum_i \hat{n}_i.$$

If the firms are not identical we can put:

$$N = \sum_i n_i \quad \forall i \quad \text{for which} \quad w/y_i'(0) < p^s$$

$$Y = \sum_i y_i(n_i) \quad \forall i \quad \text{for which} \quad w/y_i'(0) < p^s$$

(where p^s is the common supply price); and again we have that Y is a differentiable function of N.

7 The existence of equilibrium is ensured by the fact that $D^e(N)$ and $Z(N)$ are continuous and monotonic and that

$$\lim_{N \to \hat{N}} = p^e Y(\hat{N}), \quad \text{while} \quad \lim_{N \to \hat{N}} Z(N) = \infty.$$

8 The state variables of Keynes' model are the level of output and employment and the real wage rate. Therefore, the flexibility of the money wage rate is relevant to Keynesian unemployment equilibrium only in so far as the fall in the wage rate can influence the aggregate expenditure function. To deal with this problem, however, we need a wider model and therefore the issue will not be pursued here.

REFERENCES

Casarosa, C. (1978) 'Un contributo all'analisi dei fondamenti microeconomici della teoria keynesiana della domanda effettiva', *Rivista di Politica economica*, November, pp. 1371-409.

Davidson, P. (1972) *Money and the Real World*, Macmillan, London.

Keynes, J. M. (1936) *The General Theory of Employment, Interest and Money*, Macmillan, London.

Millar, J. R. (1972) 'The Social Accounting Basis of Keynes' Aggregate Supply and Demand Functions', *Economic Journal*, June, pp. 600-11.

Patinkin, Don (1976) *Keynes' Monetary Thought: A Study of Its Development*, Duke University Press, Durham, NC.

Vandenborre, H. (1958) 'An Integration of Employment Economics Within the Keynesian Theory of Money Flows', *Oxford Economic Papers*, June, pp. 205-19.

Weintraub, E. R. (1979) *Microfoundations*, Cambridge University Press.

Weintraub, S. (1966) *A Keynesian Theory of Employment, Growth and Income Distribution*, Chilton Co., Philadelphia.

Wells, P. (1978) 'In Review of Keynes', *Cambridge Journal of Economics*, September, pp. 315-25.

4

Breit, Kalecki and Hicks on the Term Structure of Interest Rates, Risk and the Theory of Investment

ALBERTO CHILOSI*

I INTRODUCTION

Marek Breit was a Polish economist of the 1930s, of the same generation of Lange and Kalecki, with both of whom he was closely associated in different periods of his brief professional career.

Born in Cracow in 1907 of a Jewish family, he got his PhD from that University in 1933, with a dissertation in monetary economics. He then went to Warsaw, where he worked, in close association with Kalecki and Ludwig Landau, in the Institute of Research on Business Cycles and Prices, which was directed by Edward Lipinski. His work at the Institute was interrupted in 1936, when, together with Landau, he was dismissed by finance minister Kwiatkowski, following a critical report they had written on the economic policy of the government. Kalecki, then in England, resigned, expressing his solidarity with Breit and Landau, and decided to stay abroad.

Breit could have very lively discussions with Kalecki even outside the Institute; but despite their friendship and their common socialist outlook, their backgrounds as economists were in fact very different.[1] Kalecki was self-taught (he never completed his university studies) and was in many ways eterodox. Breit had completed a regular university curriculum and had a firm background in the Mittel-European neoclassical economics of his age, even if, as we shall see,

* I would like to thank Tadeusz Kowalik for providing the biographical and bibliographical data on Marek Breit which are reported here, and Sir John Hicks, Giacomo Costa, Roberto Cippà and Carlo Casarosa for useful suggestions and encouragement. Of course, the above mentioned persons should not be held responsible for the contents of the present paper. Its final version was completed during a stay at St Antony's College, Oxford, which was financed under a British Academy/Wolfson Foundation research grant.

he had an innovating outlook and by no means accepted established academic teaching uncritically.

Unlike Lange and Kalecki, Breit was in Poland at the outset of the Second World War, and like so many Polish intellectuals of his generation, he was killed by the Nazis (in 1940). His main contribution is an article published in 1935 on the *Zeitschrift für National-ökonomie*,[2] which is notable for having introduced into the theory of credit and investment imperfect competitive considerations and for having stimulated the formulation of Kalecki's well-known principle of increasing risk. The other contribution for which Breit may be noted is his co-authorship of a chapter, written jointly with O. Lange (in Polish), entitled 'The Road to the Socialist Planned Economy' from a volume published by a group of young socialist intellectuals in Warsaw in 1934. This essay anticipates a number of aspects of Lange's model of a socialist economy of 1936–37, and at the same time presents a number of interesting features of its own, such as its concern with the model of a *self-managed* socialist economy.

II BREIT'S 'CONTRIBUTION TO THE THEORY OF THE MONEY AND CAPITAL MARKET

Breit's 1935 article originates in the framework of the Mittel-European monetary theory of the 1930s (namely, that kind of theory which H. S. Ellis surveyed in his lengthy 1934 book on *German Monetary Theory*). As a matter of fact, the only English economist cited is Hicks' 'Suggestion for Reconsidering the Theory of Money' and 'Gleichgewicht und Konjunktur'.[3] In those days Hicks was among the English economists especially close to continental economics (cf. Hicks, 1973, 1979). (This was to some extent a consequence of the fact that until 1935 he was at the London School of Economics, where under the chairmanship of Lord Robbins a certain symbiosis with continental economics was taking place, culminating with the nomination of Von Hayek to a chair. Later, *Value and Capital* was the mature outcome of Hicks' continental interests.)

The task that Breit sets for himself at the outset of his article is to arrive at an explanation of the relationship between short- and long-term interest rates. He starts with a lengthy discussion of Machlup's critical stand, in the background of Austrian capital theory, towards the approach, then allegedly common in monetary theory, of pairing short-run credit with the formation of circulating capital and long-run credit with the formation of fixed capital, at the same time believing that the two rates of interest become equal through some mechanism working on the side of the supply of credit. Breit's own approach is to shift the burden of the determination of the relationship between short and long interest rates on the side of the demand for credit, stressing the role performed by the possibility of substituting short and long credits for financing fixed investments, and so embracing what will later be called the 'expectation hypothesis', according to which long-run interest rates are ruled by expectations of short rates. Let us for simplicity abstract from the imperfectly competitive aspects of the credit market and so assume that the cost of credit is the same for everybody. Let us assume also that the same applies to expectation of future short rates. Then the rate of interest on long-run finance will not be higher in equilibrium than the cost of short-run finance plus transformation costs (where the latter are defined as the additional costs of using short-term credit for financing fixed investments, such as the costs of credit renewal, taking into consideration the future changes in short interest rates[4]), except when the 'whole demand until now satisfied on the capital market shifts to the money market' and 'the whole demand for formally long run credit'[5] disappear. Breit does not pay enough attention to the stock equilibrium aspects of the problem (as already expounded, in particular, in Keynes' *Treatise on Money*: Keynes, 1930, pp. 357ff.) and to how supply and demand of securities of different maturity affect the overall structure of interest rates; he is satisfied with considering the equilibrium conditions of the investors in fixed capital.[6] On the other hand, he goes beyond the usual simplifying 'hypothesis of a completely free credit market', in the sense that the conditions of credit are independent of the quality of the borrower and of the amount borrowed, as well as of the source from which finance is drawn.[7] Instead, he assumes that the cost of credit increases with its amount and that this happens with respect to each of the two markets in which the credit market is considered to be segmented. Therefore, the investor willing to undertake an investment project usually first draws credit from the capital market, until the individual rate of interest so increases that it pays to turn to the money market for financing long-term investment, because the short-term rate of interest plus transformation costs has become lower than the long-term rate. Once both the marginal short rate plus transformation costs and the long rate cease to be lower than the marginal rate of return, the investor ceases to invest. On the other hand, the possibility of the long rate being higher from the outset, because of additional risks, than the short rate plus transformation costs that applies to the last amount of credit borrowed by the investor is by no means excluded (and plays for Breit an important role in the slump). It should be noted that, following the assumption that each individual faces an individual interest curve on both markets (namely, a curve that gives the rate that the individual borrower must pay for the different amounts of credit), what enters in the transformation costs are not just the expected future short rates of interest, but 'the expectations of positive or negative changes of all elements that decide on the course of the individual interest curve'. According to Breit (1935, p. 642), it will be possible, 'taking into consideration a coefficient which corresponds to their probability', to translate these expectations 'in the form of a corresponding premium, namely in form of costs'.

The reasons why the individual rate of interest increases with the amount of credit drawn by a single investor is basically that the lender (identified by Breit as 'the bank') 'sees a close correlation between the height of his risk and the volume of the credit' (Breit, 1935, p. 641). Breit does not elaborate much on this point, but he does imply the fact that under imperfect competition the conditions of sale worsen with the amount produced and that therefore the probability of having an unfavourable outcome for a given invest-- ment project increases with its size.[8] Moreover, a further explanation is the division of risk on the part of the creditor 'among different firms and sectors' (Breit, 1935, p. 641). Beyond a certain ceiling the investor cannot borrow further resources, at any price.

From the above considerations, one could arrive at the positive effect of the accumulation of wealth on investment that characterizes Kalecki's theory of investment, and at some further conclusions, which we will consider later on, by considering the guarantee that the wealth of the borrower represents for the lender, and the fact that, potentially at least, the amount borrowed and invested is consequently bound to be an increasing function of the wealth of the investor. However, this circumstance is not mentioned by Kalecki because he concentrates his attention on the risk of the borrower, rather than, as in Breit's case, on the risk of the lender. For Kalecki, in fact, 'there are two reasons for the increase of marginal risk with the amount invested. The first is the fact that, the greater the investment of an entrepreneur, the more his wealth position is endangered in the event of unsuccessful business. The second reason making the marginal risk rise with the size of investment is the danger of "illiquidity"' (Kalecki, 1937, p. 442).[9] For Kalecki, therefore, the increasing risk influences the amount invested directly through broad considerations of portfolio selection on the part of the investor, while for Breit the influence works indirectly, through the increase in the rate of interest with the amount borrowed. Kalecki refers to Breit in his 1937 article on the principle of increasing risk, when he states that 'if, however, the entrepreneur is not cautious in his investment activity, it is the creditor who imposes on his calculation the burden of increasing risk charging the successive portions of credits above a certain amount with rising rate of interest' (Kalecki, 1937, p. 442). However, this point is not raised further by him in that article.[10] In fact, even without considering the imperfections in the credit market, and so without departing too much from the traditional approach, Kalecki is able to arrive at a number of conclusions which, with some further reasoning, could also be reached in Breit's framework, provided that the guarantee that the wealth of the borrower represents for the lender were taken into account. These conclusions are that the amount of financial resources that are drawn upon depend on the wealth of the investor because, 'the smaller is the own capital of an entrepreneur investing the amount k, the greater is the risk he incurs', so that 'the own capital is a "factor of investment"', (Kalecki, 1937, p. 443), and that, given the total or partial assimilation that Kalecki makes between capitalists, savers and entrepreneurs, savings have a positive effect on investment decisions because they bring about an increase in overall entrepreneurial wealth.[11] The above also explains why 'in a given industry at the same time large and small enterprises are started' (Kalecki, 1937, p. 442).

III RISK AND INVESTMENT IN THE SLUMP

The consideration of increasing risk allows Kalecki to solve the problem, raised in 1936 in this review article on the General Theory, of determining the size of investment projects in the case of constant returns to scale and conditions of perfect competition, a problem that remains open in Keynes, in so far as 'Keynes' theory determines only the level of investments *ex post* and does not say anything about the investments *ex ante*'.[12] It is interesting to note that in his review article Kalecki was pointing to a 'certain special hypothesis relating to entrepreneurial psychology' (Kalecki's way) or to a 'hypothesis of imperfection of the money market' (Breit's way) as the way of solving that problem.

Breit himself was concerned more with analysing the monetary factors of business cycles in general and of the slump in particular. During the latter, even if the prime rate for short-run credits is low, the amount of credit that can be obtained at that rate is greatly reduced and 'the individual interest curve' increases sharply because of the 'diffidence and mistrust' that 'dominate during the slump' (Breit, 1935, p. 651). Moreover, the gap between the prime rates on money and capital markets is particularly high, especially as a consequence of the particular impact of the risks of an 'objective' nature on long-run credit. (While the risks of 'subjective' nature 'act differently on the different economic units', 'objective risks are valued by their very nature nearly equally by all economic subjects'. The first 'determine the level where the overall supply curve starts; its further shape on the other hand is determined through the subjective risks': Breit, 1935, p. 647). Moreover, the short rate is only *apparently* low, because, in the case of borrowing short for financing the formation of fixed capital, the corresponding transformation costs are particularly high, 'following in particular the pessimistic view of the borrower with respect to the behaviour of rationing coefficients for the immediate future' (Breit, 1935, p. 650).[13]

Furthermore, the impact of risks is increased by the fact that they act twice, once on the supply curve of credit, and again on the demand curve for financing investments, so that risk is counted twice. This happens in case the borrower believes that he will repay his debt independently of the outcome of his project and the lender believes that he will be repaid only in case of a successful outcome. But even under less extreme assumptions the risk inherent in the project is usually counted more than once. During the slump 'the increase of the investment risks not only brings about an upward shift of the lower bound of the schedule of credit supply, but acts towards a reduction of the net profitability of enterprises', in so far as 'the entrepreneur must deduct from the anticipated profitability a corresponding premium for the expected risks. In this way, on *both sides* of the relationship between profitability and rate of interest the increase of risks brings about a simultaneous deflationary pressure on economic life' (Breit, 1935, pp. 654–5). It is interesting to note that in the General Theory this 'duplication of a proportion of the entrepreneur's risk, which is added *twice* to the pure rate of interest to give the minimum prospective yield which will induce the investment', is formulated in a very similar way. Keynes however came over to the same idea as Breit, independently; in fact, he asserts that 'this duplication of allowance for a portion of the risk has not hitherto been emphasized, so far as I am aware' (Keynes, 1936, p. 145).

The consideration of risk and of its variation in the course of the business cycle assumes in Breit a paramount importance, allowing him to reach conclusions that have a distinctive Keynesian flavour. He advocates public investments as a means of overcoming the slump – not because of their multiplicative effects, which Breit does not recognize, but because they bring about a reduction of objective risks and increase the profitability of existing enterprises, so that 'if the shock is strong enough the conjuncture develops itself already automatically along an increasing curve' (Breit, 1935, p. 658). The reason why this happens is that through public investments 'new, previously idle means of the credit market' are put into operation and 'in this way a new demand, that previously did not exist in the economy, is originated':

> [This,] as any new demand, shapes optimistically entrepreneurial expectations . . . and diminishes considerably the risk of investment in so far as it brings about a stabilization of delivery conditions, an improvement of solvency, the disappearance of general uncertainty, etc. In this way both the short as well as the long-run interest rates are reduced (even if the latter are reduced to a greater extent) and the net profitability (namely the profitability less the risk premium) increases to a greater extent. If the effect is strong enough, previously unprofitable combinations . . . become profitable, and in correspondence of the changed relation between the equilibrium rate and the current rate of interest a cumulative upward Wicksellian process sets in. (Breit, 1935, p. 657)[14]

Breit's considerations on risk also explain why during the slump 'the relationship of investments financed with own means to the investments which are fed with borrowed capital, seems . . . incomparably higher than in the other phases of the business cycle', in so far as, 'if the entrepreneur invests his own capital, . . . he calculates the risk only once, *and not twice*' (Breit, 1935, pp. 655–6). This intrinsic difference between own and borrowed funds, which, as Breit remarks, goes against 'the basic principle' in economic theory of 'the complete identity of own and borrowed capital', is another way that leads directly to the positive influence that savings have on entrepreneurial investment in Kalecki, and, at the same time, to his conclusion that 'business democracy where anybody endowed with entrepreneurial ability can obtain capital for starting a business venture' is an illusion, and that 'the most important prerequisite for becoming an entrepreneur is the *ownership* of capital' (Kalecki, 1954, pp. 94–5).

NOTES

1 An echo of the debates between the 'subjectivist' Breit and the 'objectivist' Kalecki can perhaps be perceived in Breit's polemical stand against 'object-ivism, which is contrary to economic theory' and in defence of the 'much more important side of subjective calculation'; these remarks in fact could be applied to much more recent debates (see Breit, 1935, pp. 637–8).

2 An Italian translation, with an introduction by the present author, has been published in the *Rivista Internazionale di Scienze Sociali,* no. 3, 1980.

3 See Hicks (1935 and 1933). The influence of section III of the latter paper, 'Risiko und Geld in Konjunkturablauf', on Breit's essay can be clearly perceived.

4 The concept of transformation costs can be illustrated as follows. Let us suppose that an entrepreneur considers undertaking an investment project $x = (x_0, \ldots, x_i, \ldots, x_T)$; $x_0 < 0$, $x_i \geqslant 0$, $i = 1, \ldots, T$. Let us suppose also that finance can be borrowed either long, for T periods, or short for 1 period, and that each credit renewal brings about a fixed cost a.

   Suppose the expected short rate of interest prevailing at time i is r_i and the long-run rate of interest is r.

   In the case of short-run financing, the effective rate of interest charged on the investment costs in the T years period is the positive solution r_L to:

$$V_T = -x_0 (1 + z)^T$$

where

$$V_T = -x_0 (1 + r_0) \ldots (1 + r_{T-1}) + a\{(1 + r_1) \ldots (1 + r_{T-1})$$
$$+ (1 + r_2) \ldots (1 + r_{T-1}) + \ldots + (1 + r_{T-1})\}.$$

   In the case of unchanged short-run rate and no transaction costs the effective rate of interest is r_0. Transformation costs may be defined as $r_t = r_L - r_0$. If $(r_0 + r_t) < r$ Breit's investor prefers short-run, otherwise he prefers long-run, finance; in the case $(r_0 + r_t) = r$ this happens because of the advantage presented by the certainty of the rate of interest applied. On the other hand, one may point (as Breit does not) to the greater flexibility of short-run finance, in so far as it allows the indebtedness to be reduced by utilizing the returns to the investment or makes easier to truncate, if possible, the process before reaching the Tth year. (Following Breit, we suppose here that the only forward markets are either for short or long lending.) Of course, a more complete and up-to-date discussion of the problem would require among other things a better specification of investors' preferences and of the nature of their expectations. Here we can content ourselves with expounding Breit's own viewpoint.

5   Breit (1935), p. 648. In the footnote on p. 643 Breit also discusses the case in which it pays to the entrepreneur to utilize long-run credit for financing short-run production. On the other hand, in the text he abstracts, for simplicity, 'from the demand for long-run finance that is based on the production of circulating capital' (p. 644).

6   Nor does Breit consider the possibility of selling one's credit. An explanation of the differences in approach lies perhaps in the different role performed by financial markets and by banks in financing capital formation in Great Britain and in central Europe, and in the much greater role performed by the financial market in the economy of the former. This corresponds to the fact that Breit, instead of speaking of the 'lender', speaks of the 'bank' (see below).

  For getting to Breit's conclusions one should assume that only new credits can be negotiated, that no old ones can be sold, and that debts can be repaid only at maturity. In this way the changes can occur only at the margin, so that the problem reduces to one of flow.

7   Breit (1935), p. 640. In the framework of 'a completely free credit market' and of a model of general economic equilibrium, a solution to the issue of the term structure of interest rates could be found four years later in Hicks' *Value and Capital.* On the other hand, on pp. 143-4 of that work Hicks points to the case that the credit market 'is not completely free' and the rate of interest increases with the amount borrowed. However, he does not develop this hint any further.

8   An analogous argument is considered by Kalecki as a possible explanation of the decrease in the marginal efficiency of investment with the amount invested (Kalecki, 1937, p. 441; cf. also Kalecki, 1954, p. 91).

9   It should be noted that the first reason refers implicitly to risk aversion on the part of the investor (his having a concave utility function), so that the gap between the marginal efficiency of investment and the rate of interest is eventually not enough to compensate for the increased possibilities of losses as the size of investment increases. On the other hand, the second reason ('illiquidity') translates itself in the greater danger of having to resort to borrowing at higher rates of interest in the future if 'too much credit has been taken', and so in a mutuation in this respect of Breit's framework. It should be noted that, as a matter of principle, the 'danger of "illiquidity"' could also be translated into the increased probability of being insolvent and of bankruptcy. This possibility, which is not explicitly taken into consideration by Kalecki, plays an important role, as we shall see, in Breit's treatment of risk.

10 On the other hand, in Kalecki (1954) the influence that the amount of entrepreneurial capital has 'on the capacity to borrow capital' figures on a par with increasing risk in limiting the size of enterprises (p. 92).

11 Cf. Kalecki (1954), p. 98. The assimilation between entrepreneurs, capitalists and savers is complete in his earlier works. In the *Theory of Economic Dynamics,* he simply assumes that 'the gross savings of firms. . . are related to total gross private savings' (p. 97).

12 Kalecki (1936), p. 25. An Italian translation of Kalecki's review article of *General Theory* can be found in Chilosi (1979), pp. 203-15.
13 It can be seen, therefore, that risk factors, alongside of the expectations of future short interest rates, were playing an important role in Breit, as they did later on in Hicks' *Value and Capital* (chapter 11, section 4), for explaining the relation between short and long interest rates.
14 One may compare Breit's reference to Wicksell cumulative process to Kalecki's in Kalecki (1936), p. 25, and Kalecki (1937), p. 445.

REFERENCES

Breit, M. (1935) 'Ein Beitrag zur Theorie des Geld-und Kapitalmarktes', *Zeitschrift für Nationalökonomie*, pp. 632-59.
Breit, M. and Lange, O. (1934) 'Droga do socjalistycznej gospodarki planowej', *Gospodarka-polityka-taktyka-organizacja socjalizmu*, Plomenie, Warsaw; reprinted in Lange, O. (1973), *Dziela*, vol. 2, PWN, Warsaw, pp. 164-83.
Chilosi, A. (ed.) (1979) *Kalecki-Antologia di scritti di teoria economica*, Il Mulino, Bologna.
Ellis, H. S. (1934) *German Monetary Theory*, Harvard University Press, Cambridge, Mass.
Hicks, J. R. (1933) 'Gleichgewicht und Konjunktur', *Zeitschrift für Nationalökonomie*, pp. 441-55.
Hicks, J. R. (1935) 'A Suggestion for Simplifying the Theory of Money', *Economica*; reprinted in Hicks, J. R. (1967) *Critical Essays in Monetary Theory*, Clarendon Press, Oxford, pp. 61-82.
Hicks, J. R. (1973) 'Recollections and Documents', *Economica*, pp. 2-11.
Hicks, J. R. (1979) 'The Formation of an Economist', *Banca Nazionale del Lavoro Quarterly Review*, pp. 195-204.
Kalecki, M. (1936) 'Pare uwag o teorii Keynesa', *Ekonomista*, pp. 18-26.
Kalecki, M. (1937) 'The Principle of Increasing Risk', *Economica*, pp. 440-7.
Kalecki, M. (1954) *Theory of Economics Dynamics*, Allen & Unwin, London.
Keynes, J. M. (1930) *A Treatise on Money*, vol. II, Macmillan, London.
Keynes, J. M. (1936) *The General Theory of Employment, Interest and Money*, Macmillan, London.

5

Temporary Equilibrium with Rationing

ROBERTO F. CIPPÀ and VINICIO GUIDI*

I INTRODUCTION

The modern theory of general equilibrium was first initiated in the 1930s with the classical articles of Wald (1936), and received its general and complete formulation with the works of Arrow and Debreu (1954), Debreu (1959) and McKenzie (1959). In this paper we discuss the Arrow–Debreu–McKenzie (A–D–M) model,[1] which, with its modifications, extensions and criticisms, forms the basis of the relevant part of the research, theoretical and applied, on the subject subsequently developed. Some short indications of its logical and analytical structure will be dealt with in the following section. In the third section, we shall discuss the most important innovations and developments that have been suggested to the original model and, in particular, we shall introduce the concept of a temporary equilibrium[2] and of equilibrium over time.[3] We shall shed light on some of the most striking limits of the theory. Finally, in the last section, we shall discuss critically some alternative models, specifically the models of temporary equilibrium with quantitative rationing, which have been recently elaborated.

II THE GENERAL EQUILIBRIUM MODEL

Basic assumptions
In the A–D–M model[4] there is a finite number of economic goods and agents, who can act either as consumers or as producers. The

* We are indebted for suggestions and comments on the first draft of this paper to Christopher Bliss of Nuffield College Oxford, and to Professor Piero Tani of the University of Florence. Especially appreciated were the remarks of all the participants in the seminar held in Trinity term 1979. Cippà's research has been supported by the Swiss Science Foundation.

former have a convex consumption set, whose elements are ordered on the basis of a complete, transitive convex and continuous preference relation. Each consumer has a strictly positive endowment of goods or productive factors, and also receives a share (which can also be equal to zero) of the profits earned by each firm. Firms are characterized by a certain production set which may show limited phases of increasing returns to scale, but such returns must be excluded at the level of social production; it is possible for a firm to be inactive. However, at the social level, it is impossible to produce something from nothing. The consumers choose commodity bundles that maximize their utility under the constraint of the budget, defined on the basis of given prices. Firms choose those combinations of inputs and outputs which, at the same prices, yield the highest profit under the constraint of the available technology. All these decisions must be carried out simultaneously; i.e., their algebraic sum must be equal to the existing resources.

The economy described by the A–D–M model is an 'atomistic' economy of perfect competition, whose agents behave as 'price-takers'. Under the assumptions made, a system of prices exists, which assures the compatibility between the supply and demand for each good (utilizing Brouwer's, or Kakutani's version, fixed-point theorem). The key elements are the parametric role of prices and their identity for the different economic agents. Other important elements are the knowledge of prices and the absence of transaction costs. It is also proved that each competitive equilibrium is a Pareto optimum and, vice versa, that for each Pareto optimum it is possible to allocate the available resources in such a way that there is a price system relative to which that optimum is a competitive equilibrium.

In order to assure the uniqueness and the stability of the equilibrium, one has to introduce some additional assumptions.[5] To date, the necessary conditions to assure uniqueness have not been found, although there are many sufficient conditions, among which the most significant is diagonal dominance.[6]

Dynamic adjustment
The problem of the stability of an economic system cannot be taken into consideration without an analysis of the dynamic adjustment process. In the A–D–M model one supposes that prices react to the excess demand, different from zero, and that the changes are accommodated by the auctioneer instantaneously.[7] Besides, no transaction is carried out when the transactions cannot be realized simultaneously (process of *tâtonnement*).

The adjustment process is said to be globally stable if every economic path approaches an equilibrium. In this case, if the equilibrium is unique, then that equilibrium is globally stable. An equilibrium is said to be locally stable when the stability of the economic system is assured for small deviations from equilibrium. Finally, a process is quasi-globally stable if every solution path approaches the set of equilibria of the economy through a Lyapounov function: after a sufficiently long lapse of time we are sure that the solution path is in the neighbourhood of an equilibrium, but it is not possible to select any particular equilibrium for which this is true.

For the stability analysis the most frequently used assumption, apart from the diagonal dominance, is gross substitutability. Such hypothesis is formulated on the aggregate demands without an explanation of what properties, in terms of preferences, technology or endowments (primitive data of the model), would give rise to it.

By distinguishing the goods according to their physical characteristics, the availability date, and availability location and the state of nature on the occurrence of which their existence depends, it is possible to extend the atemporal and certainty model to the intertemporal and uncertainty analysis (Radner, 1968, 1974; Malinvaud, 1961). The extension, however, is not costless. In fact, it is well known that, in the case of infinite temporal horizon, a competitive equilibrium is not necessarily intertemporally efficient: in the case of proportional growth paths, we know from Malinvaud (1953), Phelps (1965) and Starret (1968) that a sufficient condition is that the interest rate is higher than the growth rate.

III CHANGES AND EXTENSIONS

The removal of the assumption of the existence of competitive forward markets for all goods except one (which is assumed to perform as money) and their replacement with a vector of prices expected by each economic agent (the expectations can be, and generally are, different for the different agents), allow us to introduce the concept of temporary equilibrium. Each agent chooses his own plan of action on the basis of his price expectations and of the constraint of the past decisions and available possibilities. The only transactions carried on are those for current commodities and money. The equilibrium, which occurs only on current markets, is named temporary and does not necessarily imply the co-ordination of the expectations.[8]

The equilibrium over time is defined within the framework of sequences of temporary equilibria. At the beginning of each period the economic agents reformulate their expectations[9] and the equilibrium is obtained when all the prices, in each period, are those expected previously (Hicks, 1939, 1965). Another interpretation of the equilibrium over time is that of a situation in which both prices and quantities remain constant; such equilibrium is called stationary. It is, however, difficult in a world dominated by uncertainty, to suppose that the economic quantities remain unchanged over time. Therefore the concept of stationarity, in a statistical sense, seems much more appropriate.[10] Usually in such an analysis, one supposes that, within each period, prices react instantaneously to the fluctuations of the supplies and the demands; but if the speed of price adjustment is finite, it may well happen that, before the temporary equilibrium is reached, the economy has already shifted to the following period and therefore to another state of nature. In this case we could observe an incomplete and repetitive kind of adjustment: the economy would always (or almost always) be in a situation of disequilibrium and demand would never be equal to supply on all markets. On the whole, such a stochastic process could, however, be considered an equilibrium in the sense that it could be stationary (Green, 1973; Radner, 1974).

The sequential analysis of the economic process allows us to introduce money,[11] financial markets, the stock exchange,[12] etc. A condition for the existence of the equilibrium in a monetary economy is that money has a positive exchange value (Hahn, 1965), even if it has no value in itself. Grandmont (1974) (see also Stigum, 1969) shows that the short-period price of money is positive under the condition that the expected price for future money is positive, regardless of the current observable prices. The same result can be obtained when the agents wish to transfer their wealth in the future, and money is both a store of value and an institutional means of exchange (Hool, 1976). Also, it becomes possible to introduce specific agents, such as banks, which grant credits and act with open market operations (Grandmont and Laroque, 1975, 1976a).

Within the framework of the temporary equilibrium attempts have also been made to take into account the capital goods or the bonds (Arrow and Hahn, 1971, p. 137; Bliss, 1976). The problems arising in this context, among the others, are as follows:

(1) The economic agents, having different expectations about future profits, give a subjective estimation of the value of the firms.

(2) Each firm faces, in each period, a budget constraint which must be met (bankruptcy problem).
(3) Share-holders can be at variance with the managers.
(4) The distribution of profits at the beginning of the period or in future times is no longer indifferent.
(5) The issue of new shares or bonds is no longer bounded.[13]

The consequences of these five cases usually bring forth discontinuities in the model, hence the present impossibility to prove the existence of an equilibrium with the known techniques. These difficulties have been solved partly, but a general and satisfactory solution has not yet been proposed.

The introduction for some agents of a demand (supply) function that binds the quantities that can be sold (bought) on the market to the prices has made it possible to handle non-competitive situations within the framework of the A–D–M model (see Arrow and Hahn, 1971, ch. 7).[14] The introduction of named goods according to the person who produces or undergoes the external effects in the maximization of his utility or of his profits allows the handling of the 'externalities', hence of the public goods, in the model. In a similar way, by distinguishing retail and wholesale prices, it is possible to take into account the transaction costs and/or the costs of price formation (Foley, 1970; Starret, 1973; Hahn, 1973a); hence it follows that the existence of markets is no longer an *a priori* hypothesis: it is to be included among the endogenous variables, and therefore it is solved correctly within the model.

If we accept that, in the presence of externalities, and given the inability to exclude the lack of information, the absence of security markets and the basic characteristics of non-convexity of the external effects (Starret, 1972; Heller and Starret, 1973; Arrow, 1969), the possibility of the market failure arises and, as a consequence, there is room for other channels of resource allocation (public expenditure, taxes, etc.), then it is possible to choose a structure of taxation that, by distinguishing producer prices from consumer prices, maximizes a social welfare function whose arguments are the individual utility functions[15] (see Diamond and Mirrlees, 1971a and 1971b).

In addition to this work of generalization, a work of refining the hypotheses has been developed, i.e., less stringent conditions have been identified which can assure, within the framework of the A–D–M model, the existence of an equilibrium situation. Therefore the completeness and the transitivity of the individual preferences

(Gale and Mas Colell, 1978),[16] the convexity of the social production set and of the individual consumption set,[17] the positivity of the initial endowment, or the existence of tight inter-dependency relationships among the economic agents are no longer essential (Gay, 1978).

The extensions and generalizations just stated have been produced, basically, because of the dissatisfaction of the neoclassical economist with the original A-D-M model.[18] In fact, the sequential character-istics of the economy were not considered in this model, since the economic decisions were essentially concentrated in a single period (the first one) with a complete system of forward and contingent markets; and there was no room for the differentiation of the state of information for the economic agents;[19] there was no realistic process of price formation[20] or any significant process of change of the primitive postulates, and, further, as we have seen, there was no role for money, for the stock exchange or for other financial institutions.

Not all economists, however, have shared this kind of approach to the problems dealt with (and partly solved) in the extensions and refinements of the A-D-M model. Many of them think that the right answer can be given only by modifying the basic structure of the model.[21] Others (for example the neo-Ricardians or the neo-Key-nesians) think that the model is totally useless and that the problems must be analysed in a different theoretical context.

IV TEMPORARY EQUILIBRIUM WITH QUANTITY RATIONING

The origins
Among those economists who share the view that the A-D-M model should be modified, even if not totally rejected, we find the authors of the so-called non-Walrasian models. In these models prices are not flexible in each trading period, so that, when the economic agents formulate their net trade offers, they must take into account the quantity constraints originating from the rationing process. These models are basically short-period ones, and are included in the temporary equilibrium theory.[22]

Non-Walrasian models, of which we shall review the most interest-ing aspects soon, originate from the classic works of Clower (1965) and Leijonhufvud (1967, 1968, 1969) which meant to provide a sound microeconomic basis to the most important results of the

Keynesian analysis and, in particular, to the existence of an unvoluntary unemployment equilibrium.[23] The conclusion that one reaches comparing the A–D–M model with Keynes' work is that 'either Walras' law is incompatible with Keynesian economics, or Keynes had nothing fundamentally new to add to orthodox economic theory' (Clower, 1965). Keynes would have reverted the ranking of the price- and quantity-adjustment speeds set by Marshall.[24] This does not mean that prices are rigid: dispensing with the Walrasian auctioneer implies that the co-ordination of the individual behaviours requires time and information; it generates research costs and, once workers are unemployed, the decline in their demands produces further unemployment (this is the main feature of the multiplier).

'The deviation-amplifying, information-distorting process just described could never take place in a barter system. The Keynesian disequilibrium problem is peculiar to a system of markets in which goods are always exchanged for money and money for goods' (Leijonhufvud, 1969, p. 33). The fact that the transactions are against money prevents the transmission of the signals (in terms of goods) to the market; in other words, the price system does not communicate the necessary information. This is particularly true for future goods and prevents saving acts from being perceived as acts of future effective demand, so that 'liquidity preference will come again into play. . . preventing the decline of yields from becoming as large as required and necessitating a reduction in money income' (Leijonhufvud, 1969, p. 38). As we have seen, unemployment, which tends to persist and to amplify, is supposed to depend upon too high an interest rate, hence on too low a money value of the assets, as compared with the money wages. Then the stickiness of the capital marginal efficiency (which depends upon its long-period nature) would be responsible for the unvoluntary unemployment in a monetary economy without the auctioneer and with transaction and information costs.

The rationing models
This approach is shared by Barro and Grossman (1971; 1976).[26] Their point of view is that the statistical data do not support an important implication of Keynes' analysis, i.e. that cyclical fluctuations of employment go along with counter-cyclical fluctuations of wages.[27] They merge Clower's analysis on the consumption function with Patinkin's analysis (1965, ch. 13) on the excess supply on the output market, and they elaborate an extremely aggregated general model of disequilibrium.

This analysis has been extended to any finite number of goods by Benassy (1975 and 1976). His model (together with that one elaborated by Drèze, 1975) is a milestone for the literature of disequilibrium models. Therefore it is necessary to indicate its structure and its most significant differences as compared with Drèze's model.[28]

In Benassy's model the economic agents who control the markets fix the price of all goods at the outset of each trading period, and they modify them in the following period on the basis of perceived demand functions that embody the available information. So at given prices, each agent, based on subjectively perceived quantity constraints, expresses as effective demand for a good the corresponding element of the preferred (or at most indifferent) vector that satisfies the budget constraint and the quantity constraints for all goods except the one taken into account. If the sum of the individual effective demands for each good is not zero, a revision of the perceived constraints (which, as the realized transactions, are continuous functions of the effective demands) takes place; this goes on until the equilibrium is obtained. Furthermore, the rationing rule satisfies the property that nobody can be forced to exchange more than he wishes, and that the agents on the short side of the market realize their demands. Benassy also assumes that the agents on the long side have a perceived constraint which coincides with the realized transactions, while those on the short side perceive the possibility to increase their trades in the same direction.

In Drèze's model the auctioneer quotes a price vector selecting from a certain compact set (which can be a singleton) and assigns some quantity constraints to each agent, who chooses the preferred vector of net trades among those that satisfy the budget constraint and the quantity constraints. When the net aggregate demand for each good is not zero, a price adjustment and a change of the constraints take place until a situation of equilibrium is obtained. An important condition imposed by Drèze is that, if prices turn out to be below (or higher than) the highest (or lowest) limit, then the rationing of the demand (supply) cannot take place.

A comparison between the two models
As the effective demands are formulated in Benassy's model while ignoring the quantity constraints, we have a measure of the disequilibrium that exists in the economy. That does not happen in Drèze's model, in which the economic agents and the auctioneer do not know at all how much more (or less) the agents, who are on the short side of the market, would buy (sell) eventually if they were not

constrained.[29] However, such a knowledge of the measure of the disequilibrium is not reliable in so far as the sum of the effective demands does not satisfy the budget constraint, and it gives wrong information (except in the equilibrium) to the agents who have to fix the market prices. The effective demand, so defined by Benassy, seizes some important aspects of the economic reality: for instance, the unemployed worker who does not cease to look for a job.[30]

One of the differences between Benassy's model and Drèze's model lies in the fact that, in the latter, prices can be changed within each trading period;[31] another difference consists of the fact that Benassy's model can (while Drèze's model cannot) handle general rationing schemes. Despite these differences, it is possible to demonstrate that, under suitable hypotheses, each equilibrium of Drèze's model has a corresponding one in Benassy's model and vice versa.[32]

Various extensions

A common feature of these models is that every transaction is against money[33] (money cannot be a rationed good), this characteristic implies the inefficiency of the equilibrium.[34] In fact, we can have a situation in which it is convenient to exchange goods directly, but it is not possible to find a sequence of exchanges through money that realizes them. Consequently, there are spill-over effects on the markets, and the inefficiency is so amplified according to the lines traced by Leijonhufvud previously.

The use of the methods of game theory has made a better and wider knowledge of the process possible. Also, one can generalize and unify the analysis developed in the A–D–M model (without auctioneer) and in the rationing models, by defining the set of the transactions available to each economic agent[35] and by utilizing a concept of equilibrium in which non-cooperative elements (the possibility to sell or to buy, at given prices, less than everybody is doing), and co-operative aspects (there must be a degree of co-operation among the economic agents to decide their transactions), are blended. Furthermore, it has been proved (Grandmont, Laroque and Younès, 1978) that the rule of rationing the short side is stable in an economy with a great number of agents of limited power; this means that it is not possible for any group of agents to improve the situation of its members under the following hypotheses: (1) the exchanges occur at given prices; (2) each good is exchanged against money; (3) the re-negotiation does not concern two markets or more at the same time (i.e., it is efficient for each good taken into account separately).

Finally, it is shown by Boehm and Levine (1979) that each situation of equilibrium of such models can be considered as an equilibrium in the sense of Nash.

The analysis has been generalized supposing that the production set exhibits increasing returns to scale (Guidi, 1979) and introduces external effects. An investigation on the dynamics of a situation of equilibrium has also been started.

It is important to point out that the rationing models have given sound microeconomic basis to the theory of the accelerator and of the multiplier:

> in particular it is possible to reach a temporary equilibrium where there is an excess supply both in the market of the output of the firms and in the labour market, that is, which displays Keynesian unemployment. Both these models are able to generate other situations as well; for instance, one in which there is an excess demand for output and an excess supply for labour (stagflation or classical unemployment), or one in which there is an excess demand in both markets (repressed inflation). (Grandmont, 1977, p. 555)

V CONCLUSIONS

It should be stated that reasonable doubts have been raised on the results achieved (cf. Hahn, 1977).[36]

This aside, the weakest aspect of these models concerns the price formation process.[37] In the models we have examined the problem has been solved, fundamentally, with the introduction of non-competitive market situations, even if in this connection one can point out significant differences.[38]

For some economists (see Kurz, 1979, pp. 333–4), although the price rigidity and the quantity signals are important and realistic phenomena, they are still not the fundamental problems on which one should focus attention. The mechanisms that generate them are much more important for these authors; the rationing models can be considered, at most, as attempts to formalize such mechanisms rather than to study their economic logic. This task has been tackled in a better way by the literature on the transaction costs and by the implicit contract theory.[39]

POSTSCRIPT

In the last two years and a half, many papers have sought to extend and improve fix-price models, and interesting results have been achieved especially with regard to macroeconomic policy. We have to confine ourselves to pointing out only a few of the contributions which seem to us particularly relevant.

In a recent book (Malinvaud, 1980) medium-term evolution is analysed by introducing a linear investment function, which increases with the excess of demand over the productive capacity and with the excess of productivity over the real wage. Profit expectations, which are influenced by the demand course, costs and productive capacity, play a relevant role in the derivation of such a function. In particular Malinvaud analyses the dynamic evolution of the economic system through progressive adaptations of prices and wages, improving the analysis developed by Honkapohja (1979). In the meantime, the literature of fix-price models has investigated how to finance investments (Fourgeaud, Lenclud and Michel, 1980), how to treat international trade in a satisfactory way (Dixit, 1978; Neary, 1980) and it has begun to develop disequilibrium growth analysis. The policy implications have been enriched by taking into account bonds, which allow the government to pursue independent fiscal and monetary policies (Hool, 1980). For a useful survey of these contributions see Dehez (1980).

The role played by expectations has also been studied in a deeper way in order to answer to the criticisms raised by the 'new classical macroeconomists' (see, for instance, Barro, 1979; Grossman, 1979b) both on certain empirical aspects (such as the indetermination of the cyclical behaviour of real wages) and on theoretical ones (the different importance of transaction and information costs which are necessary to rationalize price stickiness). In a framework of rational expectations on quantity constraints, Neary and Stiglitz (forthcoming) have shown that the effectiveness of government policy can be enhanced rather than reduced, and Heller (1981) has proved the existence of a stationary long-run equilibrium with unemployment and inflation (in this case we have rational expectations on prices as well). A critical survey on the nature of expectations and on the rationality of agents' conjectures, without necessarily making imperfect competition intrinsic to the model is presented in Drazen (1980).

Hypotheses relating to the process of price setting remain unsatisfactory, even if some support for the fix-price assumption is obtained from conjectural equilibria *à la* Hahn and Negishi and from Green and Laffont's (1981) recent contribution. As regards the former John (1977) has proved that there are conjectures such that every fix-price equilibrium can be conceived as a conjectural one, supposing that on each market no agent is completely constrained. In an article published in the *European Economic Review*, Green and Laffont (1981) have developed a promising approach to the process of price setting. They assume that prices are fixed at the beginning of the period at the level which would correspond to the Walrasian equilibrium if all random factors equalled their average values; in addition, they analyse how inventories interact with prices in order to produce testable results. On the other hand, several recent contributions relating to the implicit-contract theory do not seem useful as regards the fix-price assumption because the divergence between the real wage and the marginal productivity of labour cannot be considered a signal of disequilibrium (Holmstrom, 1981).

Finally, information theory is one of the subjects which have shown a remarkable development in the literature. In fact, information plays an essential role in the debate with the 'new classical macroeconomists'. Their analyses imply that the price system reveals all the relevant information and, as far as missing markets are concerned, agents can, on average, reproduce the missing signals; there would not in general be a market failure to achieve standard efficiency and so government intervention would not be justified on these grounds. On the contrary, it is argued that 'the rational expectations hypothesis implies an incredible ability of agents to analyse the future general equilibrium of the economy' (Arrow, 1978, p. 161). Besides, there are equilibria in which prices convey no structural information and when that is the case, in the absence of a rumour, information may cause the nonexistence of a competitive equilibrium.

NOTES

1 The term A–D–M was coined by Weintraub (1979). For an outline of the historical evolution of the theory of general equilibrium, see, besides Weintraub's book, Arrow and Hahn (1971), ch. 1.

2 The concept of temporary equilibrium was first introduced by Lindhal (1939) and developed later by Hicks (1939).

3 The difference between temporary equilibrium and equilibrium over time is due to Hicks (1939). See also Radner (1974).

4 We refer here to Debreu's *The Theory of Value* (1959), which can be considered safely as the main contribution in the field of general equilibrium.

5 For an exhaustive analysis of such problems, see Arrow and Hahn (1971), chs 9, 10, 11 and 12; Arrow and Hurwicz (1977) part III, and Fisher (1978a, 1978b). For an excellent survey concerning stability see also Negishi (1962).

6 An economy has the property of diagonal dominance when the excess demand for each good is more sensitive to a change in its price than to a change in the prices of all other goods combined. This property justifies, in a certain sense, the partial equilibrium analysis: in fact, in this context the prices of the other goods are supposed constant.

7 This rule is not the only one that can be used.

8 See Grandmont (1974), Arrow and Hahn (1971), Hicks (1939), Bliss (1975a, 1976). Whenever the time-span extends over more than two periods, there arises, with the possibility of reopening the markets, the problem of speculation which can jeopardize the existence of the equilibrium. The problem has been approached with the *ad hoc* hypothesis that the transactions concerning money (or bonds) are limited, or that the price expectations are not too bound to the current prices. An analogous effect on the existence of the equilibrium may result when the present period is only a part of a sequence of periods: this is due to the possible existence of credits and debts in money inherited from the past; we may have sequences of prices for which the demand correspondence is no longer upper semi-continuous. See Grandmont (1977) and Arrow and Hahn (1971), ch. 14.

9 The question concerning the formation of the expectations is a very complex one. In order to analyse the dynamics of the economic system it is necessary to define it with a strict rule. In the literature we find the perfect foresight approach, the adaptive and the rational expectations.

10 For an outline of the stochastic processes of temporary equilibria of the Markov type with stationary probability of transition, see Radner (1974) and Grandmont and Hildenbrand (1974).

11 A role for money has been found: (a) in the existence of transaction costs also in view of restoring the Paretian efficiency (Heller, 1974); (b) in a saving of information and/or time to decentralize the transactions; (c) in an incomplete knowledge of the goods prices; finally, (d) by imposing a money constraint on the transactions (mostly *ad hoc*). See Ostroy and Starr (1974), Radner (1974), Clower (1967) and Ulph and Ulph (1975).

12 In the A–D–M model the stock market is inactive because there are no price expectations, or, if any, they are the same for all agents. The absence of a complete system of future markets for the various states of nature brings about a situation of a competitive equilibrium which is not optimal in the sense of Pareto. By introducing the stock market, attempts are made in order to see if there is a possibility to reach a kind of constrained optimum (see Diamond, 1967; Drèze, 1974; Grossman and Hart, 1979; and Friesen, 1979).

13 The problem of the unboundness of the transactions on the stock market and on the bonds market creates the most serious difficulties for the demonstration of the existence of an equilibrium. Some authors have tried to find

a solution by introducing new concepts. Bliss (1976) resorted to the figure of a 'financier'; this model has been formulated 'in the belief that the most urgent imperative facing the capital theory at the present time is to get away from steady states, long-run equilibrium, and even the "essentially time-less" Arrow–Debreu model, and to confront directly to the problems of short-run equilibrium in a world in which the future is uncertain' (p. 187). Future transactions are bounded thanks to the financier who could be considered as a notional agent, representing the opinion about the state of the market, and who has his own expectations of the future prices, according to which the action plans of the economic agent must be viable. A plausible justification for the acceptance of this kind of rationing could be found in the different states of information between the agents and the financier and a strong risk aversion arising from the lack of information.

14 In this case the optimal properties of the equilibrium are usually lost.

15 If one wishes to derive the collective choices from the individual orderings, satisfying plausible conditions, one has to face the problems well known since the appearance of Arrow's impossibility theorem (Sen, 1971). In the case of optimal taxation of goods, since it is a second-best situation, it turns out that production efficiency is a necessary condition for welfare maximization.

16 The use of a corollary of a Fan's theorem, proved by Borglin and Keiding (1976), allows us to dispense with the assumption of the preferences convexity; but it is not clear what kind of preferences satisfy their condition.

17 There is no general analysis of non-convexities, except the cases in which one uses the measure theory theorems. For instance, it is assumed that the allocations of the competitive sector are able to overcome the increasing returns to scale of the non-competitive sector (Arrow and Hahn, 1971; FitzRoy, 1974); or, if the non-convexities are limited compared with the size of the economy, there exists an approximate equilibrium whose distance from the true one remains unchanged when the number of the agents increases indefinitely; therefore the ratio of the distance to such a number approaches zero (Arrow and Hahn, 1971, ch. 7). In this case it is possible to take into account the indivisibilities due to the transaction costs (Heller, 1972).

18 On the meaning and importance of the A–D–M model see Arrow and Hahn (1971, Introduction), Weintraub (1979, chs 2, 6 and 7).

19 Radner (1974) is an exception. Here, however, two important aspects of information are not taken into account: (a) the possibility of producing non-convexities; and (b) the sequential character of its acquisitions.

20 Granted that this aspect is really a purpose of the A–D–M model (Shubik, 1976).

21 This is clear, for instance, in Shubik (1975; 1976) and in Stiglitz (1975), as the question of information is concerned in economic analysis and in the Edgeworthian models (Weintraub, 1979).

22 Little has yet been said on the dynamics or on the equilibrium over time of such models (see Solow and Stiglitz, 1968). Varian (1977) formulates a

non-Walrasian model and proves that the equilibrium, compared with an appropriate dynamic system, is stable; while the corresponding Walrasian equilibrium appears to be unstable. Laroque (1978) studied the stability of a simple model of exchange for two goods: in the neighbourhood of a locally stable Walrasian equilibrium, the agents on the short side of the market always prefer the Walrasian allocation to the disequilibrium one, while the opposite happens for the agents on the long side. It follows that the dynamics of such system appears to be a form of struggle among the various agents to impose the price: each agent, in fact, tries to modify the situation to his own advantage. For the analysis of the stability of an equilibrium with rationing, it is usually necessary to resort to the theorems and techniques of the differential topology.

23   We have no intention whatsoever of offering a global evaluation on Keynes' work, nor we are suggesting that the quoted studies succeeded in this intent; there are many doubts in this connection (see, among others, Hahn, 1977, and Grossman, 1972). It is known that in the general equilibrium model, the outcome of an unemployment equilibrium, wages being positive, is due exclusively to the rigidity (or rather to the stickiness) of the monetary wage (there is no need at all of the liquidity trap, hence of Pigou's effect). The problem of the non-existence of an equilibrium situation is naturally different: as we have seen, the existence of monetary debts or particular price expectations are sufficient to obtain such a result.

24   Many economists are sceptical about this interpretation. Marshall's quantity adjustment is, in fact, to be considered in a context that is completely different from that we have discussed here.

25   Bliss (1975b), unlike Nagatani (1978), expresses a negative opinion on this point: 'Relative prices are wrong in Keynes' unemployment state; long-run assets (i.e. capital good prices) are too low; long-run interest rates are too high. The cause is speculation in security markets which gives rise to stickiness in long-run interest rates. If I am right to think that this view is at the heart of Leijonhufvud's interpretation of Keynes, then . . . as economic analysis it appears to be wrong. One could go further and say that it is quite definitely wrong if it were conceded that Keynes is concerned with short-period equilibrium modified by wage stickiness and dual decision constraints on labour' (p. 209).

26   Later these authors strayed from it, for they held this approach only as a way to give macroeconomics a sound microeconomic basis (Grossman, 1972, p. 26).

27   In fact, Keynes accepts a production function with a decreasing marginal productivity of labour (Keynes, 1936, p. 17).

28   We refer to the version brought about by Grandmont and Laroque (1976b).

29   The knowledge of the measure of disequilibrium is very important for a possible analysis of the dynamics of the models under consideration. In Benassy's model the agents would be informed about the disequilibrium if they knew the final trades of the other agents and if some markets could

be considered as future markets. In this case, we would confront a new problem, i.e. that of the boundness of the transactions.

30 If it were supposed that the agents knew how the rationing process operates, the introduction of purchase and information costs (and more generally of transaction costs, only partially considered by Benassy, 1976), as well as the law constraints, would become possible.

31 It is this feature that draws Drèze's model closer to the A–D–M model analysed in the second section of this paper and more suitable for possible generalizations and extensions.

32 In Younès (1975) we can find a demonstration of the equivalence between his concept of equilibrium and Drèze's notion. Boehm and Levine (1979) prove the equivalence with Drèze's model and also prove that each situation of equilibrium in Benassy can be conceived as equilibrium in their model, but there is no proof of the converse. It is possible to demonstrate that every equilibrium in Drèze is an equilibrium in Benassy: the converse requires an hypothesis on the number of markets that are rationed and/or on individual preferences. (Cf. also Guidi, 1980.)

33 Even if 'Money in all of this has been a disaster from beginning to end' (Hahn, 1977, p. 38).

34 See Younès (1975) for a difference among a 'p-equilibrium', a 'p-optimum' and an 'acceptable p-equilibrium' (i.e. a situation of equilibrium which is constrained as exchanges are against money, and which must satisfy definite criteria of optimality).

35 Then it is possible, for instance, to handle the transaction costs directly.

36 It is generally recognized that the appropriate interpretation of Keynes' analysis is: flexible prices for goods, rigid money wages and rationing for labour.

37 Naturally there are other weak aspects concerning the restrictiveness of the hypotheses and the poverty of the achieved results.

38 This is clear in Benassy (1976). Hahn's model is slightly different (and more convincing). In his paper, Hahn (1978) does not make monopolistic competition intrinsic to the model. Only if the agents are rationed can they formulate conjectures, in the sense that they have to raise (or reduce) the prices in order to increase their purchases (sales). In the absence of rationing, they take the prices as given (it is not specified who fixes them). Hahn proves that there are non-Walrasian conjectural equilibria, even if they are not rational (pp. 12–13). As far as the worker is concerned, this means that he is supposed to have a perceived demand function with a corner corresponding to the previously demanded quantity and decreasing with a wage increase. By setting a further hypothesis on the elasticity, we obtain the framework in which Negishi (1978) and Futia (1977) move. A differentiation is in order: while the latter is aware of the limits of his analysis (Futia, 1977, p. 202), Negishi believes that he is studying a perfectly competitive situation with unvoluntary unemployment. Negishi and Walters (1978) introduce trade unions in the model: it becomes logically coherent but

scarcely interesting, since it is not surprising at all that, in an imperfectly competitive market, there is unemployment. Hahn outlined a new rationing model in a seminar delivered in Oxford during the academic year 1979-80. The emergence of unemployment is considered in terms of differences of behaviours and expectations between employed and unemployed workers.

39 Critical evaluations of these results have been expressed recently by Grossman (1979a) and Solow (1979).

REFERENCES

Aoki, M. and Marzollo, A. (eds.) (1979) *New Trends in Dynamic System Theory and Economics*, Academic Press, New York.

Arrow, J. K. (1969) 'Political and Economic Evaluation of Social Effects and Externalities', in *Frontiers of Quantitative Economics*, vol. I, ed. M. D. Intriligator, North Holland, Amsterdam/Oxford, pp. 3-25.

Arrow, J. K. (1978) 'The Future and the Present in Economic Life', *Economic Inquiry*, pp. 157-69.

Arrow, J. K. and Debreu, G. (1954) 'Existence of an Equilibrium for a Competitive Economy', *Econometrica*, pp. 265-90.

Arrow, J. K. and Hahn, F. H. (1971) *General Competitive Analysis*, North Holland, Amsterdam/Oxford.

Arrow, J. K. and Hurwicz, L. (1977) *Studies in Resource Allocation Processes*, Cambridge University Press.

Artis, A. G. and Nobay, A. R. (1976) *Essays in Economic Analysis*, Cambridge University Press.

Bagiotti, T. and Franco, G. (eds.) (1978) *Pioneering Economics*, Cedam, Padua.

Barro, R. J. (1979) 'Second Thoughts on Keynesian Economics', *American Economic Review, Papers and Proceedings*, pp. 54-9.

Barro, R. J. and Grossman, H. I. (1971) 'A General Disequilibrium Model of Income and Employment', *American Economic Review*, pp. 82-93.

Barro, R. J. and Grossman, H. I. (1976) *Money, Employment and Inflation*, Cambridge University Press.

Benassy, J. P. (1975) 'Neo-Keynesian Disequilibrium in a Monetary Economy', *Review of Economic Studies*, pp. 503-23.

Benassy, J. P. (1976) 'The Disequilibrium Approach to Monopolistic Price Setting and General Monopolistic Equilibrium', *Review of Economic Studies*, pp. 69-81.

Benassy, J. P. (1977) 'On Quantity Signals and the Foundations of Effective Demand Theory', *Scandinavian Journal of Economics*, pp. 147-68.

Blinder, A. S. and Friedman, B. (eds.) (1978) *Natural Resources, Uncertainty and General Equilibrium Systems: Essays in Memory of Raphael Lusky*, Academic Press, New York.

Bliss, C. J. (1975a) *Capital Theory and the Distribution of Income*, North Holland, Amsterdam/Oxford.

Bliss, C. J. (1975b) 'The Reappraisal of Keynesian Economics: an Appraisal', in Current Economic Problems, ed. M. Parkin and A. R. Nobay, Cambridge University Press, pp. 203-16.

Bliss, C. J. (1976) 'Capital Theory in the Short Run', in Essays in Modern Capital Theory, ed. M. Brown, K. Sato and P. Zaremka, North Holland, Amsterdam/Oxford, pp. 187-202.

Boehm, V. and Levine, P. (1979) 'Temporary Equilibria with Rationing', Review of Economic Studies, pp. 361-77.

Borglin, A. and Keiding, H. (1976) 'Existence of Equilibrium Actions and of Equilibrium', Journal of Mathematical Economics, pp. 313-16.

Clower, R. W. (1965) 'The Keynesian Counter-Revolution: a Theoretical Appraisal', in The Theory of Interest Rates, ed. F. H. Hahn and F. P. R. Brechling, Macmillan, London, pp. 103-25.

Clower, R. W. (1967) 'A Reconsideration of the Microfoundations of Monetary Theory', Western Economic Journal, pp. 1-8.

Debreu, G. (1959) The Theory of Value, John Wiley, New York.

Dehez, P. (1980) 'Apport de la théorie de l'équilibre temporaire en analyse macroéconomique', Recherches économiques de Louvain, pp. 27-56.

Diamond, P. A. (1967) 'The Role of the Stock Market in a General Equilibrium Model with Technological Uncertainty', American Economic Review, 57, pp. 759-76.

Diamond, P. A. and Mirrlees, J. A. (1971a) 'Optimal Taxation and Public Production', American Economic Review, pp. 8-27.

Diamond, P. A. and Mirrlees, J. A. (1971b) 'Public Production, Tax Rule II', American Economic Review, pp. 261-78.

Dixit, A. (1976) 'Public Finance in a Keynesian Temporary Equilibrium', Journal of Economic Theory, pp. 242-58.

Dixit, A. (1978) 'The Balance of Trade in a Model of Temporary Equilibrium with Rationing', Review of Economic Studies, pp. 393-404.

Drazen, A. (1980) 'Recent Developments in Macroeconomic Disequilibrium Theory', Econometrica, pp. 283-306.

Drèze, J. H. (ed.) (1974) Allocation under Uncertainty: Equilibrium and Optimality, Macmillan, London.

Drèze, J. H. (1975) 'Existence of an Equilibrium under Price Rigidity and Quantity Rationing', International Economic Review, 16, pp. 301-20.

Fisher, F. M. (1978a) 'Continuously Dated Commodities and Non-Tâtonnement with Production and Consumption', in Natural Resources, Uncertainty and General Equilibrium Systems, ed. A. S. Blinder and B. Friedman, Academic Press, New York, pp. 137-67.

Fisher, F. M. (1978b) 'Quantity Constraints, Spillovers, and the Hahn Process', Review of Economic Studies, pp. 19-31.

FitzRoy, F. R. (1974) 'Monopolistic Equilibrium, Non-Convexity and Inverse Demand', Journal of Economic Theory, pp. 1-16.

Foley, D. K. (1970) 'Economic Equilibrium with Costly Marketing', Journal of Economic Theory, pp. 276-91.

Fourgeaud, C., Lenclud, B. and Michel, P. (1980) 'Analyse des équilibres à prix fixes dans un modèle à deux secteurs', *Annales de l'INSEE*, 37.

Friesen, H. P. (1979) 'The Arrow–Debreu Model Extended to Financial Markets', *Econometrica*, pp. 689-707.

Futia, C. (1977) 'Excess Supply Equilibria', *Journal of Economic Theory*, pp. 200-20.

Gale, D. and Mas-Colell, A. (1978) 'On the Role of Complete, Transitive Preferences in Equilibrium Theory', in *Equilibrium and Disequilibrium in Economic Theory*, ed. G. Schwodiauer, D. Reidel Publishing Co., Dorchrect, pp. 7-14.

Gay, A. (1978) 'The Exchange Rates Approach to General Economic Equilibrium', *Economie Appliquée*, pp. 158-74.

Grandmont, J. M. (1974) 'On the Short-Run Equilibrium in a Monetary Economy', in *Allocation under Uncertainty, Equilibrium and Optimality*, ed. J. H. Drèze, Macmillan, London, pp. 213-28.

Grandmont, J. M. (1977) 'Temporary General Equilibrium Theory', *Econometrica*, pp. 535-72.

Grandmont, J. M. and Hildenbrand, W. (1974) 'Stochastic Processes of Temporary Equilibria', *Journal of Mathematical Economics*, pp. 247-77.

Grandmont, J. M. and Laroque, G. (1975) 'On Money and Banking', *Review of Economic Studies*, pp. 207-36.

Grandmont, J. M. and Laroque, G. (1976a) 'On the Liquidity Trap', *Econometrica*, pp. 129-35.

Grandmont, J. M. and Laroque, G. (1976b) 'On Keynesian Temporary Equilibria', *Review of Economic Studies*, pp. 53-67.

Grandmont, J. M., Laroque, G. and Younès, Y. (1978) 'Equilibrium with Quantity Rationing and Recontracting', *Journal of Economic Theory*, pp. 84-102.

Green, J. R. (1973) 'Temporary General Equilibrium in a Sequential Model with Spot and Futures Transactions', *Econometrica*, pp. 1103-23.

Green, J. R. and Laffont, J. J. (1981) 'Disequilibrium Dynamics with Inventories and Anticipatory Price-Setting', *European Economic Review*, pp. 199-221.

Grossman, H. I. (1972) 'Was Keynes a Keynesian? A Review Article', *Journal of Economic Literature*, pp. 26-30.

Grossman, H. I. (1979a) 'Employment Fluctuations and the Mitigation of Risk', *Economic Enquiry*, pp. 344-58.

Grossman, H. I. (1979b) 'Why does Aggregate Employment Fluctuate?', *American Economic Review, Papers and Proceedings*, pp. 64-9.

Grossman, S. J. and Hart, D. O. (1979) 'A Theory of Competitive Equilibrium in Stock Market Economies', *Econometrica*, pp. 293-329.

Guidi, V. (1979) 'Un Modello di Equilibrio Generale non Concorrenziale', *Giornale degli Economisti*, pp. 503-13.

Guidi, V. (1980) 'Una nota sulla nazione di equilibrio in Benassy e Drèze', *Ricerche economiche*, pp. 295-301.

Hahn, F. H. (1965) 'On Some Problems of Proving the Existence of an Equilibrium in a Monetary Economy', in *The Theory of Interest Rates*, ed. F. H. Hahn and F. P. R. Brechling, Macmillan, London, pp. 126-35.

Hahn, F. H. (1973a) 'On Transaction Costs, Inessential Sequence Economies and Money', *Review of Economic Studies*, pp. 449-61.

Hahn, F. H. (1973b) *On the Notion of Equilibrium in Economics: an Inaugural Lecture*, Cambridge University Press.

Hahn, F. H. (1977) 'Keynesian Economics and General Equilibrium Theory: Reflections on Some Current Debates', in *The Microeconomic Foundations of Macroeconomics*, ed. G. C. Harcourt, Macmillan, London, pp. 25-40.

Hahn, F. H. (1978) 'On Non-Walrasian Equilibria', *Review of Economic Studies*, pp. 1-17.

Hahn, F. H. and Brechling, F. P. R. (eds) (1965) *The Theory of Interest Rates*, Macmillan, London.

Harcourt, G. C. (ed.) (1977) *The Microeconomic Foundations of Macroeconomics*, Macmillan, London.

Heller, W. P. (1972) 'Transactions with Set-Up Costs', *Journal of Economic Theory*, pp. 465-78.

Heller, W. P. (1974) 'The Holding of Money Balances', *Journal of Economic Theory*, pp. 93-108.

Heller, W. P. (1981) 'Disequilibrium Rational Expectations', *Economics Letters*, pp. 17-24.

Heller, W. P. and Starret, D. (1973) 'On the Nature of Externalities', in *Theory and Measurement of Externalities*, ed. A. Lin, Academic Press, New York, pp. 9-23.

Hicks, J. R. (1939) *Value and Capital*, Clarendon Press, Oxford.

Hicks, J. R. (1965) *Capital and Growth*, Clarendon Press, Oxford.

Hicks, J. R. (1975) *The Crisis in Keynesian Economics*, Basil Blackwell, Oxford.

Hines, A. G. (1971) *On the Reappraisal of Keynesian Economics*, Martin Robertson, London.

Holmstrom, B. (1981) 'Contractual Models of the Labor Market', *American Economic Review*, pp. 308-13.

Honkapohja, S. (1979) 'On the Dynamics of Disequilibrium in a Macro-Model with Flexible Wages and Prices', in *New Trends in Dynamic System Theory and Economics*, ed. M. Aoki and A. Marzollo, Academic Press, New York, pp. 303-36.

Hool, B. (1976) 'Money, Expectations and the Existence of a Temporary Equilibrium', *Review of Economic Studies*, pp. 439-50.

Hool, B. (1980) 'Monetary and Fiscal Policies in Short-Run Equilibria with Rationing', *International Economic Review*, pp. 301-16.

Impicciatore, G. (1978) 'Esistenza e Stabilità degli Equilibri Non-Walrasiani', *Giornale degli Economisti*, pp. 21-47.

Intriligator, M. D. (ed.) (1969) *Frontiers of Quantitative Economics*, vol. I, North Holland, Amsterdam/Oxford.

Intriligator, M. D. and Kendrick, D. A. (eds) (1974) *Frontiers of Quantitative Economics*, vol. II, North Holland, Amsterdam/Oxford.

John, R. (1980) 'Remark on Conjectural Equilibria', *CORE Discussion Paper*, No. 8009.

Keynes, J. M. (1936) *The General Theory of Employment, Interest and Money*, Macmillan, London.

Keynes, J. M. (1937) 'The General Theory of Employment', *Quarterly Journal of Economics*, pp. 209-23.

Kurz, M. (1979) 'Review of Schwodiauer's', *Journal of Economic Literature*, pp. 531-4.

Laroque, G. (1978) 'On the Dynamics of Disequilibrium: a Simple Remark', *Review of Economic Studies*, pp. 273-8.

Leijonhufvud, A. (1967) 'Keynes and the Keynesians: a Suggested Interpretation', *American Economic Review*, pp. 401-10.

Leijonhufvud, A. (1968) *On Keynesian Economics and the Economics of Keynes*, Oxford University Press.

Leijonhufvud, A. (1969) *Keynes and the Classics*, Institute of Economic Affairs, London.

Lin, A. (ed.) (1973) *Theory and Measurement of Externalities*, Academic Press, New York.

Lindhal, E. (1939) *Studies in the Theory of Money and Capital*, Rinehart, New York.

Malinvaud, E. (1953) 'Capital Accumulation and Efficient Allocation of Resources', *Econometrica*, pp. 233-68.

Malinvaud, E. (1961) 'The Analogy between Atemporal and Intertemporal Allocation of Resources', *Review of Economic Studies*, pp. 143-60.

Malinvaud, E. (1977) *The Theory of Unemployment Reconsidered*, Basil Blackwell, Oxford.

Malinvaud, E. (1980) *Profitability and Unemployment*, Cambridge University Press.

Malinvaud, E. and Younès, Y. (1977) 'Some New Concepts for the Microeconomic Foundations of Macroeconomics', in *The Microeconomic Foundations of Macroeconomics*, ed. G. C. Harcourt, Macmillan, London, pp. 62-82.

Marshak, J. and Radner, R. (1976) *Economic Theory of Teams*, Yale University Press, New Haven, Conn.

McKenzie, L. W. (1959) 'On the Existence of General Equilibrium for a Competitive Market', *Econometrica*, pp. 54-71.

Muth, J. F. (1961) 'Rational Expectations and the Theory of Price Movement', *Econometrica*, pp. 315-36.

Nagatani, K. (1978) *Monetary Theory*, North Holland, Amsterdam/Oxford.

Neary, J. P. (1980) 'Nontraded Goods and the Balance of Trade in a Neo-Keynesian Temporary Equilibrium', *Quarterly Journal of Economics*, pp. 403-29.

Neary, J. P. and Stiglitz, J. E. (forthcoming) 'Towards a Reconstruction of Keynesian Economics: Expectations and Constrained Equilibria'. *Quarterly Journal of Economics*.

Negishi, T. (1962) 'The Stability of a Competitive Economy: a Survey Article', *Econometrica*, pp. 635-69.

Negishi, T. (1972) *General Equilibrium and International Trade*, North Holland, Amsterdam/Oxford.

Negishi, T. (1976) 'Unemployment, Inflation and the Micro Foundations of Macroeconomics', in *Essays in Economic Analysis*, ed. A. G. Artis and A. R. Nobay, Cambridge University Press, pp. 33-49.

Negishi, T. (1978) 'Existence of an Under-employment Equilibrium', in *Equilibrium and Disequilibrium in Economic Theory*, ed G. Schwodiauer, D. Reidel Publishing Co., Dorchrect, pp. 497-510.

Negishi, T. and Walters, A. A. (1978) 'Employment, Wages and Trade Unions', in *Pioneering Economics*, ed. T. Bagiotti and G. Franco, Cedam, Padua.

Ostroy, J. M. and Starr, R. M. (1974) 'Money and the Decentralization of Exchange', *Econometrica*, pp. 1093-113.

Parkin, M. and Nobay, A. R. (eds) (1975) *Current Economic Problems*, Cambridge University Press.

Patinkin, D. (1965) *Money, Interest and Prices*, Harper & Row, New York.

Phelps, E. S. (1965) 'Second Essay on the Golden Rule of Accumulation', *American Economic Review*, pp. 793-814.

Radner, R. (1968) 'Competitive Equilibrium under Uncertainty', *Econometrica*, pp. 31-58.

Radner, R. (1972) 'Existence of Equilibrium Plans, Prices and Price Expectations in a Sequence of Markets', *Econometrica*, pp. 289-303.

Radner, R. (1974) 'Market Equilibrium under Uncertainty: Concepts and Problems', in *Frontiers of Quantitative Economics*, vol. II, ed. M. D. Intriligator and D. A. Kendrick, North-Holland, Amsterdam/Oxford, pp. 43-105.

Samuelson, P. A. (1947) *Foundations of Economic Analysis*, Harvard University Press, Cambridge, Mass.

Schwodiauer, G. (ed.) (1978) *Equilibrium and Disequilibrium in Economic Theory*, D. Reidel Publishing Co., Dorchrect.

Sen, A. K. (1971) *Collective Choice and Social Welfare*, Oliver & Boyd, London.

Shubik, M. (1975) 'The General Equilibrium Model is Incomplete and not Adequate for the Reconciliation of Micro and Macroeconomic Theory', *Kyklos*, pp. 545-73.

Shubik, M. (1976) 'A Theory of Money and Financial Institutions, Part 27: Beyond General Equilibrium', *Economie Appliquée*, pp. 319-37.

Shubik, M. (1978) 'Competitive and Controlled Price Economies: the Arrow-Debreu Model Revisited', in *Equilibrium and Disequilibrium in Economic Theory*, ed. G. Schwodiauer, D. Reidel Publishing Co., Dorchrect, pp. 213-24.

Solow, R. (1979) 'Alternatives Approaches to Macroeconomic Theory: a Partial View', *Canadian Journal of Economics*, pp. 339-54.

Solow, R. and Stiglitz, J. E. (1968) 'Output, Employment and Wages in the Short Run', *Quarterly Journal of Economics*, pp. 537-60.

Starret, D. (1968) 'Contributions to the Theory of Capital in Infinite Horizon Models', *IMSSS Technical Report*, no. 16, Stanford University, Stanford, California.

Starret, D. (1972) 'Fundamental Non-convexities in the Theory of Externalities', *Journal of Economic Theory*, pp. 180–99.

Starret, D. (1973) 'Inefficiency and the Demand for Money in a Sequence Economy', *Review of Economic Studies*, pp. 437–48.

Stiglitz, J. E. (1975) 'Information and Economic Analysis', in *Current Economic Problems*, ed. M. Parkin and A. R. Nobay, Cambridge University Press, pp. 27–52.

Stigum, B. P. (1969) 'Competitive Equilibria under Uncertainty', *Quarterly Journal of Economics*, pp. 533–61.

Ulph, A. and Ulph, D. (1975) 'Transaction Costs in General Equilibrium Theory: a Survey', *Economica*, pp. 355–72.

Varian, H. R. (1977) 'Non-Walrasian Equilibria', *Econometrica*, pp. 573–90.

Wald, A. (1936) 'Ueber einige Gleichungssysteme der mathematischen Oekonomie', *Zeitschrift für Nationalökonomie*, pp. 637–70.

Wald, A. (1951) 'On Some Systems of Equations of Mathematical Economics', *Econometrica*, pp. 368–403, English Translation of Wald, A. (1936).

Weintraub, R. E. (1979) *Microfoundations: The Compatibility of Microeconomics and Macroeconomics*, Cambridge University Press.

Younès, Y. (1975) 'On the Role of Money in the Process of Exchange and the Existence of a Non-Walrasian Equilibrium', *Review of Economic Studies*, pp. 489–501.

Part Three

Macro-Foundations of Macroeconomics

6

Time as Quantum

BERNARD SCHMITT*

I INTRODUCTION

In works concerning macroeconomics, authors differentiate between *continuous time* and *discontinuous time*.

Time 'flows continuously and each variable is taken as a continuous and differentiable function of time'.

'The flow of time is divided into successive periods of constant length, taken as the time-unit' (Allen, 1967, p. 5).

Mathematical expressions of these two aspects of time are differential equations and difference equations.

When a variable is determined by time, it is said to possess a dimension in time. In this case authors consider it to pertain to periodic analysis if time is divided, or to continuous analysis if time is undivided.

Let us adopt Allen's definitions:

The aggregates of macro-economics are of two kinds. Some are *stocks*, typically the stock of capital K, and are time-less concepts – so much on hand here and now. Even in period analysis, a stock must be specified at a particular moment. Other aggregates – the majority – are *flows* such as income and output, consumption and investment. A flow variable has the time dimension t, so much per unit of time or per period. It is essential to keep time dimensions in mind when we relate one economic aggregate to another.

To show a time dimension in unmistakeable form, we write a flow variable as so much per unit of time, but for our present

---

* I am grateful to Pierre Marchand for his translation of the French manuscript.

purpose we can also multiply it by Δt to give the amount in a period of length Δt time-units. So, if Y is the constant rate of income (output) per unit of time, then the amount of income received or output produced in a period of Δt time-units is simply $Y\Delta t$. For example, with a year as time-unit, the amount is $Y/4$ in a quarter of $5Y$ over a five-year stretch. (Allen, 1967, pp. 2–3)

Let us assume, as Allen does, a constant production in time Δt. Is the output for that period $R\,\Delta t$ or R? Either answer is true, depending on the definition of R.

If R represents the activity engaged in during the period Δt, then the resulting product or output equals $R\,\Delta t$.

If R represents the result of the activity, then the product or output is R. It is obvious that $R\,\Delta t$ and R represent two identical results for the simple reason that R does not have the same meaning in both cases, representing either an activity or its result.

If R is the activity of producing, the expression $R/\Delta t$ is meaningless; if R is the result of producing, $R/\Delta t$ is the activity. In either case, the result of producing is expressed as the product of activity and time, $R\,\Delta t$ or $(R/\Delta t)\,\Delta t$.

In the expression $R\,\Delta t$, R is the activity and $R\,\Delta t$ is the measurement of its result; similarly, in the expression $(R/\Delta t)\,\Delta t$, $R/\Delta t$ is the activity and R is the measurement of its result. The activity is a flow because it occurs in time. One may conclude that activity, the act of producing, is a speed, and that its result is the product of that speed and its period of application.

II EXPENDITURES AND FLOWS

Expenditures present a specific problem; they are not flows as Allen sees them.

Let us keep R as the symbol for expenditure incurred in producing an income or the income produced in the interval Δt. However, let us use R^x for the activity – the production – and R for its result – the product:

Constant production of Δt	*Product of Δt*
R^x or $R/\Delta t$	$R^x \Delta t$ or R

If we divide interval Δt in order to reduce it to a progressively shorter period, the product $R^x \Delta t$ or $(R/\Delta t)\Delta t$ approaches zero as does Δt. At the limit, as $t = 0$, the product is nil although the instantaneous production $- R^x$ or R in each infinitesimal time unit – is positive.

For Allen, as for every economist reasoning in continuous or discontinuous time, the result of production is positive only in finite time. In other words, production is a flow because it happens in time: production is positive only if the period of implementation of the productive activity is itself positive.

Traditional theory also assumes that expenditures are velocities comparable to those of a moving body in Newton's mechanics. Division or multiplication of movement by time have been accepted at least since the seventeenth century. Baron (1969, p. 240), referring to the analysis by Barrow, who was Newton's immediate predecessor as Lucasian Professor of Mathematics in Cambridge writes:

> Time is made up either of the simple addition of rising moments, or of the continual flux of one moment. A line, being the trace of a point moving forward, may be conceived as the trace of a moment continually flowing. Time can thus be represented by a uniform right line.

Being spread through time, displacements are divided by the division of time. However, the division of displacement by time, displacement $\div$ time, is obviously not divided itself by a subsequent division of time, as both the numerator and the denominator are divided simultaneously. For this reason, the speed of the moving body does not tend towards zero as the time of implementation of that speed tends towards zero. Consequently, displacement can be expressed as the product of instantaneous displacements, or speeds, and the duration of the displacement.

Let us assume a constant action in time Δt. In every instant (of Δt) the action is positive; in every instant (of Δt) the result of the action is nil; in order to obtain a positive result, the action must take place in positive time.

Theoreticians have admitted without examination, and even without being aware that a problem exists, that expenditures are 'displacements'. Being observed during period Δt, expenditure R^x or $R/\Delta t$ results in product $R^x \Delta t$ or R. In every instant (of Δt), the result of the expenditure is nil; in order for the expended sum to be positive, the expenditure must take place in a positive time period.

Material observation does not correspond to these theoreticians' assumptions: every expenditure has an instantaneous result. The expenditure R^x or $R/\Delta t$ implies *without delay* an expended sum equal to R^x or to $R/\Delta t$. It is untrue that the implementation of the expenditure must be extended in time in order to obtain a positive result; in fact, expenditure, being an instantaneous action, has a result that is itself instantaneous.

To sum up, the difference between the cases, in that of the displacement of a moving body the action or the speed remains positive even when $\Delta t \to 0$, but the result of the action is positive only when $\Delta t > 0$. With respect to expenditures, one must also distinguish between their implementation and their results. However, the result of expenditure R^x or $R/\Delta t$ does not depend on the duration of its implementation; it *invariably equals R^x or $R/\Delta t$*, whatever duration one takes inside interval Δt – long, short or infinitesimal.

III EXPENDITURES ARE DETERMINED IN QUANTUM TIME

Let us examine the expenditure relating to production and its result.

Casual observation demonstrates that the production of an output has a relationship with time. Whether one is talking about the output from an individual, from a group or from a whole nation, it is determined in time: the output for a month, for instance, is not the same as the output for a year. In this case, Allen is right; if one takes the year as a unit of time and if production is constant, annual output is R and the value of the output is '$Y/4$ in a quarter or $5Y$ over a five-year stretch' (Allen, 1967, p. 3).

However, it is necessary to bring in the conclusion from the preceding paragraph: the result of every expenditure is instantaneously positive. Consequently, if R^x or $R/\Delta t$ defines the production of output for the period Δt, *the result of R^x in period Δt is R^x and not $R^x \Delta t$*, just as the result of $R/\Delta t$ in period Δt is $R/\Delta t$ and not R.

Let us return to the definitions of the production of Δt and of its product:

Production of Δt	*Product of Δt*
R^x or $R/\Delta t$	$R^x \Delta t$ or R

The product of Δt is equal to the production of Δt, just as the sum spent equals the expenditure. It follows that:

$$R^x = R^x \Delta t$$

or that

$$R/\Delta t = R.$$

The conclusion is that, if Δt is the time dimension of the expenditure being examined, Δt is necessarily equal to 1.

IV CONTINUOUS TIME, DISCONTINUOUS TIME AND QUANTUM TIME

This section summarizes the discussion so far.

In considering activity R^x, the production of output, it is accepted that R has a dimension in time, R being the result of R^x. The result of R^x is $R^x \Delta t$. Let us consider two propositions in order to disprove them.

(1) $\Delta t > 1$. The result would be that the output produced in period Δt, $R^x \Delta t$, would be greater than R^x, the output for that period, which is absurd.

(2) $\Delta t < 1$. This leads to the same absurdity, as the output produced cannot be smaller than the production of output.

The conclusion is that expenditure R^x has $R^x \Delta t$ as a result, where Δt is necessarily equal to 1.

The conclusion would be quite different if we were reasoning about the finite velocity, v, of a moving body and about the distance it travels per unit of time, Δt. *The expended sum is determined by the expenditure and not by the product of expenditure and time.* The distance travelled is determined not by velocity alone but by the product of velocity and time. So, in the expression $v \Delta t$, Δt is *any number*, ≥ 1. In the analysis of the finite speed of a moving body it is possible to consider time as either continuous or discontinuous, whereas in the analysis of expenditure time is logically a quantum.

Let us compare two graphs, one with the variable determined in continuous or discontinuous time (figure 6.1) and the other with the variable determined in quantum time (figure 6.2). In the case of velocity, time Δt may be any number because the result of velocity, the distance travelled, is a product of time. In the case of expenditure, time Δt is necessarily equal to the number 1 as time is included in the equivalence $R^x = R^x \Delta t$, the expended sum being already known in the expenditure.

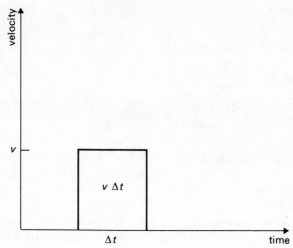

FIGURE 6.1 Variable determined in continuous or discontinuous time

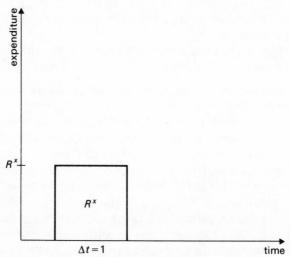

FIGURE 6.2 Variable determined in quantum time

It is interesting to search for a confirmation of quantum time in prominent theories. Let us take Samuelson's (1966) analysis (see figure 6.3). Time is shown on the horizontal axis and expenditures on the vertical axis, and the author constructs two sets of graphs in order to show the difference between the two cases, either when

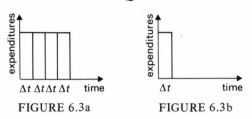

FIGURE 6.3a   FIGURE 6.3b

expenditure happens as a 'single impulse' or when it becomes continuous in time. 'Figure I will refer in every case to a sudden increase in the deficit which is thereafter maintained at a positive constant level [see figure 6.3a], while Figure II refers exclusively to a single impulse of expenditure followed by a return to the previous level [see figure 6.3b]' (Samuelson, 1966, p. 1155). The rectangle in 6.3b represents a unique impulse; the rectangles in 6.3a represent a series of impulses. It is obvious that if the rectangle in 6.3b is determined in a divisible interval of time, figure 6.3b is similar to figure 6.3a, except for the scale. Samuelson's differentiation has no meaning if interval Δt is different from the number 1.

V QUANTUM ANALYSIS HAS A PRECISE AIM: THE STUDY OF QUANTITIES WHICH INSTANTANEOUSLY PERTAIN TO A FINITE PERIOD

Take quantity G. If it is not determined in a finite period, it does not have a dimension in time and holds no interest for quantum analysis. On the other hand if, having a dimension in time, quantity G is the product of time, $G = G^x \Delta t$, in which Δt is any number, G is the subject of continuous or discontinuous analysis. However, if the time dimension of G is $G^x \Delta t$, where Δt is *necessarily* equal to one unit, that quantity can be studied only by quantum analysis.

It is easier to understand the equivalence between the quantum time unit and the number 1 if we try to show the product of an expenditure and time (figure 6.4). Let us assume that we have not yet solved this problem. The expended sum has a dimension in time; it is determined by the interval Δt of which it is the product. Being the instantaneous result of R^x, R does not correspond to any point of segment Δt. Thus, in contrast to Barrow's point, which moves, the result of expenditure R^x is not measured by time; *R is not mobile in time, although by definition, R has a dimension in time*. One can reconcile the time dimension of R with the equivalence $R = R^x$ only by writing $\Delta t = 1$. This is the only way in which the value resulting from the product of the two variables, time and R^x, will be equivalent to the sole variable R^x.

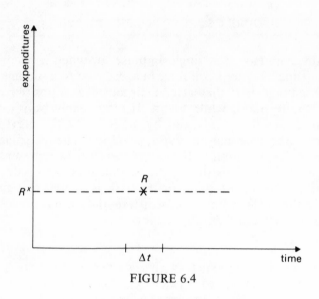

FIGURE 6.4

VI THE MEANING OF $\Delta t = 1$

This is straightforward: Δt is a definite interval in continuous or discontinuous time if, and only if, Δt is infinitely divisible. If Δt cannot be reduced to a quantity of time smaller than a given quantity, Δt is determined in quantum time. The *finite and indivisible* interval of time is equal to the number 1 in the series of natural positive numbers.

In practice, it is unnecessary to take a period Δt smaller than an interval that a physicist would already consider very long, such as a calendar day. If the day is the basic period chosen, then $\Delta t = 1$ day $= 1$. A shorter period could be considered, even a very short one, such as a second, which would be slightly preposterous: $\Delta t = 1$ second $= 1$. Whatever basic period is chosen, it is necessarily equal to the number 1, so that any sum expended is determined in the time quantum (the basic period) or in a whole multiple of that quantum.

VII PROOF BY *REDUCTIO AD ABSURDUM* THAT QUANTUM TIME EXISTS

Let us take a positive expenditure R^x. The sum expended, R, is the product of period Δt, $R^x \Delta t$. On the other hand, the sum expended equals the expenditure, $R = R^x$. This gives:

$$R^x = R = R^x \Delta t = R \Delta t.$$

When $\Delta t \to 0$, one has $R \Delta t \to 0$. Now, whatever the value of Δt, even when $\Delta t \to 0$, $R \Delta t$ equals R^x. At the limit we obtain the equation:

$$R \Delta t = 0 = R^x$$

with R^x positive.

The absurdity comes from pushing Δt towards 0. To avoid the contradiction, the analysis must be based on quantum time, Δt being a finite and indivisible time.

It is interesting to notice that every positive sum expended is infinitely divisible as such, but it is divisible only by quantum time: no sum spent is divisible either by continuous or by discontinuous time. In other words, with respect to expenditures, time is the set of natural numbers and not the set of real numbers.

This could have an amusing result in an attempt to determine a continuity of expenditures in time. Taking R^x as a positive and finite expenditure and R as its result in time Δt, let us try to divide the expended sum, R, into so great a number of expended sums that the expenditure R^x becomes a continuity in time. The solution seems attainable: it is enough for each expended sum to be infinitesimal. However, this disregards the equation $R = R^x$. It follows that, in the product of velocity (R^x) and time, *velocity tends towards zero when its time of application tends towards zero*; which does not apply to Barrow's moving body. Now, the application of nil velocity in time Δt will finally result in nil expenditure. Therefore, quantity R can be infinitely divided in itself, but can only be divided by quantum time.

VIII THE EXAMPLE OF THE HAMMER

Let us assume that a force 10 hammer blow must be struck every day. This is our problem: is it possible to spread or to 'smooth out' the hammer blow (but not the motion of the hammer) in continuous time?

It is certain that the hammer blow is infinitely divisible in itself; and as only one blow is given during the day, one can mentally divide it into *n* blows of 10/*n* force, where *n* can be an infinite number.

The real problem is elsewhere: is it possible to give *n* hammer blows through time, *throughout the day*, so that no finite time interval separates two successive blows? If this problem were solved, the hammer would remain in contact with the nail, motionless: it would exert no force. Force 10 can be obtained only through the application of a *finite* number of hammer blows of *finite* force.

Similarly, in time only a finite number of expenditures can result in a positive expenditure; an expenditure determined in continuous or in discontinuous time can give only a null result, whatever the duration of its implementation, as in each infinitesimal time interval, every continuous expenditure – and not only its result in time – is infinitesimal.

IX CONCLUSION

Since the time of macroeconomics is a quantum, the whole of macroeconomics must be rebuilt on that basis.

The example of the hammer is simple because the hammer blow has no dimension in time. The case of the expenditure is more difficult just because the sum expended is the product of time.

Until now, economic science has analysed expenditures in the same way as classical mechanics analyses the velocity and the displacement of moving bodies. This borrowing from physics is based on a false analogy because velocity and displacement are not the same, whereas the expenditure and the expended sum are necessarily equal to each other. All the difficulties of macroeconomics consist in reconciling two contradictory notions:

(1) the expended sum is the product of time;
(2) the expended sum is exactly the product of the expense.

Expenditure is a 'velocity'. If the expended sum is the product of time (1), it must equal the velocity multiplied by the time and not only the velocity, as in (2). The contradiction is avoided only by quantum time, the product of velocity and time being equal to the velocity itself if time as defined in the product is a 'bunch of instants', finite and indivisible, equal to the number 1.

Macroeconomics must explain how every sum expended is placed in finite time by an instantaneous action, the expenditure.

REFERENCES

Allen, R. G. D. (1967) *Macro-Economic Theory*, Macmillan, London.
Baron, M. E. (1969) *The Origins of the Infinitesimal Calculus*, Pergamon Press, Oxford.
Samuelson, P. A. (1966) 'Fiscal Policy and Income Determination', in *The Collected Scientific Papers of P. A. Samuelson*, vol. 2, ed. J. E. Stiglitz, MIT Press, Cambridge, Mass.
Schmitt, B. (1971) *L'Analyse macro-économique des revenus*, Dalloz, Paris.
Schmitt, B. (1972) *Macroeconomic Theory: A Fundamental Revision*, Castella, Albeuve (Switzerland).
Schmitt, B. (1973) *New Proposals for A World Monetary Reform*, Castella, Albeuve (Switzerland).
Schmitt, B. (1977a) *La Monnaie européenne*, Presses Universitaires de France, Paris.
Schmitt, B. (1977b) *Theorie des Internationalen Kreditgeldes*, Gustav Fischer Verlag, Jena.

7

The Logical Indeterminacy of Relative Prices

ALVARO CENCINI*

I INTRODUCTION

Economic theories can be divided into two main categories according to their acceptance or rejection of relative prices. Let us call *classics* the theorists who, for a given number of commodities, n, try to determine n relations of equivalence defining their *values* or *absolute prices*. Similarly, we call *neoclassics* the theorists who, for the same number of commodities n, determine only $n-1$ relations of equivalence defining *relative prices*.

The purpose of our paper is to prove that the choice between these two schools is not arbitrary: non-determination of relative prices forces us to abandon neoclassical theories. The fundamental reason for their failure lies in the lack of an objective theory of value. Now, such a theory requires the intervention of money and its integration in the real world. Here again, neoclassics does not succeed in solving the problem; real and monetary worlds being rigidly separated, commodities and money values (purchasing power) remain completely unexplained. Finally, we claim that a solution can be found in Keynes' concept of wage-units, thanks to which the basic relation between product and labour is measured in terms of money.

II THE PROBLEM

Let us begin our analysis with the works of Walras. There appears to be no money in Walras' theory: all factors and variables are real.

* I am grateful to Christine Webb for her assistance in improving the style of the English manuscript.

The fundamental determination is that of relative prices, and no money is introduced except the *numéraire*. Now the *numéraire* is in fact a commodity, so that the General Equilibrium System does not differ substantially from a barter economy. In this context, it might be interesting to try to prove that relative prices are logically undetermined.[1]

Given two agents A and B dealing with two commodities a, b, is it possible to determine the relative prices of a and b? The answer seems to be necessarily positive: the real forces of supply and demand are sufficient for this task. Starting from this first consideration, the neoclassics worked out their analysis of price determination; price is given by a system of equations relating the demand for and supply of each commodity. However, the solution proposed encounters a great difficulty: the physical heterogeneity of products. This obstacle becomes particularly evident when price determination is concerned with more than two commodities. Suppose that the economy is composed of three agents and three commodities. Transactions between the agents take place by a process of indirect exchange. Now, the number of prices to be determined is three, the same as the number of equations: the solution should be very easy. Nevertheless, this conclusion holds only if the equations can be written in spite of the physical heterogeneity of commodities. Let us prove this.

First, Walras' Law reduces the three equations to two, while the variables are similarly reduced (the price of one commodity is set equal to unity). Then, the two remaining equations relate the supply of each commodity to the supply of the others. For example, the supply of commodities b and c referred to it. Yet, to solve this equation it is necessary to reduce a, b and c to the same denominator. In other words, the physically heterogeneous products (a, b and c) must be made commensurable.

III THE NEOCLASSICAL SOLUTION: A CRITICAL APPRAISAL

The neoclassical answer to this fundamental question is well worked out. It is based on the logical equivalence between the two terms of any exchange. As was pointed out by Walras, when an exchange takes place between two commodities it defines an equivalence; i.e., no difference can exist between the commodities exchanged so that their equivalence at once solves the heterogeneity problem.

Since relative prices represent an exchange, the solution seems within easy reach. The equations can be expressed in terms of a, b and c because these commodities become commensurable once their relative prices are determined. This apparently simple analysis is in fact very subtle. Indeed, it is so subtle that it may be considered self-contradictory: relative prices are the solution of equations that can be written only on the basis of relative prices themselves. Nevertheless, the contradiction is overcome by a further consideration: the simultaneity of the equations and their solution.

Now, being strictly dependent on the exchange, the equations are verified for any level of relative prices defined by them: given the equivalence of exchange, the equality between demand and supply is assured by any realized price. Correspondingly, if the equations can exist only when the exchange is realized, they become pure identities with no explanatory power over any process of determination. The law of exchange is so powerful that the determination of relative prices becomes impossible whether we deal with two or any number of commodities. In fact, even when we have only two commodities, price is not determined by the supply and demand equation because, instead of representing a condition of equilibrium, this equation is the simple definition of any possible exchange. The equation $S_a = D_a$ is always true for any relative price of a. The fundamental reason is that every equation relating to the demand for and supply of two or more commodities can be expressed only in relation to the series of possible *realized* prices. If not, the commodities remain heterogeneous and the equations cannot even be written. Solution of the heterogeneity problem implies therefore the complete indeterminacy of relative prices.

As has been pointed out by Bernard Schmitt (1982, p. IV-11), the neoclassical impasse results from a confusion between equations and identities. Assuming that relative prices can be determined by a system of equations, the neoclassics do not take into account the difficulty represented by the heterogeneity. Equations, in fact, can exist as relationships only between homogeneous magnitudes. Before the equations are solved, the magnitudes that enter them are already homogeneous: the result is their equalization and not their identity. If, as in the case of relative prices, these magnitudes are not homogeneous, they cannot even be related to each other. An operation is needed to reduce them to the same quality. Now this reduction logically is not an equalization or an equation, which presupposes homogeneity, but a *definition*, whose result is the identity of the formerly heterogeneous magnitudes. Where applied to relative prices this means that commodities either remain heterogeneous, so that no relationship can be established between them, or are made homogeneous, through an operation that defines their equivalence. As Walras states, commodities are made homogeneous through exchange. Thus, exchange is the operation which, by reducing commodities to the same 'common denominator', defines them as equivalent. The equalization between the two terms of any relation of exchange is therefore meaningless since it would correspond to the equalization between a given magnitude and itself. Walras' equilibrium system is a set of identities that define relative prices and not a set of equations determining them.

Does the introduction of an 'auctioneer' change anything in the analysis?

If we deal with only two commodities, a solution can be found in the sense that the direct confrontation between the supplier and the purchaser, at any virtual price called by an auctioneer, can lead to an exchange of their commodities. Thus, price is determined by the real forces of supply and demand which can be directly exercised on the market. Yet, when there are more than two commodities the solution cannot be found so easily. The necessarily indirect process of exchange requires the elaboration of an equilibrium system.

Now it has been said that, when certain assumptions are respected, the General Equilibrium System can be solved and its solution is not the set of all possible prices (Debreu, 1959, pp. 83–4). Unfortunately, here again two distinct processes are being confused. The mathematical solution of the equations cannot be intermixed with the process of price determination. The result given by the General Equilibrium System is nothing other than the price defined by all the constraints put into the system. Then, it is absolutely correct to say that prices thus calculated have been constructed and not determined. In other words, price becomes a simple representation of a given set of assumptions. Any change in the assumptions implies a change in their mathematical expression and therefore in the price that is defined by them.

IV FURTHER EXPOSITION OF THE CRITIQUE

Let us present our argument once again. The basic assumption of neoclassical theory is related to the effect of exchange. According to Walras, commodities are completely heterogeneous before exchange. Nevertheless, this heterogeneity does not represent a serious difficulty since, when exchange takes place, commodities instantaneously enter into a relation of equivalence. Two main results are then obtained by the process of exchange. First, the commodities are made homogeneous; and second, supply and demand are equalized. In fact, the equality between supply and demand is not the result of exchange but its basic definition. As Aristotle had already pointed out, there can be no exchange without equivalence and no equivalence without commensurability. So, the neoclassics seem to respect that logical sequence by assuming that the commensurability is coincident with exchange. Unfortunately, this assumption does not allow any process of price determination. Demand and supply can never represent a pair of forces whose interaction determines prices because they are always identical, their measurement being possible only if the commodities are commensurables. Accordingly, no difference between supply and demand is possible since their value can be known only at exchange. A difference between these two forces is possible on one condition, which is systematically refused by the neoclassics: namely, the measurement of the commodities before their exchange. Without that, prices remain undetermined because, outside exchange, supply and demand are undetermined.

Let us suppose that any price whatsoever is proposed by the market. Only two possibilities are logically available:

(1) exchange takes place at the suggested price, in which case supply
     and demand are identical; or
(2) exchange is not realized.

In the second case, is it possible to evaluate the difference between demand and supply? The answer can be positive only if the two forces can be expressed in the same unit of measurement. Now this possibility implies their commensurability – that is, for the neoclassics, their exchange. It follows that supply and demand can never be determined outside exchange and, therefore, that no real force is available for the determination of relative prices.

Despite this negative conclusion, is it possible to rescue the analysis? Is it not true that prices can be imagined and 'called' before exchange? Corresponding to these hypothetical prices there are supplies and demands, themselves hypothetical, which can differ among each other. If this reasoning is correct, then it is also true that the commensurability based on these hypothetical prices is itself hypothetical. Consider, however, the following argument, implicitly present in many authors' analyses: even though the forces of supply and demand corresponding to a given virtual price are not realized, they are nevertheless real. Before exchange, supply and demand are desired magnitudes and, as such, they must be considered as real forces. Now, given that the identity only results from the realized exchange, desired supply and demand can be different at any level of virtual price. Hence, the equalization between desired supply and demand logically can be considered as the factor determining prices.

As can easily be seen, this analysis does not overcome the initial difficulty. Whether desired or not, supply and demand cannot be measured, since the commodities remain heterogeneous. It is certainly true that even outside exchange supply and demand are real forces, but their (economic) evaluation implies the existence of a unit of measurement capable of ordering all the commodities in the same 'field'. This unit of measurement is clearly not acceptable to neoclassical theories. Our conclusion is strengthened by a further consideration: homogenization is impossible even *within* exchange. In fact, it has been argued that the process of exchange cannot logically solve the problem posed by heterogeneity (Cencini and Schmitt, 1976, ch. V, section 2). Equivalence between the two terms of any exchange requires the existence of a single unit of account. Exchange, being a two-fold operation, can never define a single unit of measurement. Consequently, commodities that are heterogeneous before exchange remain incommensurable even during exchange.

V MONEY INTEGRATION

Another important characteristic of neoclassical analysis is the dichotomy between money and commodities, and the consequent logical indeterminacy of purchasing power. This problem seems, however, easily solvable. A mere empirical observation is sufficient. In fact, where can the relation between commodities and money be observed if not in exchange? From this simple consideration it follows that the purchasing power of money is determined by the commodity price level. The higher the price, the lower is purchasing power and vice versa. The problem has thus slipped from one level to another, from purchasing power to the price level. However, the relation between the two is *not* a causal one; purchasing power is, by definition, equal to the inverse of the price level. Their relation is nothing other than an identity, whose value has to be independently determined. Clearly, this means that the determination of purchasing power must precede the exchange in which this power is exerted.

The question remains unresolved: how can the demand for money be determined if it depends on a price level whose measure implies the explanation of the purchasing power of money? If the price level cannot be explained by the demand for money, why could it not be determined by the joint action of the demand for and supply of money? As in the case of relative prices, the solution could possibly be the result of an equilibrium in which all the variables are simultaneously determined. Then, it appears as if everything were going to be for the best in the best of all possible theories. In fact, all we have to do is to put the money equation into the General Equilibrium System and look for its solution. This is, for example, the approach adopted by Hicks. Having proved that Wicksell's theory leaves money prices completely undetermined, Hicks tries to overcome the dichotomy by introducing into his General Equilibrium Model the supply of and demand for money.

In reality, the problem is not simply a matter of equations and variables. The integration of money and commodities is not the result of an act of faith; the desire to integrate money is not sufficient to explain it. In fact, the money equation can at most be the result of the integration process: it can never be its cause. Supply of and demand for money depend on the integration and not the reverse. Now, that difficulty seems to be spurious here since all variables are determined simultaneously. There is no direct causal link between prices on one side and demand and supply on the other. Even if we accept simultaneity, however, integration still has to be explained because prices, as well as supply and demand, require the previous integration of money into the real world. In other words, we are confronted with the following question: what is the principle that guarantees the homogeneity of commodities and money?

Two logical possibilities are offered. We can answer either that the principle we are seeking is exchange or that the integration of commodities and money results from production. In the first case we are approaching the neoclassical point of view according to which money is basically nothing other than a commodity. The implication of such a theory, however, is that the whole system is reduced to a simple barter economy.[2] Furthermore, in this theoretical context the equation between supply of and demand for money becomes redundant because, according to Walras' Law, it is always necessarily included in the supplies and demands of all the other commodities. Thus, if the money equation is dropped, the system can determine only *relative* prices and the real rate of interest: Wicksell and the dichotomy triumph. We are thus left with the second case, which we shall analyse in some detail.

VI KEYNES' SOLUTION

From the last point two important results emerge, namely that exchange cannot explain integration and that money logically must be distinguished from any commodity set. The second answer to our previous question about the homogeneity between commodities and money is consistent with these two results and represents one of the most important findings of Keynes' work.

According to Keynes, the neoclassical dichotomy between relative prices and money prices is completely mistaken because, in reality, the two concepts are strictly interrelated, the price level being a function of relative prices and relative prices being themselves affected by a change on the side of money. Subsequently, he attempts to find the fundamental relationship between products and money.

In the *Treatise* the fundamental equations stress the role played by the forces of saving and investment in setting up a monetary equilibrium. Nevertheless, and according to Keynes himself, the fundamental equations do not solve the problem they lead up to: the purchasing power of money and the price level of output as a whole (Keynes, 1930, ch. 14). Keynes' interpretation of the Quantity Theory is rather interesting because it is capable of disproving the truism present in the original version of the Theory. The link between the quantity of money and the Bank rate, however, is not the solution we are seeking: the purchasing power of money must be determined before any other variable – it represents the 'necessary condition' of any monetary measure. For the same reason, equilibrium between saving and investment or between cash balances and real balances can perhaps explain the variation of a given price level, but can never determine it.

Keynes is aware of this failure and tries to overcome it in the *General Theory* (1936) by developing his analysis of the monetary definition of national income. In fact, a very fruitful suggestion is already present in his *Treatise on Money* (1930). Developing his chapter on the fundamental equations for the value of money, Keynes points out that

> Human effort and human consumption are the ultimate matters from which alone economic transactions are capable of deriving any significance; and all other forms of expenditure only acquire importance from their having some relationship, sooner or later, to the effort of producers or to the expenditure of consumers. (Keynes, 1930, p. 134)

Thus, we are led to think that the purchasing power of money must be derived from the relationship between labour and product, which results from the process of production.

Now, how is this relationship determined in terms of money? The answer is very well known to economists: money wages, expressed in wage-units, represent the homogeneous measure of labour and products. So stated, this result seems to be very similar to the classical (pre-classical in Keynes' own terms) theory of value. In fact, it differs from it on a small but very essential point: the monetary measure of labour. According to the classics, labour is measured in physical units, whereas Keynes' basic unit is a monetary one. Wages are then the objective link between money and product, a link that is the direct result of the process of creation called production.

Two main difficulties never overcome by the classics are thereby avoided, namely the physical heterogeneity of labour and the integration of money into the real world. Despite these considerations, there could be a traditional reluctance to accept this new theory of labour cost. It is worthwhile, then, to recall the reasons that persuaded Keynes to go against the mainstream represented by neoclassical thought.

Two important reasons can be found: first, the impossibility of integrating money directly into the commodity market, and, second, the necessary identity between commodities and the social cost of their creation (production). From the first argument it follows that the integration must be the result of production, whereas from the second consideration we learn that commodities are defined by the monetary payment associated with their production.

Are these two considerations sufficient to establish the identity between product and wages? The answer is undoubtedly positive if we remember that, according to Keynes, there is only *one* factor of production: labour (Keynes, 1936, pp. 213–15).[3] Commodities are determined by the monetary evaluation of their production; that is, since labour is the sole factor of production, by the wages[4] earned by the totality of labourers.

VII CONCLUSIONS

This short and intentionally provocative paper does not claim to be an exhaustive appraisal of the neoclassical analysis of price determination and money integration. We hope, however, that our critique will reactivate interest in these problems and the solutions proposed in the new Theory of Emissions (see chapters 6 and 8) based on Keynes' analysis of income determination. If physical heterogeneity and dichotomy are not avoided by the simultaneous solution of a General Equilibrium System, then the feelings of unease experienced by many authors in relation to the neoclassical theory are fully justified.

Let us conclude with the claim that Keynes' identity, Product ≡ Wages, represents the most fundamental concept of the whole of economic theory. Its acceptance is not a matter of faith but the ineluctable consequence of logical reasoning. Rejecting it requires the elaboration of a theory capable of explaining the integration of money in a world where more than one factor of production is at work. To quote Samuelson (1977, p. 789), 'Indeed, we still lack in 1972 a really adequate theoretical structure that encompasses the foundations of a money economy'. Such a theory does not yet exist. We maintain, with Keynes, that its foundations require the rejection of the neoclassical theory:[5]

The classical theorists resemble Euclidean geometers in a non-Euclidean world who, discovering that in experience straight lines apparently parallel often meet, rebuke the lines for not keeping straight – as the only remedy for the unfortunate collisions that are occurring. Yet, in truth, there is no remedy except to throw over the axiom of parallels and to work out a non-Euclidean geometry. Something similar is required to-day in economics. (Keynes, 1936, p. 16)

NOTES

1 That is, they remain unexplained. In fact, we do not introduce any distinction between determining and explaining, a logical determination of any concept implying necessarily its explanation.
2 If, alternatively, we do not include money in the commodity set, then our analysis must be consistent with the law of the circuit proposed by Bernard Schmitt (1975). One of the consequences of this law is the impossibility of deducing integration from exchange on the commodity market.
3 It is surely evident that we do not affirm that other factors such as land and capital are excluded from the process of production. However, these factors do not determine the value of the products, their influence being confined to the physical determination of production (Marx's 'use values').
4 Inclusive of indirect wages such as social securities, allowances, pensions and so on.

5 Keynes calls 'pre-classical' the theory that we call 'classical', and 'classical' the theory that we call 'neoclassical'.

REFERENCES

Cencini, A. and Schmitt, B. (1976) *La pensée de Karl Marx: critique et synthèse.* vol. I: *La valeur*, Castella, Albeuve (Switzerland).

Debreu, G. (1959) *Theory of Value*, John Wiley, New York.

Fradin, J. (1976) *Les Fondements logiques de la théorie néoclassique de l.échange*, Presses Universitaires de Grenoble, and François Maspero, Paris.

Friedman, M. (1956) 'The Quantity Theory of Money: A Restatement', in M. Friedman (ed.), *Studies in the Quantity Theory of Money*, University of Chicago Press, pp. 3-21.

Keynes, J. M. (1930) *A Treatise on Money*. vol. I: *The Pure Theory of Money*, Macmillan, London.

Keynes, J. M. (1936) *The General Theory of Employment, Interest and Money*, Macmillan, London.

Samuelson, P. (1977) 'Samuelson on the Neoclassical Dichotomy: A Reply', in *The Collected Scientific Papers of P. A. Samuelson*, vol. IV, MIT Press, Cambridge, Mass., pp. 780-9.

Schmitt, B. (1966) *Monnaie, salaires et profits*, Presses Universitaires de France, Paris.

Schmitt, B. (1975) *Théorie unitaire de la monnaie nationale et internationale*, Castella, Albeuve (Switzerland).

Schmitt, B. (1982) *Les Dépenses monétaires et le temps quantique*, Presses Universitaires de France, Paris.

Walras, L. (1874-78) *Eléments d'économie politique pure*, Corbaz, Lausanne; English translation: *Elements of Pure Economics*, ed. W. Jaffé, Allen and Unwin, London, 1954.

8

Wages and Profits in a Theory of Emissions

BERNARD SCHMITT and ALVARO CENCINI*

I INTRODUCTION

Distribution is one of the main problems with which economics has always been confronted. Are wages and profits complementary in the value of the product, or do they represent two separate issues? This question has been answered differently according to the process actually chosen as determinant. For example, Sir James Steuart defines profits as the positive difference between price and cost, thus confirming the predilection for the process of circulation. Now this analysis encounters an insurmountable obstacle. If profits are determined as the difference between price and cost, their macroeconomic value is necessarily nil, since cost represents the total amount of available income. How could it be possible to spend 150 units of money out of 100 units of income? That is the unavoidable paradox of Steuart's theory: in order to realize a positive profit of 50, the product whose cost is 100 units of money has to be sold for a price of 150; and yet only 100 units are available in the system. Steuart's 'profits upon alienation' remain inexplicable, mainly because he underestimates the role played by the process of production.

Some years later Ricardo introduces a new analysis, which establishes the complementarity of wages and profit in the value of the product. Retained and developed by Marx, this analysis aims to explain profit without introducing any discrepancy between price and cost. The solution is well known. Profits are defined as the difference between total cost of production, in terms of labour, and cost of labour-power (also in terms of labour) where labour-power is

* The authors are grateful to Christine Webb for assistance in improving the style of the English manuscript.

the only cost assumed by firms; so that profit is that part of the total cost of production which is given free of charge to the capitalist. To sell the product at a price corresponding to its value will, therefore, be sufficient for the realization of a positive profit, since

Value = Total labour   and   Total labour > Labour-power.

Now, such a transaction would be sufficient if it were possible; that is, if income were equal to the sum of wage-goods and profit-goods. However, this is not the case. Income, the money cost of production, is restricted to wages, and this implies the non-realization of profit-goods. Expenditure of wages can explain the realization of wage-goods; but where does the income corresponding to profit-goods come from, given that their production is supposed to be monetarily costless? Unlike Steuart, Marx explains profit by taking only the process of production into account. Yet the result is not fundamentally different; both theories fail in their attempt to explain profit because they maintain a dichotomous separation between production and circulation.

II THE IDENTITY OF PRODUCTION AND CIRCULATION

A substantial step towards the solution is realized by Keynes, who explicitly distinguishes between factor markets and the commodity market. On the factor markets, production is measured by its total cost, inclusive of profits. Now, Keynes recognizes the existence of only one factor of production, labour (Keynes, 1936, pp. 213–15). Accordingly, he measures income in wage-units and refutes the complementarity of profit and wages. Hence profits are originally nothing but wages. In order to explain this transformation of wages into profits, we have to introduce the commodity market. It is in fact by the interaction of the two markets that profit can be fully understood.

As Keynes proved, final expenditure of income on the commodity market is the necessary counterpart of income creation on the factor markets. Thus, wages represent the purchasing power necessary and sufficient for the final purchase of wage-goods and profit-goods. Bringing the two processes of production and circulation into identity, Keynes is able to explain profit as that part of wages which is paid for the production of profit-goods and spent for their final purchase. Profits are therefore formed and realized simultaneously, through the confusion of the two processes. Let us verify this last point by the quantum theory of expenditures.

III THE EMISSIONS

As has been shown (Schmitt, chapter 6 above), expenditures are instantaneous events defining a finite and indivisible period of time. These events can also be called *emissions*. As we shall see, monetary expenditures are emissions since they refer to a production that is itself an emission. Thus, income is defined as the exchange between two simultaneous emissions, a monetary one and a real one. Without this exchange the monetary emission would be empty and production non-existent, since purely physical goods are a collection of heterogeneous objects rather than a product.

Emissions are divided into two main categories, according to whether they relate to the production process or to the circulation process.

The first emission is concerned with payment of wages and represents the positive side of income: its creation. Imagine a process of production taking place during a given period of time. What the theory tells us is that the process and its result, the product, are one and the same thing. The determination of production and product is therefore simultaneous. Moreover, it is instantaneous since it coincides with an expenditure: the payment of wages. Thus, wages are the instantaneous definition of a production occupying a finite period of time. Let us consider them more accurately.

First, wages are a monetary expenditure and, from this point of view, can be considered a nominal emission. If we introduce the banking system, this emission can be represented as in figure 8.1. At the very instant wages are paid, money accomplishes a full circle and is recaptured by the bank that emits it. By its own nature, money

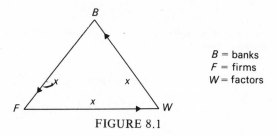

FIGURE 8.1

cannot be held by anyone; it is defined as a circular emission whose significance lies in the mark it impresses on the economy. As a result of this instantaneous operation firms are indebted to the banks, whereas factors of production are credited by the same amount. In our teminology, firms have a negative quantum deposit and workers a positive quantum deposit. Now, this monetary emission becomes meaningful once it is associated with a social production. Payment of wages is in fact related to the social activity of producing goods and services. Thus, wages are better defined as a simultaneous exchange of a monetary and a real emission. The real emission defines the product as the real content of wages and allows the transformation of the money issued by the bank into a unit of payment. As a result of this transformation, workers own the product in the form of money. Income is, therefore, the monetary form of the product created by workers. This real aspect of the first quantum expenditure can be described as an instantaneous movement of a net credit from workers to workers through firms and banks. Graphically, it can be shown as figure 8.2. Payment of wages literally creates the product. Workers are the agents of this creation, which gives an object to their financial credit (positive quantum deposit). Thus, workers are both 'emitters' and beneficiaries of the economic product. By the same operation the physical product is deposited in F, where it fills the negative quantum deposit owing to the nominal emission of wages. Newly produced goods and services are the object of the workers' positive quantum deposit, which is the economic definition of the physical product stocked in F.

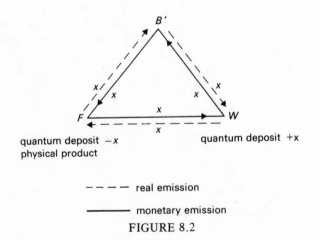

quantum deposit $-x$ quantum deposit $+x$
physical product

– – – – real emission

———— monetary emission

FIGURE 8.2

An important result of this analysis is that wages are not the monetary counterpart of the product, but the product itself. According to this analysis, in contra-distinction with previous theories, money and product are one and the same thing. Wages *are* the product, and the product is fully defined by them. Finally, the product is instantaneously determined by the quantum expenditure corresponding to the payment of wages.

The second emission is concerned with the final purchase of the product. As in the first case, this quantum expenditure is simultaneously monetary and real. When workers W spend their income, this operation is carried on by a nominal emission of money circulating instantaneously from B to B (figure 8.3). The result of this emission can be easily understood. Workers lose their positive quantum deposit, so that the final situation is one of perfect financial equilibrium (= 0) both in F and in W. At the same time, as money is emitted and recovered by B, the physical product is transferred from F to W. In spending their income, workers free the physical product from the negative quantum deposit in which it has been put, and destroy definitively its economic value.

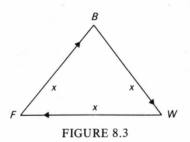

FIGURE 8.3

The first emission, which defines the creation of income, has as its exact counterpart the second emission, which corresponds to its final destruction. Analogously, this emission is an instantaneous event whose two aspects, monetary and real, are perfectly coexistent. The main point to be underlined here is the perfect correspondence between negative and positive quantum deposits. Any expenditure of income, a positive quantum deposit, destroys a negative quantum deposit of exactly the same amount and defines the final purchase of a corresponding product. Hence, the final purchase of any product implies an exchange between equal amounts of positive and negative quantum deposits. In other words, income spent for the purchase of a given product is always necessarily equal to its value: no distinction can be drawn between price and value.

In such a context, how can we explain profit? If price equals value and if wages equal product, can distribution still be accounted for?

IV INTERNAL PROFITS

We shall distinguish between two kinds of profit, which can be called *internal* and *external*. Internal profits are that part of income which is (re-)distributed as rent, interest and dividends, whereas external profits are false incomes related to a pathological working of the economic system.

Let us consider first internal profit. If the commodity market and factor markets were autonomous, the identity of price and value within a wage-units theory of production would be irreconcilable with the existence of positive profit. However, as Keynes pointed out, profit is immediately understandable once we consider the two markets in their organic unity. This means that expenditures on the commodity market are necessarily related to expenditures on the factor markets. Obviously enough, final purchase of any given commodity requires the previous creation of a correspondent income, i.e. the payment of its cost of production. In reality, the relation between those two emissions is even more significant: expenditures on the commodity market are not only based upon, but can also modify, expenditures on the factor markets. This happens when workers receive only part of the physical product in exchange for their wages. Profits, the difference between total wages and workers' purchasable product, transform the initial emission on the factor markets. Payment of wages, in its nominal aspect, is partially and contemporaneously a final purchase. In other words, a positive profit implies an expenditure of income within the payment of wages: the nominal payment of wages by F is simultaneously a final expenditure of profit. Finally, the realization of a positive profit on the commodity market must be instantaneously interpreted as an income expenditure on the factor markets. Purchases on the two markets take place respecting the identity between price and value, and yet profits are indisputably positive.

A short numerical example may prove useful. Suppose that firms F pay 100 units of wages to workers W, and that the product will finally be shared between wages and profit in a proportion of 4 to 1. Accordingly, workers receive only 80 units of the product, as a result of their spending, the remaining 20 units being captured by F. Now, these 20 units of profit represent the final expenditure hidden in the

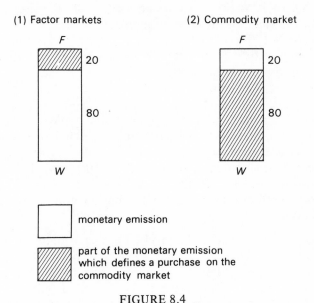

(1) Factor markets   (2) Commodity market

☐ monetary emission

▨ part of the monetary emission
which defines a purchase on the
commodity market

FIGURE 8.4

payment of wages. This may be illustrated in figure 8.4. The Keynesian identity between expenditures on (1) and (2) is fully respected, as is Marx's identity of price and value: the totality of the product is purchased by the totality of wages independently of its final distribution.

Let us analyse this once again. According to the quantum theory of monetary expenditures, the emission of wages defines the product as a whole. Its distribution between wages and profits is therefore the result of a subsequent operation taking place on the commodity market. Although correct, this observation is only the first step towards the solution. In fact, it can be proved that workers' final expenditure on the commodity market modifies retroactively the emission of wages. More precisely, the formation of a positive (internal) profit signifies the inclusion of a positive expenditure on the commodity market *within* the expenditure on the factor markets. Profits are therefore defined as a positive purchase of products, which is included in the payment of wages. In other words, workers' final transfer of income in favour of firms defines a profit that has already been spent within the emission of wages. Referring to our previous numerical example, we can see that:

(1) on the commodity market, workers' expenditure of 100 units of income is in reality a final purchase of 80, since the selling price

is equal to 125; firms acquire an income of 20 units, corresponding to the value of the remaining product;

(2) the profit of 20 units acquired by firms on the commodity market
corresponds to a final purchase of goods that has already taken
place on the factor markets.

Finally,

(3) workers' expenditure on the commodity market is the necessary
retroactive sanction of a final purchase included in the emission
of wages. Hereafter, price and value are inevitably identical:
value (i.e. the amount of wages) is 100, and 100 is also the
amount of income spent for the final purchase of the whole
product (80 on the commodity market and 20 on the factor
markets).

As a result of this process, the product is shared between wage-goods
and profit-goods. Contrary to any obvious expectation, this result is
consistent with the identity of wages and product. In fact, the
complementarity of wages and profits is verified only in real terms,
the value of the product being always identical to nominal wages.
Thus,

$$\text{Product} \equiv \text{Nominal wages}^1 \tag{1}$$

and

$$\text{Product} \equiv \text{Real wages} + \text{Real profits} \tag{2}$$

are simultaneously and consistently verified for any level of production.

V EXTERNAL PROFITS

Pathological expressions of our economic system, inflation and
unemployment, are symptomatic of a new kind of emission whose
result is represented by the external profits. Thus, the causal chain
goes from these emissions to inflation and unemployment through
the formation of profits, which are not integrated in the payment of
wages. The central point, therefore, is the existence of emissions that
allow the creation of false incomes.[2] We call these emissions *empty*,
because the monetary side is not backed by a correspondent real
emission. In other words, the payment of wages corresponding to

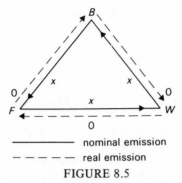

- nominal emission
- - - - - real emission

FIGURE 8.5

these empty emissions gives to the workers a product equal to zero (figure 8.5). Payment of wages defines a negative quantum deposit in F and a positive quantum deposit in W. In the case of empty emissions, however, the financial credit of W has no object. The physical product does not fill the negative quantum deposit owing to the nominal emission of wages. Obviously, this conclusion does not mean that workers' physical production of goods and services is nil. In fact, workers do produce, but their product is instantaneously appropriated by firms. Thus, external profits are clearly defined as the direct appropriation of product resulting from an emission that gives the workers a nominal wage deprived of its object.

VI CONCLUSION

The aim of this short paper is to stimulate interest in a theory whose origin can be found in Keynes' analysis of windfall profits. Based on a new conception of time in economics, this theory seems capable of giving an original answer to many still unresolved problems of our science. The conceptual and terminological difficulties, inherent in any new scientific theory, should not represent an unsurmountable obstacle to its acceptance. As Keynes (1936, p. viii) put it: 'The difficulty lies, not in the new ideas, but in escaping from the old ones, which ramify, for those brought up as most of us have been, into every corner of our minds.'

NOTES

1 Nominal wages ≡ Wages paid to the factors of production.
2 Being excluded from wages, external profits are necessarily false incomes, since wages represent the totality of income.

REFERENCES

Friboulet, J. J. (1980) *Salaires réels et profits nominaux: une nouvelle définition de l'écart inflationniste*, PhD thesis, University of Dijon.

Keynes, J. M. (1930) *A Treatise on Money*. Vol. I: *The Pure Theory of Money*, Macmillan, London.

Keynes, J. M. (1936) *The General Theory of Employment, Interest and Money*, Macmillan, London.

Schmitt, B. (1982) *Les Dépenses monétaires et le temps quantique*, Presses Universitaires de France, Paris.

Steuart, J. (1767) *An Inquiry into the Principles of Political Oeconomy*, A. Millar and T. Cadell, London; also available from Oliver & Boyd, Edinburgh and London (1966) ed. Andrew S. Skinner.

Part Four

Monetary Theory and Monetary Policy

9

The Task of Monetary Theory: The Hayek–Sraffa Debate in a Modern Perspective

MEGHNAD DESAI*

[T]he task of monetary theory is a much wider one than is commonly assumed. Its task is nothing less than to cover a second time the whole field which is treated by pure theory under the assumption of barter, and to investigate what changes in the conclusions of pure theory are made necessary by the introduction of indirect exchange. (Hayek, 1935a, p. 127)

I INTRODUCTION

In awarding the Nobel Prize jointly to Hayek and Myrdal, the Nobel Prize committee specifically mentioned their contribution to monetary theory in the early 1930s. In Hayek's case this refers to *Prices and Production* (1935a) and *Monetary Theory and Trade Cycle* (1935b) and in Myrdal's case to *Monetary Equilibrium* (1939). These, together with Keynes' *Treatise on Money* (1930) can be said to form a collection of books on the foundations of monetary theory starting from a common point of origin in Wicksell but then going on to develop different approaches along Marshallian as against Walrasian (Austrian or Swedish) lines. The advent of Keynes' *General Theory* killed this revolution in monetary theory, and only in recent years has monetary theory enjoyed the kind of attention it got in those days. This is not the occasion to evaluate these books together. I shall concentrate very much on Hayek's contribution in this abortive revolution.

* I am grateful to Adrian Winnet of the University of Bath for bringing the Sraffa article to my attention and to Sheila Verkaeren of CORE for her help in tracking down obscure books and articles.

The publication of *Prices and Production* and *Treatise on Money* almost simultaneously was an exciting event for the young generation of economists of 1931. While neither of the books gets read very much today, learned journals were then occupied with clarification of the theories and debates about their comparative merits. Not only did Hayek review Keynes, to which Keynes replied, but others, such as Hicks, Shackle, Evan Durbin, Abba Lerner and Nicholas Kaldor, joined in the debate. Many of this younger generation of economists preferred Hayek's lean and analytical (Walrasian) treatment, in almost econometric terms, of the interaction of money and production to Keynes' fundamental equations (Hayek, 1931, 1932; Keynes, 1931. For relative evaluation favourable to Hayek: Shackle, 1933. See also Durbin, 1935; Nurske, 1934. For a recent evaluation of *Prices and Production* see Hicks, 1967.) The single hostile review of Hayek was by Piero Sraffa in one of his rare forays in print. Sraffa's attack on Hayek goes to the root of the problems of monetary theory in a general equilibrium context, and hence we intend in this paper to revisit the debate (Sraffa, 1932; Hayek, 1932).

The reasons for looking at the Sraffa–Hayek debate are not only historical. Recently there has been a sustained attempt on the part of economic theorists to re-examine the foundation of monetary theory and especially to characterize a monetary economy in a General Equilibrium context. Much of this work is highly mathematical and has not yet 'trickled down'. Many of the issues raised in the Sraffa–Hayek debate are relevant to evaluating the more recent contributions. Inasmuch as the process of re-examination of monetary theory is not yet complete, such a link between the early debate and the present one may be of some interest. (The bibliography here is very large; see Hahn, 1973, Clower, 1977, and Hayashi, 1976, and the articles cited in these places.)

In section II, we briefly summarize the argument of *Prices and Production* (*PP* hereafter) supplementing it with *Monetary Theory and Trade Cycle* (*MTTC*) wherever necessary. Section III will briefly note sympathetic articles but will quickly move on to Sraffa's criticism of Hayek and Hayek's reply to it. Inasmuch as Sraffa's version is not well known (Hicks, 1967, does not cite it, nor do Shackle, 1933, or Durbin, 1935), we shall treat it in detail. Section IV will review the debate from a current point of view since we have now presumably learned more about the issues. The last section will then relate to recent developments in monetary theory.

II THE MODEL

Hayek delivered four lectures at the London School of Economics in February 1931 which were published in September of that year as *PP*. This was Hayek's first book to be published directly in English. It was reprinted within a month, and after a second reprint a second edition came out in 1935 incorporating Hayek's response to Hansen and Trout's criticism in *Econometrica* 1934. In the meantime *PP* was translated into German and Japanese and Hayek's earlier work on trade cycles appeared in English as *MTTC*. The Walrasian influence on Hayek is much more explicit in *MTTC*, and this influence is vital in understanding the concerns of *PP*. This influence is brought out explicitly in the following question where Hayek is criticizing statistical attempts to explain business cycles:

There is a fundamental difficulty inherent in all trade cycle theories which take as their starting point an empirically ascertained disturbance of the equilibrium of the various branches of production. This difficulty arises because, in stating the effects of the disturbance, they have to make use of the logic of equilibrium theory [Hayek adds in a footnote: 'By equilibrium theory we here primarily understand the modern theory of the general interdependence of all economic quantities, which has been most perfectly expressed by the Lausanne School of theoretical economics.'] Yet this logic, properly followed through, can do no more than demonstrate that such disturbances of equilibrium can come only from outside, i.e. that they represent a change in economic data and that the economic system always reacts to such changes by its well-known methods of adaptation, i.e. the formation of a new equilibrium. No tendency towards the special expansion of certain branches of production, however plausibly adduced, no chance shift in demand, in distribution, or in productivity, could adequately explain, within the framework of this theoretical system, why a general disproportionality between supply and demand should arise. For the essential means of explanation in static theory, which is, at the same time, the indispensable assumption for the explanation of particular price variations, is the assumption that prices supply an automatic mechanism for equilibrating supply and demand. (*MTTC*, pp. 42–3)

It would seem from the above (and other evidence in *PP* and *MTTC*) that in Hayek's view the Walrasian model was characterized not only by equilibrium but a *rapid convergence* to a (new) equilibrium if any disturbance occurred. Thus one could not observe, much less 'identify', periods of disequilibrium in a Walrasian economy. It should be immediately said that, while we now know about conditions for stability of competitive equilibrium, we do not know much about speeds of convergence in general. Hayek's view of the Walrasian model is much more stringent, and makes more additional implicit assumptions about the Walrasian economy, than is necessary.

Hayek moves immediately to assert that, since a Walrasian economy cannot exhibit disequilibrium, observed disequilibrium must arise from a factor not in the Walrasian economy, i.e. money. The introduction of money opens out the 'closed' Walrasian system and permits cycles to occur.

In tracing business cycles to monetary influence, Hayek was careful to reject the view of Cassel, Pigou, Fisher and others that money causes disturbance by changing the general price level. Hayek rejects in the very first lecture in *PP* the analytical validity of an aggregate price index measuring the purchasing power of money, and even remarks on the 'superfluity' of such a concept (*PP*, p. 29).[1] The crude Hume doctrine is quickly dismissed in favour of Ricardo, and especially Thornton's appreciation of the relations between demand for capital, expected profitability and the cost of credit. After mentioning the contributions of Bentham, Malthus and Walras to the concept of forced savings, he arrives at Wicksell and von Mises whom he accepts as having provided the best starting point for a monetary theory.

Hayek's attitude to Wicksell is one of a sympathetic critic. He finds Wicksell's concept of the natural rate of interest helpful, but Wicksell's definition confusing. Thus the natural rate of interest could not be at the same time one that would equilibrate the supply of real savings and the demand for capital, and one that would prevail if the transactions were carried on *in natura* in a barter economy, i.e. the rate at which the price level would be stable. As he made clear in *MTTC*,

> The rate of interest at which, in an expanding economy, the amount of new money entering circulation is just sufficient to keep the price level stable, is always lower than the rate which would keep the amount of available loan-capital equal to the amount simultaneously saved by the public, and thus, despite

the stability of the price level, it makes possible a development leading away from the equilibrium position. (*MTTC*, pp. 113-14)

Mises, on the other hand, was the first to point out but not develop the differential effect of credit received by producers as against consumers. This is the theory Hayek developed in the next two lectures forming the second and third chapters of *PP*.

Hayek starts by sketching an economy with many stages of production, beginning from capital goods produced by land and labour alone and progressing to consumer goods produced by intermediate goods plus land and labour. Land and labour are the only original means of production; all other inputs are produced. There is no fixed capital in the model, that is, no joint production.

By assumption, the structure of production or, equivalently, the Leontief input coefficient matrix is triangular. Hayek himself used a triangle with its base equal to output of consumer goods (in value terms) and the altitude representing time between the first and the final stage of production. The proportion of the area of the triangle (measuring all the intermediate production) to the base measured the period of production. By the Austrian theory of capital, then, the longer the period of production (higher the altitude), the more productive (in physical terms) was the system.

Hayek starts by assuming the system in initial equilibrium. In this equilibrium the rate of interest (implicitly on bank credit) equals the natural rate, and the length of period of production corresponds to the equilibrium of voluntary saving and demand for capital. The price margin between two successive states of production equals the interest cost of sustaining the higher stage of production. Then Hayek traces out a new equilibrium which is reached if the rate of saving goes up, for some reason. As he says, '[I]t is my conviction that if one wants to explain economic phenomena at all, we have no means available but to build on the foundations given by the concept of a tendency towards equilibrium' (*PP*, p. 34). Thus, rather than concentrate on the transition (traverse) to the new equilibrium, he describes the new equilibrium. Since the increase in savings is voluntary, the reduction in the interest rate makes it profitable to lengthen the period of production. Firms that previously produced intermediate inputs for their requirements internally now can buy them from firms that specialize in this higher stage. It becomes easier to undertake longer methods of production. Such methods are already known – blueprints exist for such production processes, and no technical change occurs. Since consumer goods prices have fallen, equilibrium is restored when the more productive methods bear fruit in terms of higher physical output which can be sold at the lower price with normal profit. Despite the reduced money expenditure on consumer goods, there will in equilibrium be a higher real consumption. Equilibrium is reached when enough demand for capital for longer methods of production has matched the higher savings. There is a short-run inventory problem for the consumer goods producers, and if factors of production (intermediate products) are specific to lower stages of production they suffer temporary loss of earnings, but non-specific factors move to higher stages of production. The convergence to new equilibrium does not cause any problems, e.g. cyclical adjustments, which Hayek thinks worth discussing. Since the sacrifice is voluntary, consumers are willing to wait till the new methods yield extra consumption goods at lower prices.

The situation is different when the savings are not voluntary but are 'forced' due to inflation. Hayek analyses this case by taking as a starting point banks lending at a rate below the natural rate. In case this may sound arbitrary, Hayek had already explained in *MTTC* why such a thing may occur in a monetary economy:

> the situation in which the money rate of interest is below the 'natural rate' need not by any means originate in a *deliberate lowering* of the rate of interest by the banks. The same effect can be obviously produced by an improvement in the expectations of profit or by a diminution in the rate of saving, which may drive the 'natural rate' (at which the demand for and the supply of savings are equal) above its previous level; while the banks refrain from raising their rate of interest to a proportionate extent, but continue to lend at the previous rate, and thus enable a greater demand for loans to be satisfied than would be possible by the exclusive use of the available supply of savings. (*MTTC*, p. 147)

In this case producers are encouraged to lengthen the period of production; i.e., new firms enter the earlier stages of production financed by borrowing, although there is no real saving to justify it. Factors are bid away from consumer goods industries though the nominal demand for consumer goods is unchanged. The resulting inflation robs the consumers of their real consumption. Now, banks need to go on extending such credit until the new methods yield fruit. But they may take a long time. 'For obvious reasons, the banks cannot continue indefinitely to extend credits. . . .' (*PP*, p. 90). On the other hand, 'there is no doubt that, if their money receipts should rise again, they [the consumers] would immediately attempt to expand consumption to the usual proportion' (*PP*, p. 57). This happens quite soon, since factor rewards are bid up by producers in the earlier stages of production (though Hayek does not make it clear whether this improves rewards in real terms as well or just in nominal terms). Thus, before the lengthening is consumated, demand for consumer goods rises so fast that the rise in consumer goods prices makes it profitable for consumer goods producers to bid away the factors and shorten the period of production. Alternatively, banks stop credit expansion or cannot keep expanding at the rate necessary to cover the factor price spiral. Many capital goods projects are abandoned incomplete and factors are unemployed. They cannot immediately be employed in consumer goods industries since the latter's demand for labour is limited by the supply of intermediate product they need to produce output. This is a crisis.

The solution to the crisis is not to extend more credit.

> The only way permanently to 'mobilise' all available resources is, therefore, not to use artificial stimulants whether during a crisis or thereafter – but to leave it to time to effect a permanent cure by the slow process of adapting the structure of production to the means available for capital purposes. (*PP*, p. 99)

Thus, cycles are caused when 'the natural' movement of prices is disturbed by the movements in the supply of money (*PP*, p. 85). Now, in a crisis, credit shrinks more than is strictly necessary in light of available supply of savings – the banking system, over-reacts. But Hayek had little faith in what may now be called fine tuning of money supply (see especially *PP*, pp. 97–8). Indeed, Hayek blamed much of the trouble on the 'elastic' currency. He recommends in the last chapter of *PP* that to be neutral – non-disturbing to the natural movement of prices – money supply, very broadly defined, should be totally invariant. Money supply is not neutral if it keeps the general price level stable. Money supply need not be expanded just because output is increasing; much rather that prices should fall and pass the fruit of technical progress to the consumer.

Such an invariant money supply may require a counter-cyclical credit policy. 'It is probably entirely utopian to expect anything of that kind from central bankers so long as general opinion still believes that it is the duty of the central bankers to accommodate trade and to expand credit as the increasing demands of trade require' (*PP*, p.

116). The problem is, however, much more complicated, since the demand for money can depend crucially on the degree of vertical integration. This leads to a crucial concept on which Hayek spends too little time – '*the coefficient of money transaction*', which is 'the proportion between the total flow of goods and the part which takes the form of an exchange against money or the rate at which goods are exchanged against money' (*PP*, p. 118). This coefficient changes over time and is different for different stages of the production cycle. Thus one may reach

> the conclusion that changes in the demand for money caused by changes in the proportion between the total flow of goods to that part of it which is affected by money or, as we may tentatively call that proportion, of the coefficient of money transactions, should be justified by changes in the volume of money if money is to remain neutral towards the price system and the structure of production. (*PP*, p. 121)

This was however not within the bounds of possibility. 'Hence the only practical maxim for monetary policy to be derived from our considerations is probably the negative one that the simple fact of an increase in production and trade forms no justification for an expansion of credit. . .' (*PP*, p. 125).

In case the audience felt a bit disappointed at such a small practical gain from four lectures, Hayek brought out for them the analytical lessons that had been learnt. One was to note the imperfect state of monetary theory, where 'even some of the most fundamental problems in the field are yet unsolved, that some of the accepted doctrines are of very doubtful validity' (*PP*, p. 126). (Such a conclusion can be drawn even today from many debates on monetary theory!) Hayek hoped to have showed that money exerted a determining influence and 'that, therefore, no analysis of actual economic phenomena is complete if the role played by money is neglected' (*PP*, p. 126). He then summarized the tasks of monetary theory quoted at the outset of this paper. The uncertain state of monetary theory also meant that there was no case yet for a radical reconstruction of the monetary system, especially to replace the Gold Standard by a managed currency.

It may have seemed to some of his audience, as it did to his socialist students, that Hayek was not drawing the obvious conclusions about the guilty party – the bankers who caused the cyclical fluctuations, according to his own analysis. Indeed, Evan Durbin drew the conclusion that only socialization of the banking system would solve the problems of monetary policy. In *MTTC* Hayek explicitly answered such questions. The theoretical analysis of the cycle was the same:

> *The determining cause of the cyclical fluctuations is, therefore, that on account of the elasticity of the volume of currency media, the rate of interest demanded by banks is not necessarily always equal to the equilibrium rate, but is, in the short-run, determined by considerations of banking liquidity.* (*MTTC*, p. 180; italicized in the original)

But there was no reason to blame the bankers for this:

> Nobody has ever asked them to pursue a policy other than that which, as we have seen, gives rise to cyclical fluctuations; and it is not in their power to do away with such fluctuations, seeing that the latter originate not from the very nature of the modern organization of credit. So long as we make use of bank credit as a means of furthering economic development, we shall have to put up with the resulting trade cycle. (*MTTC*, p. 189)

The practical conclusion is a Schumpetarian one of cycles being the price we pay for progress. The technical difficulties of defining money, of keeping it neutral in face of possible sectoral and secular fluctuations in the coefficient of money transactions, the slim chance that any solution even if it could be found would be implemented by the banking system, subject as it was to popular pressure, made a very pessimistic conclusion that cycles were here to stay. They were a feature of a monetary economy.

III DEBATE

Prices and Production, with its triangle illustrations of the structure of production, the analytical rigour of its presentation, especially the readiness of the author to pursue a theoretical argument through to its logical end, caught the imagination of the young economists. Many of these were at that time associated with the London School of Economics (LSE). In the first issue of the *Review of Economic Studies*, Shackle compared Keynes' *Treatise* with *PP*. Hayek's model of the interest rate determination, with a direct and immediate adjustment to excess demand or supply for capital, was much more logically satisfactory, according to Shackle, than Keynes' argument, which depended on the degree to which banks offset bullish or bearish behaviour of the public in the financial markets by their own actions. Shackle leaves no doubt in the reader's mind that he preferred the rigorous presentation of Hayek, with its general equilibrium background, to Keynes' rather messy argument, which seemed to get tangled up in institutional details (Shackle, 1933).

The limitations of a triangular technology matrix were noted immediately by Ragnar Nurkse (1934) and by Evan Durbin (1935). Nurkse, again in *the Review of Economic Studies*, criticized the triangularity as too restrictive and suggested what he called a circular assumption. He put forward in this respect Marx's two-departmental schema with its mutual interdependence as a better model. Durbin also appreciated the problem of purchase of lower-stage inputs by higher-stage industries, and put forth a flow chart of simultaneous purchase and sale, adding a financial sector as well. The financial sector received all savings and let out to businessmen. The market for financial assets mediated in a manner Keynes had suggested in the *Treatise*. Durbin's work, which was far-reaching in its extension of Hayek, deserves much more detailed treatment than we can give it here.

But if the Young Turks of LSE were enthusiastic, those of Cambridge were unmistakably hostile. Sraffa's review article on *PP* appeared in the *Economic Journal* of March 1932, provoking a reply by Hayek and a rejoinder by Sraffa in the June issue. Sraffa in his review immediately moved in to attack by blaming *PP* for 'unintelligibility' and saying: 'the inescapable conclusion is that it can only add to the prevailing confusion of thought on the subject' (Sraffa, 1932a, p. 12).

The problem, according to Sraffa, is Hayek's theoretical interest in the neutrality of money and his practical advocacy of it. Hayek was concentrating on money purely as a medium exchange and neglecting that it was 'also a store of value, and the standard in terms of which debts, and other legal obligations, habits, opinions, conventions – in short, all kinds of relations between men, are more or less rigidly fixed' (Sraffa, 1932a, p. 43). Thus in Hayek's model, Sraffa said, 'There are no debts, no money-contracts, no wage-agreements, no sticky prices in his suppositions.' But if money is only a medium of exchange, and all prices are flexible, the money-ness of money is assumed away. But if that were the case, failure to maintain money supply unchanged should not have any adverse consequences. Why, then, in Hayek's case are they so serious? Sraffa claims that this can be due either to logical error or to introduction of some irrelevant non-monetary consideration; and he seeks in his review to track down the answer. He first takes up the issue of 'forced saving'.

Sraffa's criticism of the 'forced saving' aspect of Hayek's theory is that Hayek fails to show why voluntary, as against forced, saving has different consequences. Sraffa rejects Hayek's idea that those whose consumption was curtailed by inflation will try and get back to initial consumption level as soon as their money receipts go up. He says:

> nothing of the sort will happen. One class has, for a time, robbed another class of a part of their incomes; and has saved the plunder. When the robbery comes to an end, it is clear that the victims cannot possibly consume the capital which is now well out of their reach. If they are wage earners, who have all the time consumed every penny of their income, they have no wherewithal to expand consumption. And if they are capitalists who have not shared in the plunder, they may indeed be induced to consume now a part of their capital by the fall in the rate of interest; but no more than if the rate had been lowered by the 'voluntary savings' of other people. (Sraffa, 1932a, p. 48)

Sraffa goes on to notice Hayek's emphasis on the problem of allocation of credit in the correct proportion between consumer and producer goods, but finds such a belief in powers of banking an irrelevant element.

> What has happened is simply that, since money has been thoroughly 'neutralised' from the start, whether its quantity rises, falls, is kept steady, makes not the slightest difference; at the same time an extraneous element, in the shape of the supposed power of the banks to settle the way in which money is spent, has crept into the argument and has done all the work.

Sraffa then examines the relation between Wicksell and Hayek and especially Hayek's criticism of Wicksell which we cited above. This is an interesting piece of debate on Wicksell in its own right, independent of other criticisms. Sraffa attributes to Hayek the notion that a divergence between the actual and the natural rate (which Hayek calls the equilibrium rate) is possible only in a monetary economy, since Hayek says that 'the quantity of [money] available for capital purposes may be arbitrarily changed by the banks' (*PP*, pp. 20–1). Sraffa then proceeds to demonstrate that in a barter economy there are as many natural rates of interest as there are commodities, but they would not be equilibrium rates. Each of the natural rates will be equal to the equilibrium rate when spot and forward prices coincide. Thus, in a non-money economy,

> when equilibrium is disturbed and during the time of transition, the 'natural' rates of interest on loans in terms of the commodities, the output of which is increasing, must be higher, to various extents, than the 'natural' rates on the commodities the output of which is falling, and . . . there may be as many 'natural' rates as there are commodities. It will be noticed that, under free competition, this divergence of rates is as essential to the effecting of this transition as is the divergence of prices from the costs of production; it is, in fact, another aspect of the same thing. (Sraffa, p. 50)

In respect of Hayek's criticism of Wicksell that the natural rate of interest could not both keep the price level stable and equate the demand and supply of capital in a growing economy, Sraffa sides with Wicksell. In times of growth (i.e. in transition to a new equilibrium) there is no unique equilibrium rate of interest – the one for producer goods being higher than that for consumer goods. But for Wicksell, one can define a weighted average of the natural rates using the same weights as for the general price level, and this will meet the dual requirements. Hayek, since he denied the validity of a general price index, cannot use such a defence. Now of course, such an average rate of interest is not unique. There is, for each composite commodity, a corresponding natural rate which will equalize the purchasing power of money saved and invested in terms of that composite commodity. Thus, a non-monetary economy with a composite commodity that is used as a standard for deferred payments will in fact be the same as a monetary economy with neutral money. Thus neutral money can be defined for a non-monetary economy as well as a monetary economy.

Sraffa's final point of criticism is regarding the smooth transition to equilibrium in a non-monetary economy when savings rise. Matching saving and investment is as much a problem in a barter economy as in a monetary economy unless plans coincide. Hayek thinks in terms of additional savings releasing a flow of finished goods that can be borrowed by investors. But this is a 'delusion'. Producers of consumer goods must anticipate the fall in demand and not produce the unwanted goods. This alone will release the resources that the producers of intermediate goods can use. Otherwise the increase in savings is abortive.

In his reply Hayek reiterated that it was his very object to distinguish between a barter and a money economy. The distinction was to be sought not in the textbook descriptions of the uses of money but in the inherent tendency of a real economy towards equilibrium and of monetary factors to lead to disequilibrium. He then explains the crisis in terms of loss of value of capital invested in producer goods industries when relative prices of consumer goods suddenly go up owing to consumers' desire to restore their consumption after a period of forced saving. In his reply Hayek makes the lag of money wages behind prices the root cause of misdirected investment. Upon injection of money, there is initially a substitution in favour of capital against labour. This is one reason for the slow growth of wages. But given the triangular technology, all must ultimately rise in proportion to the additional amount of money injected. Then, unless the increase in money supply is accelerated, the boom must come to an end. This is what causes losses of capital value (Hayek sometimes uses the word 'depreciation') for the producers.

> This means, however, not only that they must stop adding to the existing capital, but also that they will be unable to maintain and replace all the capital which is the produce of the forced saving. Except insofar as they are able, and find it profitable, to make up for this at the expense of their own increased income . . . , they will be able to replace their capital only at the same rate as before the forced saving took place, and their capital will, therefore, be gradually worn down to something approaching its former state. (Hayek, 1932b, p. 218)

Thus the fall in demand for capital goods at one stage will make the fixed capital of the higher stage of production worth less; i.e., the firms in this higher stage will accumulate unplanned inventory of finished goods, the price of the produce will fall and so will the present value of the capital equipment. Thus the producer at this higher stage has been robbed. 'Whether he likes it or not, the actions of other people have destroyed his capital' (Hayek, 1932b, p. 243).

Hayek's reply to Sraffa's demonstration about natural rates of interest in a non-money economy is to admit the multiplicity of natural rates of interest; but he adds: '[T]here might at any moment be as many "natural" rates of interest as there are commodities, all of which would be *equilibrium rates*; . . .' (p. 245). This is curious, as Sraffa pointed out in his rejoinder. The diversity of natural rates can only mean a transitional stage where the relative prices are still adjusting to a new equilibrium. They cannot all be equilibrium rates – not unless all substitution possibilities are excluded. In the latter case, Sraffa said that, since Hayek does not admit of an index of prices, the money rate would have to be equal to all these divergent natural rates.

We can say that in the debate about the natural rates Sraffa shows that a barter economy can be out of equilibrium as much as a monetary economy, and that 'neutrality of money' in an economy with money and establishing a rate of interest in terms of a composite commodity are equivalent. This is a more general proportion than the one Hayek starts with, which excludes disequilibrium in a barter economy.[2] In the debate about forced saving, Sraffa's view of inflation treats inflation as a problem of distribution of income rather than of allocation. Indeed, Keynes' remarks on the century of profit inflation between 1550 and 1650 readily come to mind when reading Sraffa on the robbery of inflation. But capital, once accumulated, is non-malleable for Sraffa and cannot be 'consumed' by the consumers.[3] Hayek, on the other hand, is thinking of capital not in its commodity (physical) form, but in terms of its money value. Thus there is a confusion of capital concepts at this juncture. But much more than these incidental matters was the central issue about what constituted a monetary economy. We turn to this question now.

IV PERSPECTIVE ON THE DEBATE

Institutional rivalry apart, what was at stake in the Sraffa–Hayek debate? While the Sraffa criticism says little constructive about monetary theory, it points to a basic problem with all attempts to integrate Walrasian models with money. The misunderstanding in Hayek's case is caused by the fact that, although he was conscious that a monetary economy was different from a barter economy, Hayek has no concept of a *monetary equilibrium* – an equilibrium in a monetary economy distinct from that in a barter economy. The analysis that sets out the basic Hayek model in chapter 2 of *PP* is an equilibrium in a barter economy, albeit a dynamic one. Thus Hayek carefully traces out the characteristics of the new dynamic equilibrium when the savings rate rises. This is done when the natural rate of interest falls smoothly until demand and supply for savings are equated. Prices follow their 'natural course' undisturbed by any monetary complication. The important element is real savings, and Hayek even talks of 'savings made in kind rather than in money' (*PP*, p. 53). The monetary economy due to elasticity of currency and the nature of the credit system never seems to attain equilibrium. The only equilibrium it could hypothetically attain (though in practical terms Hayek is dubious) would correspond to the equilibrium of the barter economy. This is where the concept of neutral money is fatal to Hayek's plan for the theory of a monetary economy.

In Hayek's view, a monetary and a barter economy are different, in that a monetary economy is never in equilibrium and a real economy is never (for long) out of equilibrium. Thus, the example of smooth adjustment to a rise in savings in chapter 2 is the ideal of a barter economy. In such an economy, bankers would have to be merely 'brokers, trading in savings'. They would receive 'real' savings and supply real investment capital. But Hayek had firmly rejected such a possibility for a monetary economy in *MTTC*. In criticizing Hawtrey's proposal for keeping total bank deposits stable, he says that it would necessitate abolition of all bank money. What is more, it would retard economic progress (*MTCC*, pp. 190–1). Thus, it was clear in Hayek's view, though perhaps he does not sufficiently make it clear in *PP*, that a monetary economy could never be in such an equilibrium. The pessimism of the last lecture in *PP* about any possible policy solution reinforces this. But then the neutrality of money doctrine once again muddles this up, and for the following reason.

We have already seen how powerfully the Walrasian model ruled in Hayek's schema. Above all, the notion of equilibrium and a tendency towards equilibrium were basic to his view of economic models. He fails, however, to specify the ways in which behavioural relationships in a monetary economy would be different from those in a barter economy. Lacking such specific details, he cannot define an equilibrium for such a monetary economy. The Walrasian model, on the other hand, is rich in specifications of economic relationships and it was very tempting to take it over, in total, to define an equilibrium. A monetary economy has no equilibrium of its own, but with neutral money the monetary equilibrium is the same as the real equilibrium. Thus, with neutral money, money does not matter any more.

Again and again, Hayek comes back to the virtual impossibility of ever attaining such an equilibrium. But he cannot admit of disequilibrium as a persistent tendency. Thus an institutional factor – elasticity of currency – keeps the monetary economy permanently out of equilibrium – an equilibrium defined by the Utopian ideal of neutral money. Thus, almost at the very end of *MTTC*, Hayek says: '[W]e have no right to assume that an economic system with an "elastic" currency will ever exhibit those movements which can be deduced from the proposition of static theory' (*MTTC*, p. 196). Again, in the same book,

> *An economic system with an elastic currency must, in many instances, react to external influences quite differently from an economy in which economic forces impinge on goods in their full force – without any intermediary; and we must,* a priori, *expect any process started by an outside impulse to run an entirely different course in such an economy from that described by a theory which only takes into account changes originating on the side of goods. (MTTC,* pp. 178–9; italics in the original)

But there is a little in the theoretical core of *PP* to justify this. To begin with, a monetary economy is never described by itself but only as an inflationary departure from a barter economy. While Hayek wanted to trace the impact of money on the production structure, the production structure is identical in the barter and the money economy. Presumably, economic motivations will also be identical. Hayek continues to use concepts for a monetary economy that are suitable only for a barter economy. (This is indeed as all – or, say, most – economists still think about money.) Consider, for example, the concept of real savings or savings in kind.

What could such a concept possibly mean? In a money economy people save by purchasing financial assets (including, for the time being, currency to allow for hoarding). Producers borrow or raise capital by selling financial liabilities. How could one save *in kind*? In classical economics with no fixed capital and only one wage-good constituting the fund for investment, saving – not consuming – corn output of today enabled more workers to be employed in future. Saving was real and so was investment. This is, however, for a Ricardian corn economy. Introduce fixed capital in such an economy, and real savings have to go through a monetary circuit (to use Marx's terminology) to become investment. (For the classical model, see Corry, 1962. Recently Hollander has challenged the corn interpretation of the Ricardian model and put forward a two-sector model: see Hollander, 1973, and the exchange with Eatwell, 1975.)

Many more complications can be introduced if we come to an economy based on specialization, fixed capital and durable consumer goods. Let us, however, illustrate one specific problem in Hayek's schema. When people use the concept of real savings, they either confine themselves to a one-good economy or mean money savings deflated by a price index. (The indefinite article bears the brunt of many ambiguities.) Now when real savings rise, according to Hayek, consumer goods prices fall. This must therefore immediately lead to real value of savings being higher than planned if the deflator is consumer goods prices. (For the saver, consumer goods prices, or rather future price of consumer goods, is the appropriate deflator.) Plans immediately need to be revised in favour of consumption, or excess real savings immediately occur. The corresponding rise in price of investment goods, if unanticipated, will lead to revision of investment plans. In the end, equilibrium may be reached, but the convergence may not be rapid – nor need it be monotonic.

In a monetary economy, money becomes a more or less temporary abode of purchasing power for consumption as well as savings. While in possession of money balances, an individual has to plan on basis of expectations of prices over the transaction interval. Whenever money intervenes, i.e. where indirect exchange rather than direct barter is the rule, the gap between a sale and a subsequent purchase is a time interval of random length. All decisions are based on expectations and hence deterministic equilibrium cannot be reached. A consumer's utility maximization decision can be carried out only in terms of expected value. Actual purchases will depart from planned purchases. If prices are expected to rise very rapidly, then money will be a very temporary abode of purchasing power. In saving decisions, the consumer has in view future consumption he could finance, but this may be so distant that he is more concerned with expected yield of financial assets in the short run. Money is one asset that, owing to its liquidity, permits the shortest gap between sale and subsequent purchase (or planned purchase and actual purchase) of all the assets. Any other asset, financial or real, has to be sold for money before one can make a subsequent purchase. The minimal stochastic time interval permitted by money is of course zero (or infinitesimally small). In many ways that need to be specified in detail, *a monetary economy precludes a deterministic notion of equilibrium. All equilibria in a monetary economy are stochastic.*

V RECENT WORK ON MONETARY GENERAL EQUILIBRIUM

We have now come to the point where we can discuss briefly some recent work in monetary theory. We argued in the last section that a monetary economy due to the intermediation between sale and subsequent purchase introduced a stochastic time interval between the two. The prospect of price change over this interval means that all decisions are based on expectations. We have to thus exclude deterministic equilibria rigorously from a monetary economy. The notion of a stochastic equilibrium has to be used in such an economy.

Starting with articles by Clower and Hahn in the 1960s, the 1970s have seen a comparatively large literature in the area of monetary theory. This work is similar to Hayek's, as it also takes as a point of departure the (Arrow–Debreu) model of Walrasian General Equilibrium. The authors are also, however, conscious, as Hayek was, that the task of monetary theory was to retrace all the steps of a Walrasian model in a monetary context. Their efforts to do this are as yet incomplete, but along the way much has been done that is of value in the basic task. We shall briefly sketch some of these results.

It should be remarked at the outset that cyclical fluctuations do not figure in these discussions. Also, by and large the emphasis is on exchange economies rather than production economies. Hayek's theory related money immediately to the production side as a way of financing production over the time-gap between input and output. By comparison, Hayek neglected consumers' demand for money and their portfolio decisions. Hayek also was aiming at dynamic theory, whereas the dynamics of recent models is usually confined to stylized cases.

Current discussion has one advantage over that of 40 years ago. We have a much greater understanding of the nature of a Walrasian barter economy and the conditions required for the existence of a competitive equilibrium. Hayek took the existence of an equilibrium as well as its uniqueness and stability as proven. We now know that Walras left this question in some doubt. The Arrow–Debreu economy is static in the sense that transactions are required only in the initial period. Future decisions can be transacted today by buying and selling forward. Uncertainty is taken care of in the notion of markets for contingent commodities. Given fairly normal assumptions on consumer preferences and production technology, a general equilibrium set of relative prices for current and contingent commodities can be established. Money plays no role whatever in this context. There is no dynamics, and time does not figure in any essential way.

Such a picture of a barter economy only emphasizes what severe assumptions are necessary for equilibrium to exist, and hence immediately leads to examination of consequences of the assumptions being not met and to modelling more realistic economies. Both these efforts are involved in the work on monetary economies. Markets for contingent commodities may not exist in the completeness that the Arrow–Debreu model requires, and hence uncertainty comes into play as a real factor. At the same time, we live in economies where markets meet in every period and where there are specified traders. The first of these considerations has led to models of sequences of temporary equilibria where no futures markets exist and money is the only store of value. (See the articles by Grandmont and his associates in this context referred to in Hahn, 1973, Hayashi, 1976, and Kurz, 1974.) The other consideration has led to models showing the efficiency of indirect exchange using money as a medium over barter (e.g. the work of Ostroy, Starr, Helwig and others: see Clower, 1977).

In the course of such discussions many propositions have been established that clarify the Hayek–Sraffa debate. Thus, it would be now agreed that, in a competitive model with flexible prices, money has no role to play. Many models have used arbitrary rules for establishing a need for money. Thus, money has been assumed to be the only (costless) store of value, or a required medium of exchange in every transaction; or, again, an assumption has been made that current income is not available for spending in the current period (called 'viscosity' assumption by Grandmont–Younes: see Hahn, 1973). Some such arbitrary scheme seems to be required in a world of flexible prices with a limited set of futures markets if consumers are to hold a positive amount of money, i.e. if money is to have a non-zero price. Unless money is made a required commodity by such *deus ex machina*, there seems no economic reason why in a Walrasian economy consumers should hold money.

Hahn has established the arbitrariness of various schemes by showing that many of these economies with money are isomorphic to an Arrow–Debreu economy where all transactions can be carried out in the initial time period. He calls such economies with sequences of temporary equilibria inessential sequence economies. In a sense, time does not significantly enter in such economies. There is no learning over time and no genuine uncertainty about prices. As Hahn puts it, 'The main content of the monetary theory of an inessential economy is implicit in its construction: there is nothing we can say about the equilibrium of a non-monetary economy' (Hahn, 1973,

p. 231). Thus, the fact that in temporary equilibrium in each period there is a binding budget constraint can be avoided by defining suitably discounted prices in the initial period in which all transactions can be carried out. Thus Patinkin's monetary theory, while an elegant version of neoclassical monetary model, concerns an inessential sequence economy.

One feature of attempts to develop the notion of a monetary economy has been the modelling of the transaction technology. Thus distinctions have to be made between consumption and purchase and between purchase price and sale price. The need for money holding has often been rationalized in terms of the difficulty of 'double coincidence' of wants. A monetary economy exhibits more interesting features than just of increased barter efficiency. A major feature is that of price and quantity uncertainty, for a buyer or a seller of any commodity and the concomitant of uncertainty is a recognition that a monetary economy operates in real time. The features of money that allow specializations in trading and production, that reduce speculative uncertainty of holding stocks of goods beyond current need, have to be rigorously developed. In modelling such an economy, however, if we assume that prices are announced and there is no uncertainty, then a monetary economy can be shown to have efficiency relative to a similar Arrow–Debreu economy. But as Hahn says, this is not surprising, as price uncertainty and sequential dynamics are absent.

> When these stringent restrictions are dropped, it will not be clear . . . how to chararacterise the equilibrium of an economy. To demand that all expections be fulfilled at each date now strikes me as leading to uninteresting conceptualisations. All the real work remains to be done here and the most promising route probably lies with Radner's idea of a statistical equilibrium. (Hahn, 1973, p. 236)

It is beyond the scope of this essay to develop any of these ideas in detail.[4] Enough has been said here, I hope, to show that grafting money into a General Equilibrium model proves to be as difficult a task today as the controversy in the Hayek–Sraffa debate indicated. A fully fledged Walrasian economy, in which prices are flexible, does not need money in any essential way. In this sense Sraffa was correct in locating the importance of money in Hayek's model to the institutional appendage of the banking system – an appendage, since it had not been worked into a Walrasian model.

The task Hayek set himself, as revealed in the quotation at the outset, can be seen to be an important and as yet unfinished task. The notion of a monetary economy as distinct from a barter economy with money is still a challenging one. To conclude with a quotation from Hahn again:

> I believe that we are only at the beginning of a theory of the economy in which money is essential. In particular I think that we have for a good long time been on quite unimportant and uninteresting track. The challenge of monetary theory is not the neutrality theorem or related results; it is the required reconstruction of our paradigm if we are to make sense of money. (Hahn, 1973, p. 241)

NOTES

1 In this respect, Keynes' approach in the *Treatise on Money*, while sceptical of any general measure of the value of money, is to go carefully into various standards by which the value of money can be measured. Keynes criticizes the quantity theory for confusing only one of such standards as the measure of value of money. See Keynes (1930), vol. I, bk II, pp. 47–84.
2 Among nineteenth-century economists, William Spence was perhaps the only one to attempt to show a barter economy could experience disequilibria: see Corry (1962).
3 Marx scrupulously maintained the differences between the money form of capital, its physical (commodity) form and its contribution to the production process (productive capital), which he measured in terms of labour values. The heterogeneity and unmalleability of capital is a feature of the physical form of capital but not of its value form or its money form: see Marx (1885), vol. II, pt I.
4 I have made a preliminary attempt to develop some of these points in Desai (1977).

REFERENCES

Clower, R. W. (1977) 'The Anatomy of Monetary Theory', *American Economic Review*, Papers and Proceedings, **67**, 206–12.
Corry, B. A. (1962) *Money, Saving and Investment in English Economics 1800–1850*, Macmillan, London.
Desai, M. J. (1977) 'The Value of Money in a Monetary Economy', unpublished MS, London School of Economics.
Durbin, E. F. M. (1935) *The Problem of Credit Policy*, Chapman & Hall, London.

Eatwell, J. (1975) 'The Interpretation of Ricardo's Essay on Profits', *Economica*, **42**, 182-7.

Hahn, F. (1973) 'On the Foundations of Monetary Theory', in *Essays in Modern Economics*, ed. M. Parkin and A. R. Nobay, Longman, London, pp. 230-42.

Hayashi, T. (1976) 'Monetary Equilibrium in Two Classes of Stationary Economies', *Review of Economic Studies*, no. 134, 269-84.

Hayek, F. (1931) 'The Pure Theory of Money', *Economica*, **11**, 270-95.

Hayek, F. (1932a) 'The Pure Theory of Money: a Rejoinder to Mr Keynes', *Economica*, **12**, 22-44.

Hayek, F. (1932b) 'Money and Capital: a Reply to Mr Sraffa', *Economic Journal*, **42**, 237-49.

Hayek, F. (1935a) *Prices and Production*, Routledge & Kegan Paul, London.

Hayek, F. (1935b) *Monetary Theory and Trade Cycle*, Routledge & Kegan Paul, London.

Hicks, J. R. (1967) 'The Hayek Story', in *Critical Essays in Monetary Theory*, Oxford University Press, London, pp. 203-15.

Hollander, S. (1973) 'Ricardo's Analysis of the Profit Rate 1813-1815'. *Economica*, **40**, 260-82.

Hollander, S. (1975) 'Ricardo and the Corn Profit Model: a Reply to Eatwell', *Economica*, **42**, 188-202.

Keynes, J. M. (1930) *A Treatise on Money*. Vol. I, *The Pure Theory of Money*, Macmillan, London.

Keynes, J. M. (1931) 'The Pure Theory of Money: a Reply to Dr Hayek', *Economica*, **2**, 387-97.

Kurz, M. (1974) 'Equilibrium with Transaction Costs and Money in a Single Market Exchange Economy', *Journal of Economic Theory*, **7**, 418-52.

Marx, K. (1885) *Capital*, II Vol., Allen and Unwin, London, 1928.

Myrdal, G. (1939) *Monetary Equilibrium*, William Hodge, London.

Nurkse, R. (1934) 'The Schematic Representation of the Structure of Production', *Review of Economic Studies*, **2**, 232-44.

Shackle, G. L. S. (1933) 'Some Notes on Monetary Theories of the Trade Cycle', *Review of Economic Studies*, **1**, 27-8.

Sraffa, P. (1932a) 'Dr Hayek on Money and Capital', *Economic Journal*, **42**, 42-53.

Sraffa, P. (1932b) 'A Rejoinder', *Economic Journal*, **42**, 249-51.

10

Neutrality and Monetary Equilibrium: A Note on Desai

ROY McCLOUGHRY*

I INTRODUCTION

Meghnad Desai (chapter 9 above) uses the Hayek–Sraffa debate to show that the problems of incorporating money into a general equilibrium framework are as great today as they were in that debate in the 1930s. The conclusion derived from the debate is that Hayek has no concept of monetary equilibrium; the only equilibrium that is determinate in his model is that determined by real variables alone (though expressed in money terms). Money can be incorporated into a General Equilibrium framework only when it is stripped of its 'moneyness', i.e. when long-term contracts, debts and sticky prices are ignored, and some story external to the model is told to explain the presence of money in the model.

Fundamental to Hayek's analysis in *Prices and Production* (*PP* hereafter) is the existence of forced saving, whereby resources are directed into production by the creation of money and not by the voluntary decisions of individuals to save. Hayek's thesis is that capital accumulated by such methods will be 'at least partly dissipated', and under certain assumptions will be completely destroyed economically, though it may continue to exist as physical capital. The story that Hayek tells to explain this 'self-reversing' effect of money is a peculiar characteristic of his theory of the trade cycle; and, as he admitted to Sraffa, 'it is upon the truth of this point that my theory stands or falls' (Hayek, 1932, p. 239). Sraffa's criticism implies that, far from being dissipated, the new capital will represent a new equilibrium position which will show no tendency to be reversed.

* I am grateful to Morris Perlman for helpful comments on this paper.

The second area of controversy in the debate relevant to monetary theory is the relationship between the natural and the money rates of interest. In Sraffa's opinion, any composite commodity for which there is a forward market can have an 'own rate' which is out of equilibrium with the 'own rates' on other commodities; and therefore disequilibrium can occur in both barter and money economies, not only in monetary economies as Hayek implies.

It will be the contention of this note that the Hayek–Sraffa debate does not provide adequate grounds for the discussion of the problems of modern monetary theory, as it is inconclusive on the major issues and confused by the fact that its participants, while apparently discussing the same model, are in fact not thinking within the same framework.

II THE DISSIPATION OF 'FORCED SAVINGS'

Forced savings are generated when the relationship between producer goods and consumer goods is changed by an injection of money which takes the form of an increase in producer credits.[1] This increases the money claims to output of producers without lowering the money claim to output of consumers. With full employment, producers can expand production only by bidding away non-specific factors from the lower stages of production (nearer to consumption). This leads to forced savings as resources are released to producers without the consent of consumers. Under voluntary saving consumers are willing to forgo current consumption in order to have increased consumption in the future; but in this case consumers retain their original time preference between present and future goods. Under forced saving there is excess demand for commodities by consumers and excess demand for factors by producers. Although the existence of unused stocks may mean that no scarcity of commodities will be felt in the very short run, it will eventually come, causing the prices of consumer goods to begin to rise and, as producers pay higher wages, altering the proportion between consumer goods and producer goods in favour of the former.

If consumers spend all their income on consumer goods, Hayek believes that *all* of the additional credit going to producers will become demand for consumer goods.

> Every individual entrepreneur can increase his real capital only by spending more on capital goods and less on labour used in

current production (or, what amounts to the same thing, more on labour which is used for a relatively long period). (Hayek, 1932, p. 242)

Capital is therefore capitalized labour, and even the money used for the purchase of new capital goods must ultimately be paid out to the factors that make these new capital goods (see Hayek, 1932, p. 242). While the increase in the money supply outstrips the increase in the incomes of factors, the producer will continue to invest in new capital. But as the increase in the money supply no longer compensates the producer for the increase in wages, the former proportion, representing the time preference of consumers, will be restored. The only real saving that can occur happens if producers invest rather than consume their excess profits in the boom period, but this cannot be sufficient to prevent the 'self-reversing' effects of money.

Sraffa's producers, on the other hand, save all of their increased money incomes 'and have no reason at a later stage to revise the decision' (Sraffa, 1932b, p. 249). It is worthwhile here looking again at a passage from Sraffa (quoted by Desai in chapter 9 above, p. 159):

One class has, for a time, robbed another class of a part of their incomes; and has saved the plunder. When the robbery comes to an end, it is clear that the victims cannot possibly consume the capital which is now well out of their reach. If they are wage-earners, who have all the time consumed every penny of their income, they have no wherewithal to expand consumption. (Sraffa, 1932a, p. 47)

As Desai notes (p. 162), Sraffa treats inflation as a problem of distribution of income rather than the allocation of resources. Yet consumers' *incomes* have not changed; all that has happened is that producers have a larger share of *output* than before.

There seem to be two misconceptions which bring this difference about. The first, as Desai points out (p. 162), is a confusion of capital concepts: '[C]apital once accumulated is non-malleable for Sraffa and cannot be consumed by the consumers. Hayek on the other hand is thinking of capital not in its commodity (physical) form but in terms of its money value.' For Hayek the recession is characterized by 'capital consumption' caused by wages being too high relative to the structure of production, elongated by an increase in the money supply. If wages are too high relative to their marginal produce, then they claim a larger share of output, profits fall in the higher stages of production, and eventually producers discontinue the maintenance of their capital, operating it at prices below costs.

> [A] decrease in capital means, in practically all cases, in the first instance only a decrease in the value of an equipment which continues to exist in an unchanged form and which only after the lapse of time leads to the diminution of part of it. The best equipped plant, the most wonderful machinery, which only a short while ago could be used with great advantage in production and which therefore represented a great capacity value, may in consequence of some change in conditions suddenly lose its value and cease to be capital. (Hayek, 1931, p. 7)

The second misconception that arises concerns the *period* over which Sraffa's 'robbery' takes place. Sraffa is concerned only with the current period in which markets clear. An increase in the money supply to producers causes them to 'steal' resources from consumers, and that is that. What happens in the next period is a completely different story. Thus there has been a permanent redistribution of incomes, with consumers suffering in a similar way to fixed income groups during inflation. But markets do not clear at the end of the current period in Hayek's model, as consumers still have an excess demand for commodities. Hayek is thinking not in the traditional long-period framework, *but in terms of intertemporal equilibrium* (cf. section III below).

As if these two misconceptions were not enough to confuse the debate, Sraffa gives an alternative account of the Hayek model in his rejoinder (1932b). Disputing that money used for the purchase of capital goods will be paid out to the factors that make these capital goods, he fixes on a footnote in which Hayek said: '(e)xcept for such amounts as may be absorbed in cash holdings in any additional stages of production' (Hayek, 1932, p. 242). Hayek seems to be referring to idle balances held by producers to accommodate their transaction demand for money. Such balances would be proportionate to the cost of production, an increase in stages leading to an increase in idle balances. But Sraffa states:

> [U]nder his assumptions such cash holdings will absorb not merely certain exceptional amounts, but the whole of the additional money raised during the inflation; . . . consequently incomes cannot rise at all, and there will be no occasion for any dissipation of capital. (Sraffa, 1932b, p. 250)

Sraffa goes on to explain that, since capital is accumulated in proportion to the increase in producer credits and the number of stage increases in proportion to the increase in capital, the quantity of payments increasing in proportion to the number of stages, then, 'as a result, the quantity of payments to be made increases in proportion to the quantity of money, and the whole of the additional money is absorbed in cash holdings for performing such payments' (p. 250). This alternative account of Sraffa's does not depend on either of the two previous misconceptions, yet does not shed much light on the model, the only possible interpretation being that entrepreneurs are buying physical capital from one another and investing the income from such sales in more physical capital. However, the equipment must be already in existence in excess stocks. Even if this were so it would require extraordinary assumptions to prevent *any* of the additional money going to labour.

In Hayek's theory of the trade cycle, the primary reason for a reversion to an equilibrium position described by value theory alone is the dissipation of the capital created by forced saving. Although such a phenomenon is legitimate only under the most stringent conditions in the barest of models, Sraffa fails to falsify Hayek's hypothesis, partly because they were talking at cross purposes as to the period involved. It is to this that we now turn.

III INTERTEMPORAL EQUILIBRIUM

At the outset of his analysis in *PP* Hayek states,

> This view of the probable future of the theory of money becomes less startling if we consider that the concept of relative prices includes the prices of goods of the same kind at different moments, and that here, as in the case of interspatial price relationships, only one relation between the two prices can correspond to a condition of 'intertemporal' equilibrium, and that this need not, *a priori*, be a relation of identity or the one which would exist under a stable price level.... If this view is correct, the question which in my opinion will take the place of the question whether the value of money has increased or decreased will be the question whether the state of equilibrium of the rates of intertemporal exchange is disturbed by monetary influences in favour of future or in favour of present goods. (*PP*, p. 26)

One of the problems in the Hayek–Sraffa debate is that Sraffa did not appreciate that Hayek was writing within an intertemporal framework. Yet Hayek had developed his concept of intertemporal equilibrium as early as 1928 (cf. Hayek, 1928). Commenting on *PP* in *German Monetary Theory*, Ellis pointed out that 'to appreciate the unique character of Hayek's version [of the trade cycle] one must begin with the concept of intertemporal equilibrium.' He also says that Hayek 'ordinarily refers to it as the ultimate proof of his main theoretical principle' (Ellis, 1934, pp. 350 and 351).

Milgate (1979) traces the origins of the concept of intertemporal equilibrium to Hayek's 1928 paper, predating Hick's formal presentation of it in *Value and Capital*, and comments specifically on its role in the Hayek–Sraffa debate.[2] Sraffa, in showing that the barter economy can be in disequilibrium, states:

> If money did not exist, and loans were made in terms of all sorts of commodities, here would be a single rate which satisfies the conditions of equilibrium, but there might be at any one moment as many 'natural' rates of interest as there are commodities, though they would not be 'equilibrium' rates. (Sraffa, 1932a, p. 49).

On this Desai comments (in chapter 9 above):

> Hayek's reply to Sraffa's demonstration about natural rates of interest in a non-money economy is to admit the multiplicity of natural rates of interest but he adds '[T]here might at any moment be as many "natural" rates of interest as there are commodities all of which would be *equilibrium rates*; . . .' (p. 245). This is curious, as Sraffa pointed out in his rejoinder. The diversity of natural rates can only mean a transitional stage where the relative prices are still adjusting to a new equilibrium. (pp. 161–2 above).

Seen within the framework of Intertemporal Equilibrium, this 'curiosity' is explained. There will be different rates of intertemporal exchange for each commodity:

> [E]xchange between different goods which become available at different points of time but which are of the same sort, will not

occur in a 1:1 relation; it is rather the case that such exchange can occur, according to the circumstances, in absolutely any other relationship. Furthermore, this exchange relation follows exactly the same laws as those which govern price formation between different goods. (Hayek, 1928, p. 43; Milgate's 1979, p. 9, translation)

The only essential point for Hayek is whether any one of these rates being out of equilibrium can have the same effect on the barter economy as the money rate being out of equilibrium in a monetary economy. If farmers could 'arbitrarily change' the quantity of wheat produced so that there was a wheat glut, then loans in terms of wheat would be made at a correspondingly low rate of interest. But that rate of interest is still a correct market signal, as wheat can be either consumed or saved. Money cannot satisfy final demand in the same way as a normal commodity, and therefore it is possible to 'artificially' increase the supply of money, thereby lowering the money rate of interest and giving a false signal to the economy. Desai, in chapter 9 above, concludes:

We can say that in the debate about the natural rates Sraffa shows that a barter economy can be out of equilibrium *as much as* a monetary economy and that 'neutrality of money' in an economy with money and establishing a rate of interest in terms of a composite commodity are equivalent. (p. 162 above; my emphasis)

But to say that a barter economy can be out of equilibrium *as much as* a monetary economy is to deny that the existence of money can exacerbate the fluctuations in a barter economy. Also, Hayek would agree that the rate of interest on neutral money is equivalent to the rate of interest on a composite commodity: what he would disagree with is that a movement *away* from such equilibrium rates would be equivalent in its *effects*.

In looking again at the Hayek–Sraffa debate, it is not obvious that Sraffa has proved his case. At crucial stages in the debate there are confusions arising from differences over the definition of capital and equilibrium. Yet because Sraffa may not have proved his case does not mean that there is not a case against Hayek to be proven. To show this we look briefly at the Dutch monetary theorist J. G. Koopmans' attempt to derive monetary equilibrium from neutrality.

IV NEUTRALITY AND MONETARY EQUILIBRIUM

In his paper 'Zum Problem des "Neutralen" Geldes' (1933), and later in a paper given at Hayek's Economic Theory Seminar at the LSE entitled 'The Problem of Monetary Equilibrium' (1936), Koopmans attempts to widen the scope of the concept of monetary neutrality to a concept called 'the wider issue of neutrality' or 'monetary equilibrium'. The narrowest concept of neutrality is constant cash balances over time or constant effective demand in money terms (MV), yet Koopmans is willing to relax these rigid definitions to allow wider applicability.

Non-neutrality arises from the introduction of money into a barter economy, thus enabling half-barter transactions to take place, in which goods sell for money but not immediately for other goods. It is this holding of money rather than the simultaneous exchange of goods that makes fluctuations possible. Fundamental to this approach is the assertion that 'time lags are the ultimate cause of the non-neutrality of money' (Koopmans, 1933, p. 265). Since money is essentially non-neutral, an active monetary policy has to be undertaken to preserve neutrality.

Such a policy is not concerned, however, with the stability of the general price level, or, for that matter, with any of the variables in Fisher's equation of exchange. Nor, when talking about monetary equilibrium, is Koopmans concerned with relative prices.

> Monetary equilibrium ... is not primarily concerned with the question whether the relative prices of the individual goods are affected or not, but with something of much greater economic importance ... namely the equivalence between *total* demand and *total* supply of goods, services and securities per unit of time. (Koopmans, 1936, p. 4)

In an economy characterized by indirect exchange, excess demand can be financed only by the creation of money or by the reduction of cash balances available at the beginning of the period; a shortfall will be characterized by the extinction of money or by the accumulation of larger balances than were available at the beginning of the period. If demand is not compensated by supply in the same period, Koopmans labels it 'pure demand', and supply not compensated by demand, 'pure supply'. In a closed full-employment economy the former is inflationary and the latter deflationary. Monetary equilibrium is the 'null point', the mid-point between the two.

Monetary equilibrium depends on the sum of four variables. It is present if the sum of the newly created money plus dishoarding is offset by the sum of money loans 'repayed' and increases in hoards during the same period. It does not matter to Koopmans which offsets which, as their monetary effect is the same. All that matters is that the sum of them is zero. This would seem to be a fairly straightforward criteria for locating monetary disturbances until it is realized that, thus defined, monetary disturbances seem to cancel one another out. Every creation of money means either the simultaneous hoarding of that money or, after expenditure, its 'extinction'. As Holtrop has commented,

> So if we find dishoarding or money creation in one group of units and hoarding or extinction of money in another, that finding in itself does not give us an answer to the question of whether a monetary disturbance has in fact taken place, or, if it took place at all, whether it started from hoarding or the extinction of money – which would make it a deflationary disturbance – or from dishoarding or the creation of money – which would make it an inflationary disturbance. (Holtrop, 1954, p. 33)[3]

Koopmans' criteria for monetary equilibrium are as difficult to use operationally as Hayek's concept of neutrality, and it was this difficulty that led Hayek to reject neutrality as a goal for banking policy. At the same time as Koopmans was attempting to *widen* the concept of neutrality, Hayek was placing additional constraints on its use, in a paper entitled 'Ueber "Neutrales Geld"' (cf. Hayek, 1933). In it he admitted that the existence of sticky prices and long-term contracts would thwart the realization of any neutral money policy. Neutrality could be achieved only if three conditions were fulfilled: the total money stream remained constant; all long-term contracts were based on a correct anticipation of future price movements; and all prices were completely flexible.

Fatal to both Koopmans' and Hayek's proposals is the concept of the barter economy with which monetary disequilibrium is compared; for if Hayek has no concept of monetary equilibrium, neither does he have any concept of barter disequilibrium, as Desai points out. The hypothetical barter economy in his model is an 'ideal type', free from frictions that would hinder the attainment of equilibrium, and this led Hayek to ignore the period of transition between equilibria when savings rise. Sraffa pointed out that the matching of saving and investment are just as much a problem in a barter economy unless actors' plans coincide.

This smoothness of adjustment was possible because of an additional assumption made by Hayek. This comes out in his reply to Hansen and Tout:

So much for the pure, or barter, theory of the subject (in the sense of the usual assumption that money exists to facilitate exchange but exercises no determining influence on the course of things, or, in other words, remains neutral – an assumption which is almost always made though not expressed in these terms. (*PP*, p. 145)

Of this, E. M. Claasen has remarked that it describes an economy,

in which money exists in so far as it is essential (both as unit of account and as medium of exchange) to the smooth functioning of the economic process, but from which it is eliminated so far as it acts as a disturbing element. (Claasen, 1968, p. 23; quoted in Lutz, 1969, p. 107)

Whether a barter economy in which 'money exists to facilitate exchange' is a monetary economy in all but name is now not clear. Maybe, as Lutz has suggested, the choice in *PP* is between 'an imperfectly working money economy as this exists in reality, and an, in some sense, ideally working money economy' (Lutz, 1969, p. 107). Monetary theory could not advance far while it depended on such an ambiguous concept.

V CONCLUSIONS

The Hayek–Sraffa debate, though important for an understanding of the wider debate that accompanied the publication of *Prices and Production*, is confused and convoluted. The fundamental issue at stake for monetary theory – the incorporation of money into a General Equilibrium framework – is clouded by the concept of monetary neutrality. The debate over forced saving and the possibility of fundamental disequilibrium in a barter economy is hampered by the participants talking at odds over capital and equilibrium. It is these confusions that lead to the generality of Desai's conclusions, 'that grafting money into a general equilibrium model proves to be as difficult a task today as the controversy in the Hayek–Sraffa debate indicated' (chapter 9 above, p. 168). Yet where there is a clash of

Weltanschaung as well as difference over economic theory, the task may well be impossible. As Joan Robinson has commented on another issue,

> I'm afraid it is a hopeless task to reconcile the Sraffa system with Bohm-Bawerk because they take different views of the operation of the capitalist system.[4]

NOTES

1 Sraffa's contention, that it is the power of the banks to settle the way money is spent that causes the crisis, must be overstating the case. The only assumption needed for the crisis to occur is that bank credit goes mainly to producers; an assumption that must have appeared reasonable in the 1930s.
2 Milgate traces Hicks' concept of Intertemporal Equilibrium only as far back as *Value and Capital* (1939), but Hicks discussed the idea extensively in Hicks (1933). There he discussed both Hayek's concept of intertemporal equilibrium and *PP*. (An English-language version is available in Hicks, 1980.)
3 Koopmans gets round this by describing it *ex ante*, but his definition of *ex ante* is difficult to follow. On this see F. de Jong (1973).
4 In a letter to Malte Faber: quoted in Faber (1979), p. vii.

REFERENCES

Claasen, E. M. (1968) *Monnaie, revenu national et prix*, Dunod, Paris.

Ellis, H. (1934) *German Monetary Theory 1905-1933*, Harvard University Press, Cambridge, Mass.

Faber, M. (1979) *Introduction to Modern Austrian Capital Theory*, Springer-Verlag, Berlin/Heidelberg/New York.

Hayek, F. A. (1928) 'Das intertemporale Gleichgewichtssystem der Preise und die Bewegungen des Geldwertes', *Weltwirtschaftliches Archiv*, **28**, 33-79.

Hayek, F. A. (1931) 'Capital Consumption' (typescript). Final draft of 'Kapitalaufzehrung', *Weltwirtschaftliches Archiv*, **36** (1932/II).

Hayek, F. A. (1932) ' "Money and Capital": a Reply to Mr Sraffa', *Economic Journal*, **42**, 237-49.

Hayek, F. A. (1933) 'Ueber "Neutrales Geld" ', *Zeitschrift fuer Nationaloekonomie*, **4**, 659-61.

Hayek, F. A. (1935) *Prices and Production* (2nd edn), Routledge & Kegan Paul, London.

Hicks, J. R. (1933) 'Gleichgewicht und Konjunktur', *Zeitschrift fuer Nationaloekonomie*, **4**, 441-55.

Hicks, J. R. (1980) 'Equilibrium and the Trade Cycle', *Economic Inquiry*, **18**, 523-34.

Holtrop, M. W. (1954) 'The Criterion for Locating Monetary Disturbances', in *Money in an Open Economy*, Sternfest Kroese, Leiden (1972), pp. 31-46.

de Jong, F. (1973) *Development of Monetary Theory in the Netherlands*, Rotterdam University Press.

Koopmans, J. G. (1933) 'Zum Problem des "Neutralen" Geldes', in *Beitrage zur Geldtheorie*, ed. F. A. Hayek, Springer, Vienna, pp. 211-59.

Koopmans, J. G. (1936) 'The Problem of Monetary Equilibrium'. Typescript of a paper read at the Economic Theory Seminar, London School of Economics, 15 June 1936.

Lutz, F. A. (1969) 'On Neutral Money', in *Roads to Freedom*, ed. E. Streissler, Routledge & Kegan Paul, London, pp. 105-12.

Milgate, M. (1979) 'On the Origin of the Notion of "Intertemporal Equilibrium" ', *Economica*, **46**, 1-10.

Sraffa, P. (1932a) 'Dr Hayek on Money and Capital', *Economic Journal*, **42**, 42-53.

Sraffa, P. (1932b) 'A Rejoinder', *Economic Journal*, **42**, 249-51.

11

The Treasury and Civil Service Committee and the British Monetarist Experiment

NICHOLAS H. DIMSDALE

I INTRODUCTION

The Treasury and Civil Service Committee, consisting of a group of 12 MPs drawn from the three major political parties under the chairmanship of Mr Edward du Cann, have undertaken a thorough investigation of British monetary policy. The Committee began its inquiries in March 1980, and in February of the following year published a report evaluating the Conservative Government's Medium-term Financial Strategy, accompanied by memoranda and minutes of evidence (House of Commons, 1980, 1981).

The Chancellor of the Exchequer, The Governor of the Bank of England, the Treasury and the Bank of England submitted evidence, both orally and in writing. In addition, the Committee consulted a group of monetary experts, both academics and bank officials. They circulated to 32 economists a questionnaire that was designed to bring the current state of academic thinking to bear on the issues raised by the British Government's monetary policy. This policy is a deliberate attempt to control inflation by a gradual reduction in the rate of monetary growth according to a pre-announced target path over a period of four years. It can, therefore, be regarded as a close approximation to the monetary gradualism advocated by Milton Friedman and other monetarists. The course and outcome of the British monetary experiment is, then, of wider interest than to observers of the British economy, since it can be regarded as a test of an important element in current monetary economics. The issues raised by such a policy are brought out in the well designed questionnaire circulated to the monetary experts. The wide range of professional opinions on matters of current controversy in macroeconomics is emphasized in the memoranda submitted by the experts in response to the Committee's questionnaire. The Committee was fortunate in having as technical advisers well-known economists, including Professors Miller, Buiter and Hendry. They assisted in preparing the questionnaire, drafting the report, and in particular in commenting on the evidence submitted by the Treasury in defence of current policies.

The questionnaire was treated by some experts as an examination paper in which all questions were to be answered. Others wrote memoranda that discussed many of the issues raised in the questionnaire. A further questionnaire on the technical aspects of econometric models was circulated to a group of central banks and to other institutions possessing such models.

The aim of the Committee was apparently to call into question the basis of the government's medium-term financial strategy. Its report (HC, 1981) was critical of official policy and concluded with a number of recommendations for changing the emphasis of policy. But the Committee had no authority to influence government policy directly, and its recommendations have been largely ignored by the Government, which has preferred to retain its financial strategy despite a welter of hostile criticism. The main interest of the Committee's report lies in its contribution to general economic discussion rather than in its direct impact on policy-making. The views of the academic experts ranged from the new classical school, or 'instant monetarists', represented by Professor Minford, to what the Committee described as 'anti-monetarists', represented by Lord Kaldor. Between these extremes lay the views of the rest of the academic and official economists. The opinions of the 'gradualist monetarists', Professors Friedman and Laidler, are of particular interest, since gradualism underlies much of the Government's approach to macro-economic policy. Monetarists of both 'instant' and gradualist varieties were broadly sympathetic to the Government's policies and to the theory underlying them. The Treasury and the Bank of England naturally defended current policy, but the 'pragmatists', represented by Professors Tobin, Dornbusch, Williamson, Artis and Hahn, remained on the whole unconvinced and on some issues strongly critical. Lord Kaldor roundly condemned both the Government's strategy and the monetarist thinking on which it is based.

Monetary policy has not been discussed so thoroughly and authoritatively in British official papers since the report of the Radcliffe Committee (1959). The memoranda submitted to the Radcliffe Committee were not presented on a uniform basis, since there was no questionnaire designed to focus on the differing doctrinal positions of experts. The recent report of the Wilson Committee (1980) concentrated upon the working of financial institutions rather than on the monetary system. Its report, although important, is rather a disappointment for those interested in monetary theory and its policy applications. The same cannot be said of the Report of the Treasury and Civil Service Committee.

II THE EXPERIENCE OF THE MEDIUM-TERM FINANCIAL STRATEGY

The Committee was collecting evidence shortly after the unveiling of the Conservative Government's medium-term financial strategy, which was introduced in March 1980. The strategy provided for a gradual reduction in the rate of growth of the money stock, measured by M3 sterling (including currency and all sterling bank deposits held by UK residents) from a target range of 7–11 per cent for the financial year 1980–81 to 4–8 per cent for 1983–84. In the intervening years the upper and lower limits of the target ranges were reduced by 1 percentage point per annum. The monetary target was accompanied by an announcement of the planned public sector borrowing requirement (PSBR), which was to be reduced as a percentage of nominal GDP to 3.75 per cent in 1980–81, compared with 5.5 per cent in 1979–80; it was then to fall to 1.5 per cent by 1983–84 without a definite target being set for each year. Targets for the growth of M3 and limits on the PSBR were not in themselves an innovation, since they have been set annually since the negotiations with the IMF during the sterling crisis in November–December 1976. What was new in the medium-term financial strategy (MTFS) was the declaration of policy intentions for the next four years. The Government was providing the private sector with information about its intentions which was intended to bring about a reassessment of inflationary expectations. The Government sought to create a climate of opinion in which expectations of a decline of the rate of inflation would be generated and fulfilled.

Members of the Committee were attempting to evaluate a policy that had not been in operation for a full year, although the Chancellor had announced his intention to check monetary growth in late 1979. It may, therefore, be argued that some of its judgements were premature. The introduction of the MTFS followed on the second major rise in oil prices, which affected the UK as an oil producer in a different way from other industrial economies. The strong demand for sterling as a petro-currency and the high level of UK interest rates, compared with those in other financial centres, strengthened the exchange rate during 1980 and weakened the competitiveness of British industry. The upsurge in the exchange rate had not been foreseen by the authorities any more than the subsequent decline of the sterling–dollar rate during 1981. Judged by the appreciation of sterling, the level of interest rates and the severe financial pressures on the corporate sector, monetary policy was tight during 1980–81. However, the growth of monetary aggregates, as measured by the Government's chosen indicator M3 sterling, was 18.6 per cent compared with the target range of 7–11 per cent in the MTFS. Even if an adjustment is made for the re-intermediation arising from the removal of the 'corset' restriction on the growth of the banks' interest-bearing eligible liabilities, the growth of M3 is only reduced to about 16 per cent. This is more rapid than other measures of the money supply, both narrower and broader than M3, but all measures were well in excess of the upper limit of the monetary target for 1980–81 of 11 per cent, except for M1.

There was a massive overshooting of the PSBR, which came out at £13.5 billion, compared with £8.5 billion envisaged in the Government's financial strategy, reflecting both higher-than-planned public expenditure and a deeper-than-expected recession, which depressed tax receipts. Faced with the undermining of its targets during the first year of its policy, the Government expressed a determination to continue the general thrust of the MTFS. The Committee's comment that the Government had accepted a cyclically fluctuating budget deficit turned out to be premature (HC, 1981, *Rep.*, p. xxiii). The 1981 Budget tightened fiscal policy despite the severity of the recession. The Government intends to reduce the PSBR to £10.5 billion during 1981–82 by means of the tax increases announced in the 1981 Budget. This still implies an increase in the ratio of the PSBR to GDP to 4.2 per cent against 3.0 per cent provided in the financial strategy.

The Government is, therefore, keeping to the spirit of its policy, despite the embarrassment of having grossly exceeded its estimates for monetary growth and the budget deficit during 1980–81. It has, however, had greater success in the attainment of its stated primary objective of reducing the rate of inflation. The annual rate of increase of the retail price index reached a peak of 21.5 per cent in 1980 (II) compared with the same quarter in 1979; but this has declined to 11.8 per cent comparing 1981 (II) with 1980 (II). The fall in the rate of inflation has been assisted by the appreciation of the exchange rate during 1980. Since reaching a peak early in 1981, the exchange rate has declined steeply, so limiting the scope for further reduction in the rate of inflation. The reduction of inflation has been associated with deepening recession and unemployment rising from 6.2 per cent of the labour force in 1980 (II) to 10.4 per cent in the same quarter of 1981.

Time seems to be running out for those who take a relatively optimistic view of what can be achieved by a disinflationary mone-tary–fiscal policy. While the rate of inflation has declined, the cost in terms of output has been high. Whether inflation rates will rise again when demand revives remains uncertain.

III INTERMEDIATE TARGETS AND EXPECTATIONS

This paper will examine the response of experts to some of the questions put to them in the Committee's questionnaire. The questions were divided under three broad headings of objectives of: economic policy, instruments and effects of policy, and the conduct of policy. The principal interest lies in the second category of questions, which is further subdivided into the money supply, interest rates and the PSBR, and money, the exchange rate, inflation and output. (The questionnaire is reproduced in the Appendix.)

The answer submitted by the Treasury to a general question (Q A1) on the aims of economic policy is of interest (HC, 1980, *Mem.*, p. 8). It confirms that current policy is subordinating other objectives to the Government's predominant concern of reducing the rate of inflation. The Treasury was sceptical of its ability to achieve the postwar Keynesian objectives of high and stable employment and economic growth. This response represents a remarkable narrowing of the vision of policy-makers and confirms the lower sights that the Government is setting itself in the light of the policy disappointments of the 1970s.

On the policy for intermediate targets, the Treasury and the Bank of England favour the setting of targets for intermediate variables because they are more readily controllable than final objectives (Q A5) (HC, 1980, *Mem.*, pp. 8 and 18). But it is not clear that this is a really satisfactory criterion, since setting target values for nominal GDP may be more appropriate if it is more closely related to final goals. The money supply may be controllable by the authorities, but it is not necessarily closely related to nominal income over relatively short periods of time. For this reason Tobin would prefer the principal target to be nominal income rather than a monetary aggregate (HC, 1981, *Mins*, pp. 216–17).

On the question of whether the exchange rate or the money supply should be the intermediate target, the Treasury and the Bank of England favoured the money supply (Q A6) (HC, 1980, *Mem.*, pp. 8 and 19). The nominal exchange rate may well not be controllable because it is influenced by factors other than monetary policy, such as those causing variations in the real exchange rate. The Bank pointed to the problem of lack of consistency between targets for the exchange rate and the money supply. If the exchange rate rises above the target level, intervention in the foreign exchange market and/or reduction of domestic interest rates are likely to involve a breach of the target for the monetary aggregate. Similarly, an increase in interest rates designed to rein in monetary growth within the agreed target will strengthen the exchange rate, and could, therefore, conflict with the exchange rate target. Faced with a choice between a target for a monetary aggregate and a target for the exchange rate, the British authorities would prefer a monetary aggregate, since this is more closely related to the control of inflation. Adoption of an exchange rate target would imply linking the domestic price level to the highly volatile behaviour of world prices, as Minford pointed out (HC, 1980, *Mem.*, p. 140).

Professor Artis favoured the use of targets for the exchange rate and put the case for a conditional target in which a switch is made under pre-announced circumstances between one target and another (HC, 1980, *Mem.*, vol. II, p. 41).

The role of expectations in reducing the rate of inflation was emphasized in the memoranda of both the Treasury and Minford (HC, 1980, *Mem.*, pp. 9 and 139–40). The Government believes that, if it can convince the private sector that its announced strategy will be strictly adhered to, the private sector will modify its expectations about inflation. Thus, if employers and workers believe that the MTFS will be effective, they will adjust their behaviour in the setting of wages and prices. In this way the reduced rate of growth of monetary demand will be associated with a lower rate of inflation and a minimal loss of real output and employment. Minford (HC, 1980, *Mem.*, pp. 140 and 142) emphasized the need for the authorities to comply with policy announcements, which must be both simple and credible. By following this course of action the rate of inflation can be reduced rapidly and relatively painlessly. This view contrasts with the less extreme position of the gradualist monetarists, such as Laidler

(HC, 1980, *Mem.*, p. 51), who envisaged a gradual adjustment of inflationary expectations in response to a decline in monetary growth. Pragmatists, such as Tobin, were more sceptical of the ability of pre-announced targets to influence expectations. Tobin commented that such announcements are 'a threat to everybody in general and nobody in particular' (HC, 1981, *Mins*, p. 212), since general statements about monetary targets are not immediately relevant to agents who are concerned with the behaviour of individual markets at the microeconomic level.

IV THE PSBR AND THE MONEY SUPPLY

The Treasury argued that there is a direct connection between monetary growth and the size of the budget deficit (QB1) (HC, 1980, *Mem.*, p. 9 and App. 3). The relationship between the PSBR, the change in the money supply and the rate of interest is triangular, in the sense that, if interest rates do not vary, the money supply must grow broadly in line with the PSBR. The mechanism that the Treasury envisaged is that a budget deficit, financed domestically, implies an increase in the net assets of the private sector. As the wealth of the private sector rises, so will the demand for all assets, including money, bonds and real assets. The relative yields will adjust to induce asset-holders to absorb the available stock of assets into their portfolios. If wealth is being increased mainly by the issue of bonds, the yield on bonds must rise relative to those on other assets. The relative yield on bonds will be increasing so long as other assets are growing more slowly than the stock of bonds, given the asset preferences of the public. To preserve portfolio balance, it will therefore be necessary to increase the money supply.

There are a number of difficulties with this argument. Since it is based on the notion of long-run portfolio balance, it may apply only over a considerable period of time. The Treasury officials admitted in their oral evidence that they did not look for a direct connection between the PSBR and the money supply except in the very long run (HC, 1981, *Mins*, p. 111). This contention may not, however, have much force over the four to five-year period of the Government's financial strategy. The Treasury appears to have transported a valid long-run relationship into the medium term, where its relevance is open to question.

The Treasury view was stated in a stronger form by Minford. He argued that, since there is a long-run constraint linking the PSBR and monetary growth over the medium term, monetary targets also imply targets for the PSBR (HC, 1980, *Mem.*, p. 140).

Since the Treasury argument relates to the growth of real wealth and its implications for the demand for assets, it would appear that the PSBR should be measured in real rather than nominal terms (Q B7). If the new issue of bonds just offsets the erosion of the real value of the stock of outstanding bonds, then the real value of the public's bond holding is unchanged. Other witnesses, including Friedman (HC, 1980, *Mem.*, p. 56), emphasized the significance of the real PSBR, adjusted for the effects of inflation on the stock of bonds, rather than the nominal PSBR. A similar view was taken by the Bank of England, which had first drawn attention to the importance of this distinction. The Treasury was, however, reluctant to concede the importance of the real PSBR, emphasizing the significance of the PSBR as a nominal quantity which has to be financed and related to other nominal aggregates such as the money supply (HC, 1980, *Mem.*, p. 10). This argument is surprising in view of their emphasis on real-wealth effects acting through the PSBR.

Monetarist gradualists, such as Friedman and Laidler, were unwilling to accept a close link between the PSBR and the money supply. Laidler argued that there was a considerable degree of flexibility over the way in which a budget deficit may be financed. Only if the deficit was really substantial in relation to GDP would the needs of government finance require an increase in the money stock. Such a situation may have occurred in the UK during 1975, when the ratio of PSBR to national income was about 10 per cent (HC, 1980, *Mem.*, pp. 53–4). A similar view was expressed by Friedman, who was severely critical of the Treasury's Green Paper *Monetary Control* (1980) for its suggestion that the money stock should be controlled by fiscal policy and interest rates. Friedman claimed that one reason for the alleged close connection between the budget deficit and the growth in the money supply was the defective method of monetary control used in the UK. If alternative techniques were used to control the money supply, the authorities would have greater flexibility over the finance of the PSBR (HC, 1980, *Mem.*, pp. 57–9). This may well be correct, and the issue of monetary control will be discussed later. However, Friedman's proposals might cause substantial variations in interest rates, which he would find acceptable but the Treasury and the Bank of England might not.

Dornbusch (HC, 1980, *Mem.*, p. 69) also denied a close connection between changes in the money supply and the budget deficit on the basis of annual comparisons for the UK and the USA, while Kaldor showed that the correlation between the PSBR and the growth of M3 was negligible (HC, 1980, *Mem.*, p. 119). In neither case was an attempt made to allow for the effects of interest rates, and so the outcome of the discussion is uncertain. One might reasonably conclude that the Treasury had not made a convincing case for there being a close connection between the PSBR and the money supply over the period of the MTFS, whatever may be true in the long run. Tobin has commented forcefully that it is inherently undesirable to fix targets for a variable that is as highly sensitive to the cyclical state of the economy as the PSBR (HC, 1981, *Mins*, p. 209). Friedman reached a similar conclusion because of the problems of measuring the PSBR which is distorted by inflation.

One possible explanation for the close connection in official thinking between the PSBR and the money supply is hinted at in the Report, which notes that for the 'instant' monetarists 'the budget imbalance must equal the anticipated "inflation tax" associated with the monetary policy' (HC, 1980, *Rep.*, p. xxxiv). This would imply that the PSBR would decline with the fall in the expected rate of inflation and the notional yield of the inflation tax on the nominal value of government debt. Such an argument might explain the apparent relationships underlying the Government's financial strategy. It is unfortunate that this contention was not given greater emphasis by the Committee, since it would have been interesting to observe official reactions to the notion of an 'inflation tax'.

The experts were asked about the impact of the 'crowding-out' effect occurring when the PSBR increases and the money supply is unchanged (Q B6). This issue has been extensively discussed in the literature. There is little disagreement about the displacing of resources from the private sector when public expenditure is increased in a fully employed economy. What is less clear is the impact of increased public spending with a constant money supply in an economy with unutilized capacity. The higher government spending and accelerator effects on investment tend to raise activity, while the tightening of monetary conditions and decline in the value of public sector debt associated with higher interest rates operate in the opposite direction. In an open economy with a flexible exchange rate, the rise in interest rates may appreciate the exchange rate and so tend to restrict the increase in activity. The Bank of England concluded that the issue can only be resolved empirically (HC, 1980, *Mem.*, pp. 22–4), while the Treasury found the econometric evidence on 'crowding-out' in the UK economy ambiguous and hard to interpret (HC, 1980, *Mem.*, p. 10). In general, the empirical evidence suggests that positive accelerator effects on industrial investment are likely to be more powerful than negative financial effects.

It should be noted that the rise in the relative yield on government bonds owing to a continuing budget deficit with a closely controlled money stock need not raise the required return on investment in real assets. This conclusion depends on whether bonds are good substitutes for real assets. If they are not good substitutes, the private sector may wish to add to its holding of real capital, bidding up the prices of existing assets and encouraging the production of new capital goods. Thus the Treasury's theoretical model of portfolio balance does not yield unambiguous results on the long-term effects of 'crowding-out'.

Both the Treasury and the Bank of England agreed that the PSBR should be permitted to vary over the cycle (Q B9), a larger deficit being acceptable in a year of recession, when the PSBR would be acting as a built-in stabilizer to the economy (HC, 1980, *Mem.*, pp. 10–11 and 25). This view was endorsed by the academic experts with the possible exception of Minford, who is not explicit on this question. What is not clear is whether the Government, in tightening fiscal policy in the 1981 budget, following the overshooting of the PSBR in 1980–81, took account of the contribution of the unexpected severity of the recession to the deficit. The Government apparently showed greater concern for the credibility of its medium-term strategy than for the loss of output owing to the unexpected depth of the recession. It therefore tightened fiscal policy and reduced the stabilizing properties of the fiscal system.

The Committee suggests that the Government should allow the monetary target to be exceeded in a depression, as well as limits on public borrowing (HC, 1980, *Rep.*, p. liii). The case for such relaxation arises from the strong demand for credit from the corporate sector, squeezed between a high exchange rate and the rising labour costs. Such a proposal strikes at the basis of the medium-term strategy. It is one of the inherent defects of the Government's policy that it reduces the ability of the authorities to respond to unanticipated shocks. This point is emphasized by the Deutsche Bundesbank, which considers it 'inadvisable to set monetary growth targets for medium term periods of up to five years in advance' because of the uncertainty surrounding economic developments at home and abroad (HC, 1980, *Mem.*, vol. II, p. 13). The Bundesbank manages to maintain a credible anti-inflationary monetary stance without committing itself to medium-term targets, and therefore preserves an important measure of discretionary flexibility. It is unfortunate that the Bank of England cannot do the same.

V CONTROL OF THE MONEY SUPPLY

When asked about methods of controlling the money supply (Q B2 and 3), the Bank of England and the Treasury expressed doubts about the use of direct controls on the banking system. Their answers were based on British experience of the distorting effect of restricting bank lending through both limits on bank advances and quantitative restrictions on the rate of growth of interest-bearing deposits (the 'corset'). In addition, the abolition of exchange controls in 1979 made the restriction of the growth of bank deposits, through restrictions such as the 'corset', ineffective because of the ease of arranging loans via the Euro-sterling market. The official view was that control of monetary aggregates such as M3 could be achieved by a combination of fiscal policy through control of the size of the PSBR and interest policy (HC, 1980, *Mem.*, pp. 11 and 21). The Treasury admitted that, in order to achieve control of monetary aggregates over relative short periods of about six months, it may be desirable to move towards a system of monetary base control as discussed in the Green Paper on *Monetary Control* (1980). But this would involve greater variation in interest rates than under the present system.

The official views on controlling the money supply were strongly criticized by Friedman (HC, 1980, *Mem.*, pp. 57–9). Fiscal control methods were in effect being used to deal with a problem that was created by inappropriate techniques of monetary control. Friedman recommended the redefinition of reserve assets to exclude the range of assets included in the 12½ per cent reserve ratio introduced in 1971 under Competition and Credit Control (*Bank of England Quarterly Bulletin*, December 1971). Reserve assets should be defined as liabilities of the central bank and therefore be restricted to currency and bankers' deposits at the Bank of England. Second, he suggested that Bank of England intervention in the money market should take the form of open market operations in bills rather than by fixing short-term interest rates. The behaviour of interest rates should then be left to market forces. Finally, Friedman recommended the issue of index-linked government debt to reduce the cost of public borrowing. It was inconsistent for the authorities to issue securities paying high nominal rates, when they were also indicating to the market that they expected inflation and interest rates to decline, because of reduced rates of monetary growth.

While the Bank of England cannot be expected to be converted overnight to the doctrine of monetary base control, it is interesting to note that it has modified its techniques in the direction recommended by Friedman in his memorandum. The former reserve asset ratio has been abolished, and discussions are taking place about the size of the cash ratio and the institutions that should be required to comply with it. What is not yet clear is whether the Bank of England intends to use the newly defined reserve ratio as a fulcrum for control of the money supply. The Bank has also altered its techniques in the money market, through the abolition of minimum lending rate (MLR) and the substitution of quantitative intervention in the bill market for lending at the discount window (*Bank of England Quarterly Bulletin*, December 1980, p. 428; March 1981, p. 38; September 1981, pp. 333 and 347).

Third, the Government has introduced index linked gilt-edged securities and extended the availability of index-linked National Savings media. While these changes do not involve a radical change in the monetary mechanism, they do represent a change of emphasis which could be of considerable significance. The Bank of England now has a framework within which a move towards monetary base control would be feasible. It can also test whether official fears about excessive volatility in short-term interest rates under such a system are justified. If these misgivings prove to be groundless, the case for tightening control through the cash ratio will be strengthened.

Both monetarists and 'pragmatists' agreed that monetary policy should be used to combat inflation, but they differed on whether the authorities should rely exclusively on monetary methods. 'Pragmatists', such as Tobin, urged less formality over the setting of monetary targets and reliance upon alternative policies such as wage–price guide-posts as additional devices for combating inflation (HC, 1981, *Mins*, pp. 216–17). Only Lord Kaldor was totally opposed to monetary policy, arguing that the money supply could be controlled only by reducing the level of economic activity through a deflationary fiscal policy. He claimed that the only way to control the monetary stock in a credit economy was to reduce the demand for money by fiscal deflation (HC, 1980, *Mem.*, pp. 87–104).

The observed correlation between the rise in nominal income and the money supply could be accounted for by an accommodating monetary policy as readily as by the effect of a growing money stock in raising nominal incomes. If the former case applies, then reduced monetary growth should be associated with laxer monetary conditions, since the demand for credit will have contracted. If the latter applies, a check to monetary growth would be associated with a tightening of monetary policy and rising real interest rates. Deflation in the UK appears to be following the second course, which suggests that a reduction in the rate of growth of the money supply is reducing the growth of nominal incomes rather than vice versa.

Kaldor is, however, right to emphasize the difficulties that arise in controlling a broad aggregate, such as M3 sterling, which has a large interest-bearing component (HC, 1980, *Mem.*, p. 106). When interest rates are raised, the demand for M3 sterling may also rise, unless the authorities can operate on the relative yield of money and non-money assets. Thus, yields on longer-dated securities have to rise relative to the competitive short-term rates payable on much of M3. The memorandum of the Bank of Canada notes that broad monetary aggregates are not readily responsive to interest rates (HC, 1981, *App.*, p. 122). This suggests that a central bank should employ several monetary targets in framing policy. It should not permit itself to be tied to a single target, such as M3 sterling, which is particularly resistant to short-term control.

VI THE EXCHANGE RATE AND THE COMPETITIVENESS

There was widespread agreement among the experts that the exchange rate provides a major transmission mechanism for monetary change in an open economy with a floating exchange rate (Q B11). Friedman dissented by referring to the exchange rate as a facilitating process rather than a transmission mechanism (HC, 1980, *Mem.*, p. 61). But he did not disagree on the substantive issue that a monetary change will affect the exchange rate, with subsequent impacts on output and prices.

There was, however, a difference of opinion over the transmission process between the 'instant' monetarist (Minford) and the others (Q B12, 13). For those who believe in rational expectations, combined with flexibility of all prices and wages, the loss of competitiveness owing to a rise in the exchange rate, following a tightening of monetary policy, is not a matter of particular concern. The process of adjustment to a higher exchange rate will be accomplished rapidly. The temporary decline in competitiveness will be associated with a reduction in export prices and wages so that the effects on output are minimal. There will be no output loss if the rise in the exchange rate and associated monetary contraction are expected, since workers, thinking in real terms, will revise their wage demands downwards to take account of the expected lower rate of inflation. It is only if there are errors in expectations that there will be a temporary loss of output and employment (HC, 1980, *Mem.*, pp. 132, 142).

The view of the 'instant' monetarists contrast with those of the other schools of thought, who expect a tightening of monetary policy and the associated rise in the exchange rate to cause a decline in output and employment. The 'gradualist' monetarists are relatively optimistic about the process of adjustment to a lower rate of inflation (HC, 1980, *Mem.*, pp. 51, 61). It will, however, take time for wage-earners to adapt their expectations to a lower rate of increase of prices. This will not happen quickly enough to prevent unemployment in export and import-competing industries, but adjustment should take place over about two to three years. When workers have accepted that expectations must be revised downwards because of the lower rate of inflation, there will be no lasting damage to the economy beyond the temporary loss of output. The views of the 'gradualists' were echoed by the Treasury and the Bank of England, although the latter explained in detail the problem of choosing between rival theories that attempt to explain how the exchange rate is determined (HC, 1980, *Mem.*, pp. 26–7).

The 'pragmatists' were considerably less optimistic about the long-term costs arising from the operation of monetary policy via the exchange rate. Dornbusch (HC, 1980, *Mem.*, pp. 71–2) pointed out that the loss of competitiveness could have serious consequences for the structure of export industries; and a similar view was expressed by Artis (HC, 1980, *Mem.*, vol II, pp. 44–5) on the possible adverse effects on productivity growth. But there is something to be said on the other side: squeezed between an overvalued exchange rate, reflecting the influences of North Sea oil, tight monetary policy and high labour costs, British industry has had a strong incentive to raise productivity and to economize on labour. These changes may bring long-run benefits, if a trend towards higher productivity becomes firmly established. The structural argument is not yet settled, but the 'pragmatists' are right to insist that deflation may have lasting real effects.

VII CONTROL OF THE EXCHANGE RATE

The concern of 'pragmatists' over the undesirable effects of extreme movements of the exchange rate led to suggestions for a conditional exchange rate target. According to Artis' proposal (HC, 1980, *Mem.*, vol II, p. 41) the authorities would announce that their money supply target would be replaced by an exchange rate target in the event of the floating rate moving beyond a prescribed range. Practical support for such a policy was found in the memoranda submitted by the Bundesbank and the Bank of Canada. Both central banks have revised their monetary targets to take account of the behaviour of the exchange rate; in particular, they have relaxed domestic monetary targets when the exchange rate has been in danger of considerable overvaluation. Tobin argued that, if the British Government would not relax its monetary target in these circumstances, it should, as an alternative, follow a more expansionary fiscal policy to lower the exchange rate and stimulate domestic demand (HC, 1981, *Mins*, pp. 210–11).

Dornbusch was particularly concerned about the danger of an excessive appreciation of the exchange rate seriously weakening competitiveness ((Q B14) (HC, 1980, *Mem.*, p. 27). This could occur if a rise in domestic interest rates created the expectation of an appreciation of the exchange rate. Inward capital movements could be encouraged by the anticipation of both a favourable interest differential and exchange rate appreciation, creating the prospect of a substantial real gain. To offset an unwanted rise in the exchange rate, in these circumstances he recommended the imposition of an interest equalization tax on foreign-held deposits. But this recommendation was rejected as administratively impracticable by the Bank of England because of the complexities of the London capital market (HC, 1980, *Mem.*, p. 28).

VIII THE TRANSMISSION MECHANISM IN AN OPEN ECONOMY

There was a high degree of consensus among the experts about the transmission process. A loss of competitiveness owing to appreciation of the exchange rate will curb inflation through a reduced rate of increase of the prices of traded goods. The check to output in the international sector will moderate wage settlements particularly in manufacturing, and in due course wage increases will be reduced in the non-traded goods sector. In addition, the tightening of monetary policy will cut back domestic demand because of the increase in real interest rates, while expectations of price increases will be revised downwards following the reduction in the rate of inflation.

There did not seem to be major disagreement between 'gradualists' and 'pragmatists' on the processes that are at work, but there are differences of emphasis in the transmission mechanism envisaged,

and on the costs of deflation (Q B16 and 17). While gradualist monetarists and the British authorities admitted that there would be a loss
of output and employment, expectations could play an important
role in bringing down the rate of inflation once the process of
disinflation was well under way (HC, 1980, *Mem.*, pp. 13, 29–31,
51–3). They were cautious in providing quantitative assessments of
the short-run trade-off between unemployment and inflation. Laidler
tentatively mentioned that his models suggested that inflation would
fall by 5 percentage points for an increase of 1 percentage point in
unemployment (HC, 1980, *Mem.*, p. 51). He added suitable qualifications to this estimate, but one is left with the impression that a
highly favourable trade-off is envisaged.

'Pragmatists' placed considerable emphasis on the costs of a
deflationary policy and did not look for a favourable trade-off
between inflation and unemployment. Tobin suggested, on the basis
of US evidence, a fall of $\frac{1}{2}$ to $\frac{1}{3}$ per cent in the inflation rate for a 1
percentage point rise in unemployment (HC, 1981, *Mins*, p. 212).
The Report of the Committee includes simulations with the Treasury
model, which came out with broadly similar results for the UK, but
the outcome depended upon how demand is reduced (HC, 1980,
Rep., pp. lxxiv–lxxvi). It is worth noting that the results of the
Treasury model were more pessimistic than the Treasury memorandum
on the costs of deflation. When questioned on this point, Treasury
officials argued that the parameters of their model were not invariant
with respect to the policy being followed; more might be achieved by
the MTFS than by previous deflationary policies, because of its
emphasis on modifying expectations through announced financial
targets. This implies that economic policy rests on an act of faith
rather than empirical evidence (HC, 1981, *Mins*, pp. 99–106).

There is ample econometric evidence on the determination of
wages and prices in the UK. With the exception of the rational
expectation studies of Minford, investigators have generally found
that wages and prices do not adjust rapidly when demand is reduced.
Prices are determined primarily by labour and import costs, with
little evidence of the direct influence of demand conditions. Wages
may be explained by the notion of a target real wage modified by the
pressure of demand in the labour market, or alternatively by some
form of expectations-augmented Phillips curve. A major problem
with these empirical studies is that there is no strong evidence of
unemployment moderating inflation (HC, 1981, *App.*, pp. 17–19).
On the other hand, it is difficult to deny that unemployment is
having an important effect on the moderation of wage settlements

in the recession of 1980–81. The Committee expressed concern that any recovery of demand will lead to a revival of wage inflation, thus admitting that demand factors may have played a part in reducing wage settlements (HC, 1980, *Rep.*, p. lxxvii).

The high cost in terms of output and employment of monetary deflation led 'pragmatists' to consider alternative policies. Tobin argued for the introduction of a system of wage and price guidelines, which would not be open to the criticism levelled at previous income policies (Q B19) (HC, 1981, *Mins*, pp. 219–21). There should be co-ordination between monetary targets and the wage and price guideline, so that incomes policy would be consistent with the stance of monetary and fiscal policy. The distorting effects of incomes policies would be mitigated through taxing, rather than prohibiting wages and price increases in excess of the guide posts. Gradualists, such as Laidler, showed some sympathy for incomes policies, but rejected them after careful consideration, since they need to be arbitrary to be effective (HC, 1980, *Mem.*, p. 52). 'Fair' policies must be fully discussed before implementation and will be anticipated by the labour market, leading to anticipatory wage increases.

Whatever the merits of Tobin's proposals, it is not surprising that they did not commend themselves to British policy-makers. The Treasury and the Bank of England rejected incomes policies because of their indifferent record in the British economy (HC, 1980, *Mem.*, pp. 13 and 31). Any check to wage increases achieved during the operation of the policy has been quickly offset by 'catch-up' increases taking place after its termination or collapse. British experience suggests that incomes policy is only a temporary palliative and no permanent cure for inflation; but this does not mean that some future British government will not wish to give serious consideration to Tobin's proposals.

IX A PRELIMINARY ASSESSMENT OF THE MONETARIST EXPERIMENT

The Report argues that there has been no true monetarist experiment in the UK because the authorities did not keep to their plans for restricting the PSBR in 1980–81 and did not raise interest rates sufficiently to check monetary expansion in excess of the target for M3 in the same financial year (HC, 1980, *Rep.*, p. xxviii). This judgement seems rather premature, since the Government has maintained the thrust of its policy into the next financial year. It has tightened

fiscal policy in a recession to contain the growth of the PSBR in the
1981 Budget and allowed nominal interest rates to rise to 16 per cent
later in the year. The decline in the rate of inflation to about 11 per
cent per annum implies that real interest rates have turned sharply
positive. The monetary target for 1981–82 may not be greatly
exceeded, and the revised estimate for the PSBR of £10.5 billion
(4¼ per cent of GDP) may well be achieved. Provided there is no
policy U-turn before 1983–84, Britain will have provided an excellent
example of a gradualist monetarist experiment. The modifications
made to the MTFS are relatively modest and do not affect its underlying logic. Friedman's general commendation of the policy is still
relevant; although his final requirements have not been strictly
observed:

> I strongly approve of the general outlines of the monetary
> strategy outlined by the Government: taking monetary growth
> as the major target; stating in advance targets for a number of
> years; setting targets that require a steady and gradual reduction
> in monetary growth; and stressing the Government's intentions
> of strictly adhering to these targets. (HC, 1980, *Mem.*, p. 56)

The course of the strategy has been disturbed by unexpected events.
It is unlikely that the Government had foreseen the massive appreciation of sterling between 1978 and the first quarter of 1981. The
unprecedented loss of competitiveness has been estimated by the
Bank of England at over 40 per cent. Other factors were at work here
(such as the impact of the increase in oil prices on sterling as a petro-
currency) in addition to the rise in the UK interest rates. Similarly,
the authorities did not foresee the decline in the sterling–dollar
exchange rate in 1981, owing mainly to US monetary policy; this
threatens to prevent the attainment of single-figure inflation, which
Friedman expected by 1982 (HC, 1980, *Mem.*, p. 61). The possible
impact of disturbances originating outside the economy on the
outcome of a gradualist programme was noted by Laidler in his
carefully worded memorandum (HC, 1980, *Mem.*, p. 51).

If the basic structure of the strategy remains valid, so do the
fundamental doubts about it expressed by Tobin:

> [T]he U.K. has embarked upon a very interesting and, if I may
> say so, risky experiment in macroeconomic policy and monetary
> policy. . . . The hope of the protagonists of that policy is that it
> will so melt the existing core of inflation in the economy that

the response to it will be much quicker than one might have expected in the past. It has not really been done before. It is a kind of speculative thing as to how fast that might work; whether it would actually work faster than previous recessions have succeeded in reducing on going inflation. From that point of view I must say that the United Kingdom is a very interesting laboratory experiment for economics. (HC, 1981, *Mins*, pp. 208–9)

Commenting on the progress of the experiment, Tobin stated that judgement on its success could presumably be made in the second half of 1981. It would appear that, while progress has been made in reducing inflation, the cost in terms of unemployment has been unacceptably high. Even this judgement is open to question, since much of the rise in unemployment can be attributed to the world recession, rather than to the particular macroeconomic policy being followed by the British Government. The achievements to date (November 1981) have been greater than a 'pragmatist' might have feared, but less than a gradualist monetarist might have hoped. 'Instant' monetarists will have to do some hard thinking to reconcile their doctrines with recent British experience. While something has been achieved by making the control of inflation the overriding aim of macroeconomic policy, it is reasonable to ask how long this should continue. With persistent unemployment at levels not experienced since the interwar period, the case for some relaxation of the Government's monetary and fiscal targets grows steadily stronger. Limits on public borrowing could be eased to some extent without endangering the credibility of counter-inflation policy or 'crowding-out' private investment. The benefits of deflation will not have been negligible if the process has stimulated the long-term growth of productivity in British industry, but there is not yet sufficient evidence to judge this important issue.

To conclude, the Committee has encouraged its experts to produce a great variety of interesting arguments on the working of monetary policy. Its report has helped to clarify what issues are reasonably well agreed, and where acute differences remain among the various schools of monetary thought.

REFERENCES

House of Commons (HC) (1980) Third Report of the Treasury and Civil Service Committee, Session 1979/80, *Monetary Control*: vol. I, *Report* 713-I; *Memoranda on Monetary Policy*, 720; *Memoranda on Monetary Policy*, vol. II, 720-II, HMSO, London. (Citations given as *Mem.* indicate the main volume of *Memoranda*, unless qualified by 'vol. II'.)

House of Commons (HC) (1981) Treasury and Civil Service Committee, Session 1980/81, *Monetary Policy*: vol. I, *Report* 163-I; vol. II, *Minutes of Evidence*, 163-II; vol. III, *Appendices*, 163-III, HMSO, London.

Radcliffe Committee (1959) *Report of the Commission on the Working of the Monetary System*, Cmnd 827, HMSO, London.

Treasury (1980) *Monetary Control* (Green Paper), Cmnd 7858, HMSO, London.

Wilson Committee (1980) *Report of the Committee to Review the Functioning of Financial Institutions*, Cmnd 7937, HMSO, London.

Appendix

Questionnaire on Monetary Policy

This questionnaire, drafted by the Committee's specialist advisers, was sent to a number of institutional and academic witnesses on 24 April 1980.

Introduction

The Committee is shortly starting an enquiry into monetary policy as it is evolving in the United Kingdom while taking into account the experience of other mature economies. The attached questionnaire, which has been drafted by its specialist advisers, indicates the ground the Committee wishes to cover.

This questionnaire is being sent to the attached list of experts in the United Kingdom and other countries.

The Committee would welcome replies to the whole questionnaire from the Treasury and Bank of England (with supporting evidence in due course). The Committee recognise that while some of the other recipients may wish to address themselves to all the issues raised, a number of experts will probably wish to concentrate on those topics in which they are particularly interested. This of course would be entirely acceptable to the Committee and suggestions are being made to individual experts where appropriate, but they should feel entirely free to bring in other topics than those mentioned in the questions if they consider them relevant. The Committee suggest that the questions should be regarded not as an examination paper but as a way of eliciting expert views which some may prefer to set out as a memorandum.

The Committee is concerned to establish how far the views and theories put forward are well based in the evidence and would therefore particularly welcome empirical evidence whether from the UK or other countries. The attention of witnesses submitting empirical evidence is drawn to the Appendix on Econometric Evidence. Witnesses wishing to submit empirical evidence may choose to submit answers to the relevant questions in sections A to C with the aid of their econometric equations. This would assist the Committee in its work.

The Committee may wish to publish experts' replies to this questionnaire with their Report. May they assume that there would be no objection to their doing so?

The Committee would be most grateful if experts were to send their replies to the Clerk, if possible, by 30 May 1980. Thereafter the Committee will invite certain of the experts who have submitted written evidence to give oral evidence in amplification of their views, probably in the course of June and July. It may be that further evidence will be taken in the autumn. The Committee's present intention is to report to the House of Commons at about the turn of the year.

A. *Objectives of Economic Policy*

(i) THE PRINCIPAL OBJECTIVES

The Chancellor wrote in a recent letter[1] to the Committee that "the main objectives of the Government's economic strategy are to reduce inflation and to create conditions in which substantial economic growth can be achieved", adding later that, "overriding priority must be given to reducing inflation and to strengthening the supply side of the economy".

Q1. In the past, economic policy in the UK was guided by objectives in respect of (a) the level and stability of aggregate employment, (b) the level and composition of the balance of international payments, (c) the rate of inflation, and (d) the rate of economic growth. Should the Government still pursue these objectives?

Q2. If it is assumed that the Government's policy of "strengthening the supply side" of the economy refers to efforts to increase the incentives to work by reducing direct taxation, the real value of unemployment benefits and trade union powers, does this require modifying or suspending employment and balance of payments objectives? How do you expect a low level of demand to affect the supply side of the economy?

Q3. How do you expect the change in the objectives of economic policy, indicated in the letter from the Chancellor, to affect economic performance? Specifically, is there any risk that ending the post-war commitment to high employment may permit a return to pre-war conditions of unemployment?

Q4. Are there significant costs in terms of economic performance of periodic changes in government objectives? How can they be minimised?

(ii) INTERMEDIATE TARGETS

Given its objectives for inflation and growth and for improving the supply side of the economy, the Government has proceeded to formulate declining medium term targets for the growth of the money supply and for the Public Sector Borrowing Requirement (PSBR) as a percentage of Gross Domestic Product (GDP); see Part II of the enclosed *Financial Statement and Budget Report*, especially Tables 5 and 9. The paths given are as follows:

Medium Term Financial Strategy

	1980/81	*1981/82*	*1982/83*	*1983/84*
Growth of £M3	7–11	6–10	5–9	4–8
PSBR (as a % of GDP)	3¾	3	2¼	1½

In discussing how policy might respond to deviations in world trade, oil prices, productivity, earnings etc from the paths presently anticipated, the Chancellor specifically asserts that "there would be no question of departing from the money supply policy, which is essential to the success of any anti-inflationary strategy" (Part II, para 16).

Q5. What is the rationale for pursuing the objectives of economic policy by setting up target paths for *intermediate* variables (such as the money supply, the Public Sector Borrowing Requirement or the exchange rate)?

Q6. Would you recommend the exchange rate as an alternative intermediate target to the money supply—or some compromise where the money supply target is modified in a known way in response to deviations of the exchange rate? Can the exchange rate be controlled without undesirable loss of control over the appropriate monetary target?

Q7. What role do expectations of government policy have on private sector behaviour, and how should this affect government policy and policy announcements?

Q8. On balance, do you think it advisable to announce intermediate targets and if so for which variables, over what interval of time and in what form?

[1]Memoranda on Monetary Policy and Public Expenditure, February 1980, HC (1979–80) 450.

B. *Instruments and Effects of Policy*

(i) MONEY SUPPLY, INTEREST RATES AND PSBR

Speaking at a conference in January 1980, the Financial Secretary to the Treasury made the following observations on the PSBR:

"Let me start with two simple facts. The first is a statistic. The PSBR is at present about 4½ per cent of total gross domestic product (GDP)—compared with an average of only 2½ per cent in the 1960s. The second is an economic relationship. That is, the PSBR and the growth of the money supply and interest rates are very closely related. Too high a PSBR requires either that the Government borrow heavily from the Banks— which adds directly to the money supply; or, failing this, that it borrows from individuals and institutions, but at ever-increasing rates of interest, which place an unacceptable squeeze on the private sector."

Q1. What is the "economic relationship" between the money supply, interest rates and the Public Sector Borrowing Requirement, and what does it imply for the conduct of fiscal and monetary policy?

Q2. Is the use of the basic weapons of fiscal policy, gilt-edged funding and short-term interest rates adequate for control of the money supply on a year-to-year basis, or is there a case for direct controls on credit, for example, through lending ceilings?

Q3. Has the short-run volatility of the broad monetary aggregate been excessive? Are there feasible techniques whereby the central bank can gain control over the broad money aggregate in the short run by operating on the supply of reserve assets? What implications do such techniques have for the volatility of short-term interest rates and the stability ˆ the banking system?

Q4. Is controlling the money supply a mechanism for controlling the economy or does the economy have to be controlled in order to control the demand for money?

Q5. How has the abolition of exchange control affected:

(a) the Government's ability to control £M3,
(b) the significance of £M3?

Q6. What grounds are there in theory, and what evidence in practice, that public borrowing "crowds out" private expenditure, particularly private capital formation?

Q7. Do you agree that the "inflation adjusted" PSBR (which measures the real increase in borrowing by the public sector[1]) is more relevant in assessing the danger of crowding out than the PSBR without such adjustment?

Q8. If borrowing for capital formation in the public sector is included in the measure of the PSBR which the Government is aiming to reduce, will this not lead to either the crowding out of public sector capital formation or inflation in nationalised industries' prices?

Q9. What is the desirable trend path of the PSBR (appropriately defined) relative to GNP? Should the PSBR be allowed to vary from this path over the cycle? How, if at all, should the PSBR target be modified in response to a change in the personal savings ratio?

Q10. Should Government interest bearing debt be indexed?

(ii) MONEY, THE EXCHANGE RATE, INFLATION AND OUTPUT

Q11. Do you agree that, for the UK under floating exchange rates, the principal "transmission mechanism" between monetary policy actions and the ultimate targets is via changes in the exchange rate? If so, which of the channels by which exchange rate changes can affect output and inflation do you consider important for the UK?

---

[1]See Bank of England Discussion Paper No. 6 *"Real" National Saving and its Sectoral Composition*, C T Taylor and A R Threadgold.

Q12. What is the effect of the money supply on the exchange rate? What other factors affect the exchange rate?

Q13. Should the loss of price competitiveness on British exports and against foreign imports and/or the squeeze in profit margins because of the strong £ be of concern to the authorities in their conduct of monetary policy?

Q14. Would the conduct of monetary policy be assisted by limiting the opportunity or incentive for international financial capital movements (for example, by taxing the interest paid on foreign deposits as has been the practice in West Germany and Switzerland)?

Q15. What are the major immediate determinants of wages and prices in the UK? Which of these determinants can be affected by monetary policy, and over what time horizon?

Q16. What evidence is there that the announcement of medium term targets for the money supply has a direct effect on inflation expectations in labour markets? What evidence is there for the effects of inflation expectations on wage and price behaviour?

Q17. If the announcement and pursuit of monetary targets does not have prompt and significant effects on wage and price inflation via changes in the exchange rate and in inflation expectations, will the reduction of inflation have to come through unemployment and excess capacity? If so, what will be the mechanisms causing the contraction in output and, in particular, is the link via the cash flow and the liquidity position of the corporate sector an important part of the transmission mechanism?

Q18. What evidence is there of the magnitude of output and employment reduction required to achieve a reduction of inflation from its current level to single figures by 1982? What will be the effects on investment and the potential for future growth?

Q19. Do you see any role for incomes policies as a substitute for, or complement to, monetary policies? What evidence is there of the effectiveness of incomes policies?

C. *The Conduct of Policy*

Q1. The limits on the growth rate of the money supply for the next few years announced by the Government should substantially reduce the uncertainty about future policy, but they limit the freedom of the authorities to respond to unforeseen events. Do you expect the benefits to exceed costs?

Q2. Are there more flexible policies of the "feedback" type, that combine the advantage of being easily understood by the private sector with that of being able to respond to changes in the economic environment, which you would recommend?

Q3. Do you believe that formal or explicit policy optimisation using a range of econometric models can be an aid in the design of macroeconomic policy?

Q4. Do you think it desirable and/or feasible to have policies that are "robust" in that they will deliver acceptable outcomes under a range of external and domestic disturbances, and under a variety of different specifications of how the world works?

Q5. Do you think that the pursuit of "structural" objectives (such as reducing the size of the public sector and improving incentives) must rule out the use of government expenditure and tax policy for "stabilisation" purposes?

Q6. Do you believe the policies for the money supply and the PSBR announced by the Chancellor are consistent with achieving the stated objectives of his economic policy? Should the monetary targets not be modified in response to significant upward pressure on sterling due to oil revenues?

Q7. Can you think of alternative policies which are likely to achieve the ultimate objectives (or do so more quickly)?

Q8. Can you think of alternative policies which would reduce any unpleasant "side effects" that the planned anti-inflation strategy may have for output, unemployment and the balance of payments?

12

A Monetary Model of Exchange-Rate Determination Applied to the Italian Experience with Flexible Exchange Rates

MARIO BIAGIOLI*

I INTRODUCTION

In recent years the monetary approach to the theory of the balance of payments adjustment mechanism has gained wide support among theoreticians and policy-makers.[1] When applied to the regime of flexible exchange rates (or, more precisely, the regime of 'managed floating') into which the international monetary system has evolved in the 1970s, the monetary approach can be synthetized by a model of exchange-rate determination, whose reduced form is derived and tested in this paper for the Italian experience from 1973 to 1978.

It is shown in the following sections that whenever income growth in Italy has exceeded the average rate of growth of other industrial countries, the exchange rate has depreciated. This result contradicts the central hypothesis of the monetary approach that real changes can affect the external balance of a country only by changing the demand for money and producing a potential (*ex ante*) imbalance in the money market which is eliminated through changes of the external payments position of the country. Hence, macroeconomic effects other than 'neutral' inflation seem to have been induced by the depreciation of the Italian lira that has occurred in the period under investigation, which has prevented exchange-rate flexibility from 'allowing' Italian policy-makers 'to pursue the mixture of unemployment and price trend objectives they preferred, consistent with international equilibrium', contrary to what Johnson (1969,

* I am grateful to Christopher Allsopp, Salvatore Biasco and Andrea Boltho for useful comments and helpful suggestions.

p. 18) suggested to be the major advantage of moving to a flexible exchange rates regime.

II THE MONETARY APPROACH IN A REGIME OF FLEXIBLE EXCHANGE RATES

The monetary approach regards balance of payments disequilibria as originating from potential imbalances in domestic monetary markets, which spill over into the external sector and produce both the external imbalances and the processes through which such imbalances are eliminated. Accordingly, the monetary approach highlights the importance of the monetary aspects of payments imbalances and undermines the role of 'real' variables in the adjustment process.

The theoretical foundation on which such an analysis is based is the monetarist point that money demand is a stable, linearly homogeneous function of real income, with elasticity equal to 1. The process through which *ex ante* imbalances in domestic money markets are transformed into external payments' imbalances goes as follows. Any excess supply of (demand for) money makes expenditures exceed (fall short of) receipts. The excess of expenditures would bring about, in a closed economy, a proportional increase in prices. In open economies this is not possible since domestic prices are eventually determined by world prices through the process summarized by the 'purchasing power principle'.[2] If prices are determined at a world-wide level, the only way people can get rid of the potential excess of expenditures over receipts is by buying foreign commodities, services and assets. Conversely, any excess of receipts over expenditures can be matched only by net exports of commodities, services and assets. The potential excess of supply of (demand for) money is eventually offset by a balance of payments deficit (surplus) of the same size.

Thus, 'the main characteristic of the monetary approach can be summarized in the proposition that ... since the money account is determined by the excess flow demand for money ... the balance of payments is essentially a monetary phenomenon' (Frenkel and Johnson, 1976, pp. 21 and 22).

Under flexible exchange rates, monetary imbalances cannot produce external payments imbalances since, if the monetary authorities refrain from intervening in the exchange market, the official settlements balance cannot but be balanced. Consequently, under flexible exchange rates a potential excess (shortfall) of money demand over money supply, which would produce a balance of payments deficit (surplus) under fixed rates, induces the exchange rate to deteriorate (appreciate) until the monetary imbalance is eventually eliminated.

Exchange rate changes automatically adjust the money market imbalance by causing domestic prices to change. Thus, when applied to a regime of flexible rates, the monetary approach 'shifts the focus of the analysis from the determination of the balance of payments to the determination of the exchange rate' (Frenkel and Johnson, 1976, p. 29). The exchange rate becomes the key variable of the process through which monetary imbalances are eliminated.

This process is usually modelled by examining how the foreign exchange market connects the monetary markets of different countries.[3] The conditions of equilibrium in the monetary markets of two countries – Italy and the rest of the world (indicated from now on with the subscripts It and RW) – are obtained by equalizing demand for and supply of money. Thus,

$$M_{It}^d = P_{It} \cdot L_{It}(i_{It}; Y_{It}) = M_{It}^s \tag{1}$$

and

$$M_{RW}^d = P_{RW} \cdot L_{RW}(i_{RW}; Y_{RW}) = M_{RW}^s \tag{2}$$

where M^s indicates the supply of money that is assumed to be exogenously determined by monetary authorities; M^d is money demand, which is defined as the product of the purchasing power of money and the liquidity preference function, L. The former is usually measured by an index of consumer prices, as these are regarded by monetarists as a correct 'proxy of the underlying monetary conditions' (Frenkel, 1976, p. 204). The latter is supposed to depend upon real output, Y, and interest rate, i, with partial derivatives positive and tending to 1 in equilibrium with respect to real income, and negative and tending to 0 under non-inflationary conditions with respect to the interest rate. With inflation the elasticity of money demand with respect to the interest rate becomes negative, since it measures the cost of holding money, whose purchasing power is depreciating, rather than buying commodities.

The two markets of money are connected through the process of arbitrage between domestic and foreign commodities, whose equilibrium condition is expressed by the 'purchasing power parity principle':

$$P_{\text{It}} = ER \cdot P_{\text{RW}} \tag{3}$$

where ER is the exchange rate, which indicates the price of a unit of foreign currency expressed in terms of the domestic country's currency.

The system composed by the three equations above represents the monetarist model of exchange rate determination. By substituting (1) and (2) into (3), the system can be solved to provide the following reduced-form equation of exchange rate determination:

$$ER = \frac{M_{\text{It}}^{\text{s}}}{M_{\text{RW}}^{\text{s}}} \cdot \frac{L_{\text{RW}}(Y_{\text{RW}}; i_{\text{RW}})}{L_{\text{It}}(Y_{\text{It}}; i_{\text{It}})}. \tag{4}$$

This states that the rate of exchange is an endogenous variable and its long-run dynamics are determined by changes of the money supply, real income and interest rates at home and abroad.

The following specification of the money demand function is assumed:

$$M_i^{\text{d}} = P_i \cdot k_i \cdot Y_i \cdot i_i^{e_i} \tag{5}$$

where the subscript i indicates a generic country (either Italy or the rest of the world); k_i is the money multiplier (inverse of the velocity of circulation of money, which is supposed by monetarists to be a constant); and e_i measures the interest elasticity of money demand. (Since this is assumed to be negative, the term $i_i^{e_i}$ divides, rather than multiplies, the other terms of the formula.) Finally, the income elasticity of the demand for money is supposed to be equal to 1.

Making the key assumption of the monetary approach that the demand for money is a stable function of real income, homogeneous of degree 0 in nominal variables and with income elasticity equal to 1, and substituting (5) into (4), the following expression is obtained:

$$ER = \frac{M_{\text{It}}^{\text{s}}}{M_{\text{RW}}^{\text{s}}} \cdot \frac{k_{\text{RW}} \cdot Y_{\text{RW}} \cdot i_{\text{RW}}^{e_i}}{k_{\text{It}} \cdot Y_{\text{It}} \cdot i_{\text{It}}^{e_i}} \tag{6}$$

testable by transforming all variables into natural logarithms and estimating the elasticity of coefficients:

$$\log ER = a_0 + a_1 \cdot \log(M_{\text{It}}^{\text{s}}/M_{\text{RW}}^{\text{s}}) + a_2 \cdot \log(Y_{\text{RW}}/Y_{\text{It}})$$
$$+ a_3 \cdot \log(i_{\text{It}}/i_{\text{RW}}) + u \tag{7}$$

where u indicates the error term, and interest rates have been passed from the numerator to the denominator and vice versa to take into account the negative sign of the money demand to interest rate elasticity. It should be noticed that the ratio between nominal interest rates measures only the difference between inflationary expectations at home and abroad; in real terms domestic interest rates are assumed to be equal to world interest rates, since assets denominated in different currencies are assumed to be perfect substitutes, and then to provide equal gains and to entail equal risks. The equilibrium conditions of perfectly competitive international financial markets are either the 'interest rate parity principle' (which states that the difference between forward and spot exchange rates is equal to the difference between domestic and foreign interest rates on assets with maturity at the same date as the forward contract) or the so-called 'Fisher open principle' (which states that the difference between domestic and foreign interest rates measures the differential of inflation, and then the amount of depreciation expected over the time-span up to the maturity of the assets: Aliber, 1976, derived such a principle from Fisher, 1930). Whenever such principles hold, the economic interpretation of interest rates as pure proxies for expected inflation given above is correct, since no role is played by the interest rates as determinants of the portfolio choice of investors between assets denominated in different currencies.

The hypothesis to test is that the four elasticities are equal to the 'theoretical' values specified above:

(1) a_0 should not be significantly different from 0. If true, the model is correctly identified;
(2) a_1 and a_2 should not be significantly different from 1,
(3) a_3 should be positive.

It should be noticed that estimating the sign of a_2 is a means of discriminating between the monetary and the elasticity absorption approaches to the balance of payments theory. In fact, according to the monetary view, an exogenous increase of real income is supposed to increase the demand for money and, with other things constant, is expected to bring about both a net improvement of the balance of payments and exchange rate appreciation. Conversely, according to the elasticity absorption approach, an increase in real income induces increased imports, a deterioration of the balance of trade and exchange rate depreciation.

Neither the estimate of a_1 nor the estimate of a_3 can discriminate among different views despite the fact that the roles that these variables are supposed to play by authors using different approaches is completely different.

III TESTING THE MONETARY MODEL

The model developed in the previous section is tested here under the following specification:

$$\log EER = a_0 + a_1 \cdot \log(M^s_{RW}/M^s_{It}) + a_2 \cdot \log(Y_{It}/Y_{RW})$$
$$+ a_3 \cdot \log(i_{RW}/i_{It}) + u \qquad\qquad (8)$$

which differs from equation (7) in so far as the effective exchange rate (*EER*, which measures the price of the domestic currency expressed in terms of foreign currencies weighted with the share of international trade through and from Italy and each country) has been substituted for the bilateral exchange rate entered in equation (7).

Two estimates of the ratio (M^s_{RW}/M^s_{It}) have been calculated. The first has as its numerator the index of money expansion in the rest of the world; whereas the second uses the index of money expansion in the other industrial countries.[4]

Two estimates of the variable Y_{RW} have also been calculated:

(1) Y_{IC}, which is a weighted average of the indices of real income in the main six industrial countries weighted according to the size of their GNP in dollars;
(2) Y_{Comp}, which is a weighted average of the same indices, but which uses OECD trade weights proportional to the share of each country in Italian trade flows (weights indicated in OECD, 1978).

The variable i_{RW} has been calculated as a weighted average of the money market interest rates of the four countries to which Italian trade is mainly directed (Germany, France, USA and UK), with weights proportional to the shares of these countries in Italian foreign trade. The rate on short-term government bonds has been used as a measure of it, as it is usually considered to be the most representative indicator of the short-term interest rate in Italy and, thus, the best proxy of inflationary expectations.

Four ordinary least squares estimates which combine the different specifications of the variables of equation (8) are calculated on quarterly data over the period (1973(I)–1978(IV)). The results are shown in table 12.1, where R^2 is the coefficient of determination;

DW is the Durbin–Watson statistics; s.e. is the standard error of the equation; and the numbers in brackets beneath the coefficients are *t*-statistics, whereas F indicates the values of the F-statistics (ratio of the explained variance over the unexplained variance). (Under brackets beneath the values of the F-statistics the numbers of independent variables and the degrees of freedom are recorded.)

TABLE 12.1 Estimates of the monetary model of exchange rate determination

Constant terms	Elasticities of the following variables:					R^2	F-stat. (3, 20)
	M^s_{RW}/M^s_{It}	$M^s_{IC\text{-}It}/M^s_{It}$	Y_{It}/Y_{IC}	Y_{It}/Y_{Comp}	i_{RW}/i_{It}		
Equation (1)							
0.123		0.712		−0.740	0.159	0.9589	155.43
(3.032)		(9.177)		(−2.136)	(5.678)		
DW stat. = 1.282			s.e. = 0.0396				
Equation (2)							
0.137	1.069			−0.676	0.225	0.9477	120.75
(2.819)	(7.868)			(−1.735)	(8.474)		
DW stat. = 1.457			s.e. = 0.0447				
Equation (3)							
0.117		0.714	−0.714		0.160	0.9583	153.24
(3.000)		(9.044)	(−2.056)		(5.691)		
DW stat. = 1.270			s.e. = 0.0399				
Equation (4)							
0.121	1.061			−0.567	0.227	0.9455	115.72
(2.789)	(7.608)			(−1.447)	(8.337)		
DW stat. = 1.446			s.e. = 0.0401				

The test yields two conclusions, which are in accordance with the theoretical assumptions of the monetary approach. First, relative credit expansion is shown to be a significant determinant of the exchange rate, even though the elasticity of the money supply with respect to that of other industrial countries is rather lower than 1. Second, relative interest rates are positive, as expected by the monetarists. However, tests on the constant term and on real income do not conform to the assumptions outlined in the previous section. Particularly damaging to the acceptance of the monetary theory is the finding that all the coefficients of relative income have negative signs, contrary to what is assumed by the monetary approach. Thus, the only test that is able to discriminate between monetarist and other views of balance of payments readjustment is favourable to the latter. The level of significance of these coefficients is rather lower than the significance of the other coefficients, although relative income is significant in equation (1) at the 5 per cent level of significance, in equations (2) and (3) at the 10 per cent, and in equation (4) at the 20 per cent level.

All constant terms are significantly different from 0, and first-order autocorrelation of residuals is shown by some estimates. (Durbin–Watson statistics range from 1.27 to 1.46; autocorrelations can be excluded at the 5 per cent level of significance in none of the equations, and can be excluded at the 10 per cent level of significance only in equations (2) and (4).) Both of these latter findings indicate that the model is probably mis-specified. A possible source of such a mis-specification is indicated in monetary literature. The monetary model has been developed as a reduced-form condition of equilibrium.

Reaching equilibrium could take a longer span of time than the quarterly unit of observation used in the equations estimated above. If the time of adjustment is longer than a quarter, a simultaneous equation bias occurs (supply and demand functions are not properly identified), which impairs the test.

However, it is highly questionable whether the money supply, real income and the exchange rate could be regarded as independent for periods longer than a quarter in the Italian experience. Italian monetary authorities seem to have tailored their interventions to the support of real income, while avoiding the insurgence of major imbalances (as it has been reported in several Annual Reports of the Bank of Italy). A test with a longer unit of observation would suffer from a different, and probably more serious, simultaneous-equation bias, as exogenous variables have not been independent.

The test performed here shows that in the short run real income has affected the external payments position and the exchange rate in a way systematically opposite to that suggested by the monetary approach. Thus, although the monetary model accounts for 95 per cent of the variation of the exchange rate, the failure of the test on relative real income and the indication that the model is mis-specified both suggest that it should be rejected.

IV TESTS OF THE 'PURCHASING POWER PARITY PRINCIPLE' AND OF THE 'INTEREST RATE PARITY' AND 'FISHER OPEN' CONDITIONS

In this section the two building blocks of the monetary approach – the 'purchasing power parity principle' and the condition that domestic and foreign assets are perfectly substitutable after discounting different expectations as to domestic and foreign changes of prices – are tested in order to obtain a better insight on the causes that prevented the readjustment mechanism indicated by the monetary approach from working. Both conditions originate from the principle of arbitrage, which implies that domestic markets are integrated within international markets so that domestic and foreign prices are highly correlated. The 'purchasing power parity' applies the principle of arbitrage to the markets of commodities; the 'interest rate parity' and 'Fisher open' conditions, to the markets for assets.

The 'purchasing power parity principle' regards the exchange rate as an endogenous variable determined by the differential of inflation rates between countries.[5] An empirical test has been performed on the following specification of the principle:

$$\log EER = a_0 + a_1 \cdot \log(P^c_{Comp}/P^c_{It}) + u \tag{9}$$

where P^c_{Comp} is an average of foreign countries' indices of consumer prices weighted with the share of each country's trade with Italy.[6]

The hypothesis to test is that the constant term a_0 is not significantly different from 0 and that the coefficient a_1 – which measures the elasticity of the exchange rate with respect to the differential between foreign and domestic prices – is not significantly different from 1.

The ordinary least squares (OLS) estimates of equation (9) over the period 1972(IV)–1978(IV) are recorded in table 12.2. The abbreviations used to indicate the tests performed are the same as those used in table 12.1. Since serial correlation of residuals was indicated by low values of the Durbin–Watson statistics, this has been eliminated by using the iterative Cochrane–Orcutt technique; such an estimate is indicated as CORC. For the CORC estimate the value of the first-order autoregression coefficient is recorded under the indication 'Rho'. The test has also been performed entering lagged values of relative consumer prices. The latter test has been performed using a distributed, four-period lag technique; such an estimate is indicated by PDLCORC.

TABLE 12.2 Estimates of the 'purchasing power parity principle'

Technique of estimation	Constant term (t-stat. beneath coefficients)	Elasticity of the exchange rate with respect to relative consumer prices	R^2	F-statistics (no. of indep. variables and degrees of freedom under brackets)	DW stat.
(a) OLS	−1.632 (−6.422) s.e. = 0.0395	1.338 (23.210)	0.9590	538.47 (1; 23)	0.601
(b) CORC	−1.155 (−2.399) s.e. = 0.0272	1.227 (11.136)	0.9787	1012.01 (1; 22) rho = 0.6404	1.491
(c) PDLCORC	−0.922 (−1.819) s.e. = 0.0860	1.180*	0.9775	455.62 (2; 21) rho = 0.6315	1.565

* The overall elasticity has been obtained as the sum of the following lagged elasticity values (t-statistics are recorded underneath, in parentheses):

Over the same quarter	With a 1-quarter lag	With a 2-quarter lag	With a 3-quarter lag
1.226 (4.112)	0.619 (5.879)	−0.029 (−0.267)	−0.676 (−2.176)

These results would suggest the rejection of the hypothesis that exchange rate changes have offset the differential between domestic and foreign consumer prices.[7] Although the coefficient of determination is high in all the estimates and the coefficient significant, some disturbing characteristics appear. The relative price elasticity of the exchange rate is significantly higher than 1, which indicates that exchange rate changes systematically overadjusted the changes of relative prices. The constant term is significantly different from 0. Residuals are autocorrelated: the Durbin–Watson statistics is too low to reject the hypothesis that residuals are serially correlated at the 5 per cent level of significance. The latter two findings indicate that the model is probably mis-specified.[8] When the Cochrane–Orcutt technique is used to get rid of serial correlation, the statistical fit of the estimate increases but coefficients are still significantly different from the theoretical values 0 and 1.

The monetary approach assumes that international markets for assets are efficient, i.e. that the activity of well informed arbitrageurs and speculators makes the interest rates on assets denominated in different currencies equal after covering the expected exchange rate changes for the period from now up to the date of maturity of the assets. This condition, known as 'interest rate parity principle', was first propounded by Keynes (1923) and has recently been reviewed by several authors with major contributions by Sohmen (1969) and Aliber (1976). It is synthetized by the following equality:

$$\frac{F-S}{S} = i_d - i_f \qquad (10)$$

where S indicates the price of a unit of foreign exchange for immediate delivery expressed in domestic currency; F is the price of a unit of foreign exchange for delivery at a future time t; i_d and i_f are the interest rates of the least risky domestic and foreign securities with maturity at time t.

The rationale behind the 'interest rate parity' condition is the principle of covered arbitrage, according to which transactors try to equalize the rates of return on domestic and foreign securities while covering the risk of losses from changes of the exchange rate in the market for foreign exchanges.

The two sides of equation (10) are usually interpreted as indicating two different forecasts of future exchange rates: the left-hand side indicates the forecasts provided by the market for forward exchanges, and the right-hand side the forecasts provided by domestic and foreign money markets. According to monetarist authors, relative prices, interest rate differentials and exchange rates adjust completely (i.e. are linked by a one-to-one relationship) to the difference between the rates of domestic and world credit expansion.

The 'interest rate parity principle' becomes in such a perspective a condition of consistency between predictions of the same magnitudes coming from different sources. The 'interest rate parity condition' has been estimated with OLS over fortnightly data[9] from April 1973 to December 1978, obtaining the following estimate:

$$\frac{F-S}{S} = 1.246 + 1.216\,(i_{It} - i_{US})$$
$$(1.276)\quad(8.889)$$

$R^2 = 0.3744$; F-stat. $(1; 132) = 79.006$; DW stat. $= 0.6164$;
s.e. $= 5.859$.

The hypothesis that assets markets are 'efficient' predictors of future exchange rate's changes, suggested by the monetary approach, implies that the constant term is not significantly different from 0, that the coefficient is not significantly different from 1, and that residuals are serially uncorrelated.

The estimate provided shows that the constant term is not significantly different from 0 and the coefficient of the independent variable is significant and rather close to 1. Nevertheless, since the coefficient of determination is rather low and residuals are serially correlated, we conclude that this test suggests a rejection of the 'interest rate parity condition'.

When markets for forward exchange rates are not large enough to allow for the amount of speculative activities required to stabilize the exchange rate to be carried out, as has been the case in the Italian experience,[10] the assumptions that international financial markets are 'efficient' and competitive and that domestic and foreign assets are perfect substitutes are expressed by the so-called 'Fisher open principle', according to which the differential between domestic and foreign interest rates measures the change of the exchange rate expected during the span of time up to the maturity of the assets:

$$\frac{S^e - S}{S} = i_d - i_f \tag{11}$$

where S^e is the price in domestic currency of one unit of the foreign currency in which the foreign asset is denominated expected at the date of maturity of that asset. When financial investors operate according to the 'Fisher open principle', arbitrage is said to be 'uncovered', meaning that the investors do not cover their position in the foreign currency and, then, bear the exchange risk.

The 'Fisher open principle' has been investigated by calculating S^e on the basis of the values of two foreign rates,[11] and testing the hypothesis that such S^e provides correct and unbiased forecasts of the exchange rate that will be fixed in the market at the date of maturity of the assets. The formula tested is:

$$\log S^e_{t/3} = a + b^{\cdot}\log S_{t+3}. \tag{12}$$

The null hypothesis is that the coefficient a is not significantly different from 0, whereas the coefficient b is close enough to 1 and errors are not serially correlated.

Two equations have been estimated using the two measures of i_f described in n. 11 to calculate S^e. When US interest rates are used, the expected exchange rate is indicated by $S^e_{(t/3)\text{US}}$, whereas when Euro-dollar rates are used the result is indicated by $S^e_{(t/3)\text{EUR}}$.

The ordinary least squares estimates over monthly data from January 1973 to December 1978 were:[12]

$$\log S_{t+3} = 0.744 + 0.888 \log S^e_{(t/3)\text{US}}$$
$$(3.440) \quad (27.12)$$

$R^2 = 0.9131$; F-stat. $(1, 70) = 735.45$; DW stat. $= 0.4235$;

s.e. $= 0.0468$

and

$$\log S_{t+3} = 0.835 + 0.875 \log S^e_{(t/3)\text{EUR}}$$
$$(4.000) \quad (27.65)$$

$R^2 = 0.9161$; F stat. $(1, 70) = 764.18$; DW stat. $= 0.4363$;

s.e. $= 0.0460$.

Both constant terms are significantly different from 0. Both elasticities are rather lower than 1. The Durbin–Watson statistics indicate the presence of a very serious degree of first-order autocorrelation of residuals.

This test, like the one on the 'interest rate parity', is not consistent with the hypothesis that Italian and foreign assets have been perfect substitutes. Also, this result runs against the monetary approach.

V CONCLUDING REMARKS

There are two main implications of the monetary approach for policy-making. First, the only possible remedy to external imbalances (either deficits in external payments or a depreciation of the exchange rate) is a reduction of the rate of credit expansion. Second, exchange rate changes are assumed not to have any long-lasting effects on real variables. Then, exchange rate changes *per se* are regarded as an ineffective means to improve the external position of the country. However, the evaluation of flexible exchange rates advanced by

monetarist authors is usually positive, since they regard floating as a
'second-best' measure for restoring the possibility of decreasing real
wages when nominal wages are sticky.[13]

For the monetarist conclusions to hold, complete arbitrage between
domestic and foreign commodities and assets should occur. The tests
performed in this paper suggest that the degree of arbitrage has not
been, in the Italian experience, as large as it is usually assumed by the
monetarist approach. In fact, they do not support the monetarist
view that all sources of imbalance eventually operate through the
monetary market, though they suggest that domestic credit expansion exceeding the average increase of money supply abroad has been
one of the main determinants of the depreciation of the lira during
the 1970s.

This analysis of the Italian experience with floating exchange rates
does not dismiss the effectiveness of depreciation as a way to facilitate the adjustment of external imbalances. Nevertheless, it warns
against focusing the analysis of the expected results of depreciation
on only one of the two channels through which the foreign payments
position affects, and is affected by, domestic conditions. On the one
hand, depreciation produces monetary effects that can decrease and
occasionally impair its effectiveness. These monetary effects were
often underestimated in the literature of the 1950s and 1960s. It is
a major contribution of the monetary approach to have provided a
theoretical framework apt to analyse them. On the other hand,
depreciation cannot be considered simply as a 'second-best' policy
measure for restoring the downward flexibility of the domestic structure of costs and prices, since it is induced by real factors and affects
real variables.

In this respect the evidence expounded above reaches results
similar to the ones provided by most of the empirical investigations
that have been carried out on other experiences of managed floating
in the 1970s.[14] Moreover, it seems to indicate that in the Italian
experience real aspects have been extremely important, so that the
simplistic monetary model is unable to account for the main
peculiarities of the floating of the lira.

NOTES

1 Although its theoretical foundations can be traced back to Hume's statement of the quantity theory of money, the monetary approach was
   developed in the 1970s as an extension of the monetarist counterrevolution

in macroeconomic theorizing. The main contributions to the monetary approach are contained in two collections of readings edited by Frenkel and Johnson (1976, 1978) and one by the IMF (1977). Major *ante litteram* contributions to the development of the approach have been Polak (1957), Johnson (1958) and Mundell (1967, 1971). A survey of the criticisms against the monetary approach is contained in Whitman (1976). See also Grubel (1976).

2 Such a process is composed of a two-step arbitrage. The first works directly in the markets for commodities, services and assets internationally traded, and makes domestic prices for tradeables equal to world prices (both expressed in the same currency). The second affects the exchange rate only indirectly and makes the structure of prices in any single economy inter-dependent by equalizing the prices of similar factors of production. Through the 'purchasing power parity principle', then, the monetary approach extends to the international setting the quantity theory of money – according to which money expansion is 'neutral', i.e. produces no effects on real variables – and claims that also depreciation is 'neutral'. Hence, for the 'purchasing power parity principle' to hold, the two conditions for money neutrality (changes in credit conditions should be the only source of exo-genous disturbance; and the function of money demand should be homo-geneous of degree 0 in nominal variables) should hold as well. (On money neutrality see Patinkin, 1965, and Niehans, 1978a, ch. 2.) For extending to exchange-rate changes the hypothesis of neutrality, another condition is required: policy-makers should be unable to sterilize in the long run the changes in liquidity conditions brought about by changes of international reserves. (Cassell, 1922, and Niehans, 1978b, clearly outline the derivation of the 'purchasing power principle' from the 'quantity theory of money'.)

3 The monetarist model of exchange rate determination is developed and dis-cussed in Frenkel (1976) and Bilson (1978a, 1978b). Magee (1976) and Kreinin and Officer (1978) survey the empirical evidence so far accumulated.

4 The two indices have been indicated respectively as M^s_{RW} and M^s_{IC-It}. Since the original series of data (coming from the *International Financial Statistics* of the International Monetary Fund) refer to credit expansion in industrial countries and in the world (in both cases including Italy), a correction to exclude the share of money supply due to credit expansion in Italy has been applied.

5 'Purchasing power parity does not imply a causal relationship in either direction between domestic and foreign prices, but an association between endogenous variables jointly influenced by a common cause, namely monetary changes' (Niehans, 1978b, p. 4). Two extensive surveys of the 'purchasing power parity principle' are provided by Officer (1976) and Katseli-Papaefstratiou (1979). Less extensive, though general, treatments of the principle are provided by Haberler (1961) and Isard (1978). A symposium on the principle was held in Athens in 1976, the proceedings of which have been published in the *Journal of International Economics*, May 1978.

6 Such indices have been calculated in a study by OECD (1978) in which the techniques of estimation are exposed. That study presented data from 1963 to 1977. More recent data have been kindly provided by the Balance of Payments Division of the OECD.

7 The validity of the 'purchasing power parity principle' in the Italian case has been rejected, using data and periods of estimation different from the ones used in this study, by Ulizzi (1976) and Krugman (1978).

8 Conversely, an OLS regression over relative export prices has. provided results thoroughly consistent with the 'purchasing power parity principle':

$$\log EER = -0.175 + 1.039 \log(P^x_{Comp}/P^x_{It}) \qquad R^2 = 0.9731$$
$$(-1.339) \ (28.846)$$

F-stat. $(1; 23) = 831.93$; DW stat. $= 1.065$; s.e. $= 0.0320$

This finding indicates that arbitrage between Italian and foreign commodities has mainly occurred in the sector of internationally traded goods.

9 Three-month forward rates of the lira–dollar exchange rate have been used since the market for three-month dollars is the most indicative market of forward exchange rates. No indicator of domestic interest rates, however, has been found which could represent the situation of the Italian market for three-month assets over the whole period. Interest rates on Treasury bills have been used since January 1976; but, since such assets did not have a large market before 1976, interest rates on long-run government bonds have been used for 1973 and short-run bank rates (prime lending) for 1974 and 1975. Interest rates on analogous assets in the US have been used to indicate foreign rates.

Sources of data: *The Economist* for 1973, and *Financial Statistics* of the Chase Manhattan Bank for data covering the period 1974–1978.

10 The characteristics of the markets for forward lire are examined in Ferro (1978).

11 The following formula has been applied to calculate S^e:

$$S^e_{t/3} = S_t \cdot (1 + i_d - i_f)^{1/4} \qquad (13)$$

where i_d and i_f are interest rates on three-month Treasury bills in Italy and, alternatively, either interest rates on short-term government bonds in the USA or interest rates on three-month deposits in the Euro-dollar market. S indicates the price in lire of 1 dollar; 3 is the number of months on which expectations are calculated. All data come from the *International Financial Statistics* of the IMF.

12 No technique has been used to eliminate the first-order serial correlation of residuals that is present in both estimates, since the test on autocorrelation is one of the most important tests for accepting or rejecting the 'Fisher open principle' in so far as it tests the hypothesis that expected exchange rates are unbiased forecasts of future rates.

13 Friedman (1953) and Johnson (1969) based the case for flexible exchange rates on this alleged effect of floating, and the monetarist view has not basically changed since.

14 A careful survey of the empirical and theoretical works on the impact of flexible exchange rates on the conduct of macroeconomic policy in the 1970s is provided by Goldstein (1980).

REFERENCES

Aliber, R. Z. (1976) 'Equilibrium and Disequilibrium in the International Money Market', *Weltwirtschaftliches Archiv*, pp. 73-90.

Bilson, J. F. O. (1978a) 'The Monetary Approach to the Exchange Rate: Some Empirical Evidence', *IMF Staff Papers*, March, pp. 48-75.

Bilson, J. F. O. (1978b) 'Rational Expectations and the Exchange Rate', in *The Economics of Exchange Rates: Selected Studies*, ed. J. A. Frenkel and H. G. Johnson, Addison Wesley, Reading, Mass.

Cassel, G. (1922) *Money and Foreign Exchange after 1914*, Constable, London.

Ferro, O. (1978) *I Cambi a Termine in Regime di Cambi Flessibili*, Cedam, Padua.

Fisher, I. (1930) *The Theory of Interest*, Augustus M. Kelley, New York.

Frenkel, J. A. (1976) 'A Monetary Approach to the Exchange Rate: Doctrinal Aspects and Empirical Evidence', *Scandinavian Journal of Economics*, pp. 200-4.

Frenkel, J. A. and Johnson, H. G. (eds) (1976) *The Monetary Approach to the Balance of Payments*, University of Toronto Press.

Frenkel, J. A. and Johnson, H. G. (eds) (1978) *The Economics of Exchange Rates: Selected Studies*, Addison Wesley, Reading, Mass.

Friedman, M. (1953) 'The Case for Flexible Exchange Rates', in *Essays in Positive Economics*, University of Chicago Press.

Goldstein, M. (1980) *Have Flexible Exchange Rates Handicapped Macroeconomic Policy?* Special Papers in International Economics, no. 14, Princeton University Press.

Grubel, H. G. (1976) *Domestic Origins of the Monetary Approach to the Balance of Payments*, Essays in International Finance no. 117, Princeton University Press.

Haberler, G. (1961) *A Survey of International Trade Theory*, Special Papers in International Economics no. 1, Princeton University Press.

International Monetary Fund (1977) *The Monetary Approach to the Balance of Payments*, International Monetary Fund, Washington.

Isard, P. (1978) *Exchange-rate Determination: A Survey of Popular Views and Recent Studies*, Studies in International Finance no. 42, Princeton University Press.

Johnson, H. G. (1958) 'Towards a General Theory of the Balance of Payments', in *International Trade and Economic Growth*, Unwin University Books, London.

Johnson, H. G. (1969) 'The Case for Flexible Exchange Rates, 1969', *Federal Reserve Bank of St Louis Monthly Bulletin*, June, pp. 12-24.

Katseli-Papaefstratiou, L. (1979) *The Re-emergence of the Purchasing Power Parity Doctrine in the 1970s*, Special Papers in International Economics no. 13, Princeton University Press.

Keynes, J. M. (1923) *A Tract on Monetary Reform*, Macmillan, London.

Kreinin, M. E. and Officer, L. H. (1978) *The Monetary Approach to the Balance of Payments: A Survey*, Princeton Studies in International Finance no. 43, Princeton University Press.

Krugman, P. L. (1978) 'Purchasing Power Parity and Exchange Rates: Another Look at the Evidence', *Journal of International Economics*, pp. 397–407.

Magee, S. P. (1976) 'The Empirical Evidence on The Monetary Approach to the Balance of Payments and Exchange Rates', *American Economic Review*, (Papers and Proceedings), **68**, 163–70.

Mundell, R. A. (1967) *International Economics*, Macmillan, New York.

Mundell, R. A. (1971) *Monetary Theory*, Goodyear, Pacific Palisades, California.

Niehans, J. (1978a) *Theory of Money*, Johns Hopkins Press, Baltimore.

Niehans, J. (1978b) 'Purchasing Power Parity under Flexible Exchange Rates', unpublished paper presented at a conference in Christ Church College, Oxford.

OECD Balance of Payments Division (1978) 'The International Competitiveness of Selected OECD Countries', *OECD Economic Outlook: Occasional Economic Studies*, July, pp. 35–52.

Officer, L. H. (1976) 'The Purchasing-Power-Parity Theory of Exchange Rates: a Review Article', *IMF Staff Papers*, March, pp. 1–60.

Patinkin, D. (1965) *Money, Interest and Prices*, Harper & Row, New York.

Polak, J. J. (1957) 'Monetary Analysis of Income Formation and Payments Problems', *IMF Staff Papers*, pp. 1–50.

Sohmen, E. (1969) *Flexible Exchange Rates*, Chicago University Press.

Ulizzi, A. (1976) 'Exchange Rate, Relative Inflation and Competitiveness: the Italian Case', *Review of the Economic Conditions in Italy*, pp. 241–7.

Whitman, M. N. (1976) 'Global Monetarism and the Monetary Approach to the Balance of Payments', *Brookings Papers on Economic Activity*, pp. 491–555.

Part Five

Growth and Income Distribution

13

The New View of the Ricardian Theory of Distribution and Economic Growth

CARLO CASAROSA*

I INTRODUCTION

The traditional 'fix-wage' interpretation of the Ricardian system is based on the idea that Ricardo examined the working of the economic system and the process of growth on the assumption that the wage rate remained constantly at its natural (or subsistence) level. According to this view,[1] Ricardo recognized that the market wage rate might diverge from the natural wage rate, but considered this a wholly transitory situation, since he believed that the population mechanism would rapidly force the market wage rate to converge towards its natural equilibrium level. Therefore he described the process of economic growth *as if* the wage rate remained constantly at the natural level.

In the last few years the fix-wage interpretation has been challenged on the ground that it is incapable of explaining some of Ricardo's most important results, and an alternative interpretation has been put forward.[2] The main elements of evidence against the traditional interpretation are the following Ricardo's propositions, which clearly cannot be accounted for in a fix-wage framework.

(1) During the process of economic growth the wage rate remains above its natural level (Ricardo, 1821, pp. 94–5).
(2) In the early stages of growth the wage rate may rise, but from some point onwards both the wage rate and the rate of profit will certainly fall and will keep falling until the economy becomes stationary (Ricardo, 1821, pp. 98, 101–4, 112–14, 120, 124–6).

* I should like to thank Sir John Hicks for very helpful discussions and comments on an earlier draft and A. Chilosi and A. Gay for useful remarks.

The new formulation of the Ricardian system is an attempt to build a Ricardian model consistent with propositions (1)–(2) and other propositions related to them.[3] The basic idea is that in Ricardo the evolution of the wage rate over time is determined by the contemporaneous working of the population mechanism and of the process of capital accumulation, so that there is no reason why the wage rate should converge towards the natural level unless capital is stationary. Moreover, since capital accumulation depends on the rate of profit, and population growth on the wage rate, and since the rate of profit and the wage rate are (inversely) correlated, it emerges that there is a general interdependence among the economic variables. More precisely, the wage rate, the rate of profit and the rates of growth of population and capital are simultaneously determined by the interplay between the distributive variables, population growth and the accumulation of capital.

In this paper we present a brief outline of the new view of the Ricardian theory of distribution and economic growth and discuss some of the problems it raises, on the basis of a simple one-commodity model.

II THE MODEL

The model is built on the following 'Ricardian' assumptions.

(1) There are decreasing returns to labour in agriculture.
(2) The marginal product of labour is divided between wages and profits only; rent is the surplus that remains out of total production once workers and capitalists have obtained their income.
(3) Workers accept any wage rather than be unemployed.
(4) Workers and landowners consume all their income.
(5) Entrepreneurs employ labour only if they obtain at least a minimum rate of profit. They save and invest out of profits only if the rate of profit is above the minimum.
(6) There is a natural wage rate which keeps population stationary. Population's growth is an increasing function of the difference between the market and the natural wage rate.

To simplify we assume, further, that the system produces only one commodity – corn – and that labour and land are the only inputs to production.

The model consists of six equations:

$$X = f(N) \tag{1}$$

where $X =$ amount of corn produced; and $N =$ number of workers employed; with

$$f'(\ ) > 0 \tag{1a}$$

$$f''(\ ) < 0 \tag{1b}$$

$$f'(0) > w_s(1 + r_s) \tag{1c}$$

$$f'(\infty) < w_s(1 + r_s) \tag{1d}$$

where $w_s =$ natural wage rate; and $r_s =$ minimum rate of profit.

$$W = wN \tag{2}$$

where $W =$ total wage bill and $w =$ wage rate.

$$K = W \tag{3}$$

where $K =$ stock of capital; with

$$K \leqslant f'(N) N/(1 + r_s). \tag{3a}$$

$$r = \{f'(N) - w\}/w \tag{4}$$

$$N/N = G\{(w - w_s)/w_s\} \tag{5}$$

where $r =$ rate of profit; with:

$$G(0) = 0 \tag{5a}$$

$$G'(\ ) > 0. \tag{5b}$$

$$\dot{K}/K = F(r - r_s) \tag{6}$$

with:

$$F(0) = 0 \tag{6a}$$

$$F'(\ ) > 0 \tag{6b}$$

if it does not violate (3a). Otherwise:

$$K = f'(N) N/(1 + r_s).$$

Equation (1) is the production function for corn, which we assume twice differentiable with positive, but decreasing, returns. (1c) allows the system to grow and (1d) ensures that economic growth cannot go on indefinitely.

Equation (2) is definitory.

Equation (3) says that capital consists entirely of the wage bill. The meaning of (3a) is the following: since entrepreneurs employ labour only if they obtain at least the minimum rate of profit, for each level of employment there is a maximum wage rate, $\hat{w}$, they are willing to pay. In our model:

$$\hat{w} = f'(N)/(1 + r_s). \tag{7}$$

Correspondingly, for each level of employment there is a maximum amount of capital, $\hat{K}$, that entrepreneurs are willing to invest; from equations (2), (3) and (7) we have:

$$\hat{K} = f'(N) N/(1 + r_s). \tag{8}$$

Condition (3a) says that the amount of capital the entrepreneurs employ cannot be higher than the amount that yields the minimum rate of profit.[4]

Equation (4) follows directly from the Ricardian theory of rent.

The last two equations are the laws of motion of the system. Equation (5) is the so-called law of population, that is, the relationship between the wage rate and the rate of growth of population. Equation (6) summarizes the rules followed by the entrepreneurs as far as the accumulation of capital is concerned. It says that, if the rate of profit that entrepeneurs obtain from the capital they have advanced is just equal to the minimum rate of profit, they do not save at all and therefore keep their capital constant; while, if the rate of profit is higher than the minimum, their propensity to save (and invest) is positive and is an increasing function of the difference between the rate of profit they have obtained and the minimum rate of profit. However, if the observance of these rules implied the 'advance' of an amount of capital higher than the maximum amount the entrepreneurs are willing to invest at the new level of employment, they will advance just the maximum amount and consume the rest. Otherwise they would get a rate of profit lower than the minimum they are willing to accept.

III THE WORKING OF THE SYSTEM

We can now study the working of our system in the (N, w) plane (see figure 13.1).[5] We draw the loci $w = w_s$ and $w = \hat{w}$ (or $r = r_s$). The locus $w = w_s$ is a horizontal line, while locus $r = r_s$ slopes downwards since $\hat{w} = f'(N)/(1 + r_s)$. By (5), on the $w = w_s$ locus population is stationary; above it population grows; and below it population declines. By (6) on the $r = r_s$ locus the rate of capital accumulation is either 0 or negative and below it, positive. Points above this locus are never reached, since in this case the entrepreneurs would get a rate of profit lower than the minimum they are willing to accept.

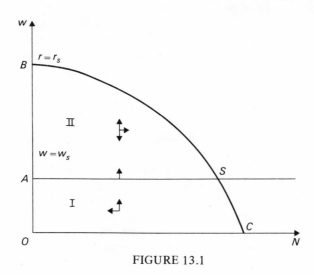

FIGURE 13.1

The two loci intersect when $f'(N)/(1 + r_s) = w_s$. Such a point exists since the loci are continuous and we have assumed $f'(0) > w_s(1 + r_s)$ and $f'(\infty) < w_s(1 + r_s)$. At the intersection point, S, population is obviously stationary. Then capital is also stationary.

What about the wage rate? We first notice that, since from equations (2)–(3) we have $w = K/N$, the rate of change of the wage rate is given by:

$$\dot{w}/w = \dot{K}/K - \dot{N}/N. \tag{9}$$

Now, in region I (below the $w = w_s$ locus) population declines and capital grows. Therefore the wage rate rises. In region II (between the two loci) both population and capital grow. Hence the wage rate may either rise or fall according to which of the two grows faster.

On the $w = w_s$ locus to the left of S the wage rate rises, since population is stationary and capital is growing. On the $r = r_s$ locus to the left of S the wage rate declines, since population is rising and capital remains stationary or declines;[6] to the right of S the wage rate rises, since population declines and capital either is stationary or declines at a lower rate than population.[7] Finally, at S the wage rate is stationary.

We are now ready to describe the possible trajectories of our system. We notice, first, that S is a steady-state position. It is, in fact, the stationary state, since capital, population and the wage rate (and hence also the rate of profit) are all constant.

If we start from a point in region I, population declines and the wage rate rises; the system moves upwards and to the left until it hits the $w = w_s$ locus. Here population becomes stationary but the wage rate goes on rising, so that we enter region II.

We now show that if the system is in region II it cannot get out, and moves continuously to the right until it reaches the stationary state. We have already seen that the system cannot break through the $r = r_s$ locus. But it cannot break through the $w = w_s$ locus either, since when the economy gets on such a locus the wage rate increases and the system goes back to region II. Actually, we can show that once the system is in region II it will never reach the $w = w_s$ locus at a point to the left of S.[8] In fact, let us assume that we are in region II, but that the wage rate is declining, because the rate of capital accumulation, although positive, is lower than the rate of growth of population. As the wage rate gets closer to w_s the rate of growth of population declines towards 0, while the rate of capital accumulation rises. Therefore at some $w > w_s$ the rates of growth of population and capital will be equal and the wage rate will stop falling. Hence, as long as we are not in the stationary state, the wage rate cannot be at the natural level and the system moves continuously to the right.

We can therefore conclude that:

(1) the stationary state is globally stable;
(2) after the wage rate has become higher than the natural wage rate, both capital and population keep growing and the wage rate remains above its natural level until the economy falls in the stationary state.

IV THE DYNAMIC EQUILIBRIUM PATH

The results we have just obtained are obviously important for a better understanding of Ricardo's theory. In fact, from the working of our model we have explicitly derived the first of Ricardo's propositions mentioned in the introductory section. Moreover, since we have shown that the process of economic growth must end up in the stationary state, and that during the process of growth the wage rate remains above the natural level, we have also shown that, at least in some neighbourhood of the stationary state, the wage rate must fall. The latter result is clearly consistent with Ricardo's proposition (2) even if we must admit that proposition (2) is more specific, since it says that the wage rate must fall all along during the process of growth, with the possible exception of an initial phase, while in the model we have just considered the wage rate might go up and down several times before falling to the natural level.

Can we get closer to the Ricardian results?

Some of the proponents[9] of the new formulation of the Ricardian system have found the answer in the notion of dynamic or balanced equilibrium path, that is, a path along which capital and population change at the same rate. Formally, this implies the addition to the system (1)–(6) of the following equation:

$$\dot{K}/K = \dot{N}/N. \tag{10}$$

From the analysis of the previous paragraph, we know that this condition can be satisfied only in region II and at the stationary point. And since in region II the rate of growth of population is positive, we can use (5) and (6) to rewrite the dynamic equilibrium condition as:

$$F[\{f'(N) - w\}/w - r_s] - G\{(w - w_s)/w_s\} = 0. \tag{10'}$$

$(10')$ is an equation with two unknowns, w and N, and therefore it gives us, for every N, the level of the wage rate that ensures that capital and population grow at the same rate. We may call it the dynamic equilibrium wage rate, w^*, and from what we have said above it is clear that:[10]

(a) as long as $f'(N)/(1 + r_s) > w_s$, $w_s < w^* < f'(N)/(1 + r_s)$;
(b) when $f'(N)/(1 + r_s) = w_s$, $w^* = w_s$.

Moreover, by differentiating $(10')$ and solving, we have:

(c) $dw^*/dN < 0$.

Therefore the dynamic equilibrium path of the wage rate is a downwards-sloping curve such as *DS* in figure 13.2.

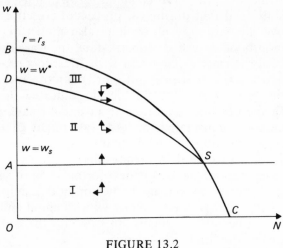

FIGURE 13.2

As for the evolution of the other variables along the dynamic equilibrium path, it should be evident from equations (5), (6) and $(10')$ that, as employment increases, the rate of growth of capital and population and the rate of profit must all fall.

According to some authors,[11] the dynamic equilibrium path is a path that can be followed by the economic system during the process of growth and can be shown to be stable. If this view were correct our task would be completed, since the dynamic equilibrium path complies fully with both of Ricardo's propositions mentioned in the introductory section. Unfortunately our Ricardian system cannot move along the dynamic equilibrium path. In fact, when the economy is on such a path the market wage rate remains constant (see equation (9)), while the dynamic equilibrium wage rate falls. Therefore the system gets off the dynamic equilibrium path.

One way to save the dynamic equilibrium analysis is to assume that the marginal productivity of labour in agriculture decreases not continuously but in steps, and that the steps are sufficiently long.[12] As long as the marginal product of labour remains constant, the dynamic equilibrium wage rate is also constant and therefore the system can move along the dynamic equilibrium path. As we pass from one step to the following the dynamic equilibrium wage rate declines to a new level and the economic system gets off the equilibrium path. However, it can be shown that the dynamic laws of the system bring about its convergence to the new dynamic equilibrium position. The possible trajectories followed by the economic system are of the type indicated by the arrows in figure 13.3. Hence we can describe the motion of the system over time as a sequence of dynamic equilibria (the last of which is the stationary state), even if the economy cannot be in dynamic equilibrium all the time.

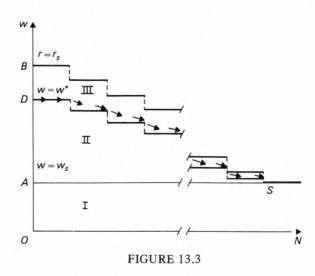

FIGURE 13.3

If we are not ready to make the step assumption we must give up the idea of describing the motion of the system as a steady equilibrium motion. This does not mean, however, that we must abandon the notion of a 'dynamic equilibrium' path altogether, since it can still be useful to restrict the possible trajectories followed by the system in the course of growth. Let us see how.

The dynamic equilibrium path divides the region between the $w = w_s$ and the $r = r_s$ loci into two regions (see figure 13.2). In region II (below the dynamic equilibrium path and above the $w = w_s$ locus) the wage rate is lower than the dynamic equilibrium wage rate and hence the rate of profit is higher than the dynamic equilibrium rate of profit. Therefore the rate of capital accumulation is higher than the rate of growth of population. Consequently the wage rate rises. In region III (above the dynamic equilibrium path and below the $r = r_s$ locus) it is the other way round and the wage rate falls.

Now, if the system starts from a point in region II, it moves upwards and to the right and sooner or later reaches the dynamic equilibrium path. Here the system moves horizontally to the right and therefore gets into region III. In region III the system moves downwards to the right. It may well converge towards the dynamic equilibrium path, but in no case can it break through the dynamic equilibrium path and move into region II, since, if the system reached the dynamic equilibrium path, it would be repelled back into region III. Actually, we could easily show that, once in region III, the system cannot go back to the dynamic equilibrium path before the stationary state.

We can therefore say that in the initial stages of growth the wage rate may rise for a while, until the system reaches the dynamic equilibrium path. Thereafter it falls and keeps falling until it gets into the stationary position.

For the other variables of the system we come to similar results: once the economy has crossed the dynamic equilibrium line, the rate of profit and the rates of growth of capital and population go on falling until the economy enters the stationary state.

These results are obviously stronger than the ones we were able to establish without the dynamic equilibrium notion and, what is more important, are exactly the same as Ricardo's results contained in proposition (2).

At this point the presentation of the new view of the Ricardian system is practically completed. However, before concluding, we would like to point out the possibility that the dynamic equilibrium path plays, in the analysis of the motion of the economic system, an even more central role than the one we have just considered.

From our analysis we know that, if the economy is initially below the dynamic equilibrium path, the actual path rises towards the former and at some point crosses it, while, when the economy is above the dynamic equilibrium path, the actual path slopes down to the right as the dynamic equilibrium path does. Now, if in region III the actual path were everywhere steeper than the dynamic equilibrium path, we could well work *as if* the system moved along the dynamic equilibrium path, especially if the initial position of the economy were below the dynamic equilibrium path or not very far from it. In fact, in this case the economic system would most of the time be in a very close neighbourhood of the dynamic equilibrium path, and clearly it would not work very differently with the actual path or with the dynamic equilibrium path.

The question is, of course, whether we can assume that in region III the actual path is everywhere steeper than the dynamic equilibrium path. Since both paths must end up in the stationary state, there is surely at least one phase in which the actual path is steeper. But this is not enough for our purpose. However, since the slope of the dynamic equilibrium path depends on the slope of the marginal product curve, while the slope of the actual path depends on the difference between the rates of growth of capital and population, we can say that, the stronger the influence of the rate of profit on the propensity to accumulate, and the flatter the slope of the marginal product, the higher the probability that the actual path will approach continuously the dynamic equilibrium path. This, of course, should be expected from what we have said in the framework of the 'step' model.

V CONCLUDING REMARKS

The traditional fix-wage interpretation of the Ricardian theory is incapable of explaining some of Ricardo's most important results. For this reason a number of economists have recently proposed to abandon the fix-wage assumption and to accept the idea that in Ricardo the evolution of the wage rate during the process of growth is determined by the simultaneous working of the mechanisms of population growth and capital accumulation.

In this paper we have presented a simple model of the new formulation of the Ricardian system and discussed the two main approaches that have been followed: the market equilibrium and the dynamic equilibrium approach. We have shown that, although the Ricardian economy cannot move along a steady growth path because of decreasing returns, the notion of dynamic equilibrium turns out to be quite useful to restrict the possible trajectories that the economic system might follow during the process of growth. We have even shown that, if the marginal product of labour decreases slowly enough, the actual path of the economic system is likely to remain most of the time in a very close neighbourhood of the dynamic equilibrium path, so that we could describe the motion of the system *as if* it followed the dynamic equilibrium path.[13]

From the analysis of the working of our model we have derived Ricardo's results which are incompatible with the traditional fix-wage interpretation of his theory. We therefore conclude that the new formulation of the Ricardian system should supersede the traditional one on the ground of its greater explanatory capacity.

NOTES

1 The most rigorous account of this approach is to be found in Pasinetti (1960).
2 Casarosa (1974, 1976, 1978), Levy (1976), Hicks and Hollander (1977), Costa (1977), Hicks (1979a, 1979b) and Hollander (1979). Johansen (1969) might perhaps be considered the forerunner of the new view of Ricardo, even if his concern was the classical school as a whole. See also Samuelson (1978).
3 Among these the following appear to be particularly important:
   – a reduction in the price of wage-goods, brought about by technical progress or foreign trade, benefits both capitalists and workers (Ricardo, 1815, p. 35; 1821, pp. 79–80);
   – taxation causes a reduction both of the wage rate and of the rate of profit (Ricardo, 1821, pp. 222, 225, 226).
4 Condition (3a) has been generally overlooked even by those who admit that in Ricardo the rate of profit is the motive behind the accumulation of capital. As a result it is admitted that the rate of profit might be lower than the minimum even in a circulating capital model. But this is clearly absurd in a system in which the entrepreneurs stop accumulating 'when their profits are so low as not to afford them an adequate compensation for their trouble, and the risk which they must necessarily encounter in employing their capital productively' (Ricardo, 1821, p. 122). In fact, why should such entrepreneurs be ready to advance their (circulating) capital at a wage rate that does not leave them at least the minimum rate of profit? The introduction of condition (3a) disposes, at least for the circulating capital model, of the 'exception' pointed out by Hicks and Hollander (1977, pp. 357–9) and of similar results obtained by Costa (1977). With fixed capital the problem is much more complicated and will not be pursued here.
5 This is the approach followed by Hicks and Hollander (1977). The obvious alternative, adopted by Johansen (1969), is to work in the (K, N) plane. Johansen's approach has been followed by Costa (1977).
6 Capital declines when $d\hat{K}/dN < 0$.
7 In fact, if capital declines (and here it happens when $d\hat{K}/dN > 0$) the economy moves along the $r = r_s$ locus. See equation (6).
8 See Hicks and Hollander (1977, p. 354).
9 See, in particular, Casarosa (1974, 1976, 1978), Levy (1976) and Samuelson (1978).
10 Caravale and Tosato (1974, 1980) presented a model very similar to the dynamic equilibrium model, but made the surprising assumption that the wage rate that keeps capital and population growing at the same rate (which they call the natural wage rate) remains constant in the course of growth. As we have just seen in the text, with decreasing returns the wage rate that keeps capital and population growing at the same rate *cannot* remain constant and actually must continuously fall as growth proceeds. Therefore the assumption of a constant natural wage rate is incompatible with the other features of the Caravale–Tosato model.

11 Samuelson (1978, pp. 1422 and 1427-8).
12 Casarosa (1978). For a discussion of this 'solution' see Hicks (1979a; 1979b, p. 54). The step model has been adopted also by Pasinetti (1981).
13 It should be noticed that the role played by the dynamic equilibrium path is in this case exactly the same as the role played by the natural equilibrium path in Pasinetti's model.

REFERENCES

Caravale, G. and Tosato, D. (1974) *Un modello ricardiano di sviluppo economico*, Boringhieri, Turin.

Caravale, G. and Tosato, D. (1980) *Ricardo and the Theory of Value, Distribution and Growth*, Routledge & Kegan Paul, London.

Casarosa, C. (1974) 'La teoria ricardiana della distribuzione e dello sviluppo economico', *Rivista di Politica Economica*, August–September, pp. 959–1015.

Casarosa, C. (1976) 'Imposte e distribuzione del reddito nell'analisi ricardiana', *Giornale degli Economisti*, March–April, pp. 171–200.

Casarosa, C. (1978) 'A New Formulation of the Ricardian System', *Oxford Economic Papers*, March, pp. 38–63.

Costa, G. (1977) 'La convergenza allo stato stazionario di un'economia di tipo ricardiano', in *Saggi di economia in onore di Antonio Pesenti*, ed. F. De Cindio and P. Sylos Labini, Giuffrè, Milan.

Hicks, J. and Hollander, S. (1977) 'Mr Ricardo and the Moderns', *Quarterly Journal of Economics*, August, pp. 351–69.

Hicks, J. (1979a) 'The Ricardian System: a Comment', *Oxford Economic Papers*, March, pp. 133–4.

Hicks, J. (1979b) *Causality in Economics*, Basil Blackwell, Oxford.

Hollander, S. (1979) *The Economics of David Ricardo*, Heinemann, London.

Johansen, L. (1969) 'A Classical Model of Economic Growth', in *Socialism, Capitalism and Economic Growth, Essays in Honour of M. Dobb*, ed. C. H. Feinstein, Cambridge University Press, pp. 13–29.

Levy, D. (1976) 'Ricardo and the Iron Law: a Correction of the Record', *History of Political Economy*, Summer, pp. 235–51.

Pasinetti, L. (1960) 'A Mathematical Formulation of the Ricardian System', *Review of Economic Studies*, February, pp. 78–98.

Pasinetti, L. (1981) 'On the Ricardian Theory of Value: A Note', *Review of Economic Studies*, October, pp. 673–5.

Ricardo, D. (1815) 'An Essay on the Influence of a Low Price of Corn on the Profits of Stock', in *The Works and Correspondence of David Ricardo*, ed. P. Sraffa, Cambridge University Press, 1951, vol. IV.

Ricardo, D. (1821) *On the Principles of Political Economy and Taxation*, in *The Works and Correspondence of David Ricardo*, ed. P. Sraffa, Cambridge University Press, 1951, vol. I.

Samuelson, P. (1978) 'The Canonical Classical Model of Political Economy', *Journal of Economic Literature*, December, pp. 1415–34.

14

A Comment on the 'New View' of the Ricardian Theory

LUIGI L. PASINETTI

Professor Casarosa, in chapter 13 above, does me the honour of considering my article on Ricardo (Pasinetti, 1960) the most rigorous account of the traditional interpretation of the Ricardian system. At the end of his paper, however, Casarosa pleads for the abandonment of such traditional interpretation and for its replacement with the 'new view', which he presents, and which, as he says, is shared by Professors Hicks and Hollander (1977) and others. I may therefore be allowed to make few comments.

It is difficult to say which view of the Ricardian theory is the really 'traditional' one, as Ricardo's theory has been the subject of lengthy discussions and frequent 'new' interpretations since its appearance 160 years ago. I shall therefore refer here almost exclusively to my own interpretation, which came as a direct outcome of Piero Sraffa's edition of Ricardo's *Works*.

Let me try first of all to eliminate what seems to me a major misunderstanding. The Pasinetti–Sraffa view – if I may be allowed the presumption of calling it so – of the Ricardian system is *not* a 'fix-wage interpretation', as Casarosa says. Two notions of the wage rate are explicitly considered: a 'natural' wage rate, which is an exogenous magnitude (and which, by the way, is *not* a subsistence wage rate, but is defined as the wage rate that induces workers to reproduce themselves 'without either increase or diminution' – see Pasinetti, 1960, p. 80); and a 'market wage rate', which is an observable magnitude and emerges from the interaction of the forces of supply and demand. It is true that, in some simplified, yet notable, formulations of the Ricardian system (for example Kaldor, 1956; Samuelson, 1959), the market wage rate has been neglected, for simplicity, and the natural wage rate has been given a privileged position. However, these have been simplified versions, aimed at stressing fundamental Ricardian features, and as such are quite justified. They must be intended as first approximations, and their implications cannot be pushed to the extreme. But, in my own formulation, the two notions of the Ricardian wage rate are clearly formulated and play a distinctive role. The growth of population is considered as a (positive) function of the difference between the market wage rate and the natural wage rate. It follows – as a strict logical consequence – that, in an economy with population growth and constant technology, as it is considered by Casarosa, the actual wage rate will normally be *above* its 'natural' level, which in turn will itself normally be above the subsistence level.

From all this we may conclude immediately that there is no incompatibility between the passages from Ricardo's *Works*, quoted at the beginning of Casarosa's paper, and the Pasinetti–Sraffa version of the Ricardian system. I should add something more. If Casarosa's analysis is intended in what I would consider an appropriate way, it itself raises no incompatibility with the Pasinetti–Sraffa version of the Ricardian system. Casarosa concentrates his efforts on defining a particular path of the actual (i.e. market) wage rate, and no objection can be raised to that. In other words, I would consider Casarosa's analysis as aimed at depicting in detail one particular dynamic path of the market wage rate that is compatible with Ricardo's theory.[1] This analysis has nothing to do with the properties of the 'natural' wage rate. Moreover, there are *other* dynamic paths, covered by Ricardian theory (and, by the way, also covered by my own formulation of the Ricardian system), that are not covered by Casarosa's analysis.[2] I would venture therefore to conclude that the Pasinetti–Sraffa version of the Ricardian system is more general than Casarosa's.

But there is another side of the coin. Casarosa's type of analysis, if not appropriately understood, is open to the danger of an extreme interpretation which would be opposite to, and would have far less justification than, the one given by Kaldor (1956) and Samuelson (1959). More specifically, by concentrating all emphasis on the Ricardian notion of *market* wage rate, Casarosa's approach is open to the danger of neglecting – or reducing to irrelevance – the much more fundamental Ricardian notion of a *natural* wage rate. This is in fact the trap into which – it seems to me – Hicks and Hollander (1977) have fallen. In their analysis, the 'natural' wage rate plays no role. To begin with, they confuse it with the 'subsistence' wage; and second, they relegate the latter to play the external role of a boundary 'floor'. All their attention is concentrated on the *market* wage rate.

I should like to point out that an interpretation of Ricardo's analysis that magnifies his hints at the forces of supply and demand is in fact no novelty at all. The pre-Sraffa economic literature is full of attempts aimed at reconciling Ricardo with marginal economic theory. And all these attempts have been focused on emphasizing Ricardo's hints at the market forces and de-emphasizing his much more fundamental notions of natural wage rate and natural prices in general.

It seems to me that one of the merits of Sraffa's edition of Ricardo's works has been precisely that of exposing the inaccuracy and unhelpfulness of such interpretations of Ricardo's theory. The simplifications used by Kaldor (1956) have perhaps overstressed the change of view. But the fact that, as a first approximation, some authors have given exclusive attention to the natural wage rate, and have neglected the market wage rate, can be no excuse for now doing the opposite, and returning to an *old* (and inaccurate) view by calling it 'new'.

NOTES

1 At least, this was the sense of my comments and suggestions, in spite of what may be inferred from the wording of Casarosa's acknowledgments, when I saw an early draft of his previous paper (Casarosa, 1978).
2 Consider, for example, a growth process generated mainly by technical progress.

REFERENCES

Casarosa, C. (1978) 'A New Formulation of the Ricardian System', *Oxford Economic Papers*, pp. 38–63.
Hicks, J. and Hollander, S. (1977) 'Mr. Ricardo and the Moderns', *Quarterly Journal of Economics*, pp. 351–69.
Kaldor, N. (1956) 'Alternative Theories of Distribution', *Review of Economic Studies*, pp. 83–100.
Pasinetti, L. L. (1960) 'A Mathematical Formulation of the Ricardian System', *Review of Economic Studies*, pp. 78–98.
Ricardo, D. (1951–73) *The Works and Correspondence of David Ricardo*, ed. Piero Sraffa, Cambridge University Press.
Samuelson, P. A. (1959) 'A Modern Treatment of the Ricardian Theory', *Quarterly Journal of Economics*, pp. 1–35 and pp. 217–31.

15

Can the Life-Cycle Theory Help in Explaining Income Distribution and Capital Accumulation?

MAURO BARANZINI*

I INTRODUCTION

The question relating to capital accumulation, income distribution and profit determination, has always occupied a prominent place in modern economic theory. When, in the late 1930s and the 1940s the first macroeconomic models of economic growth were developed, the theory of income distribution was caught in an *impasse*, represented by the well-known Harrod–Domar equilibrium condition $s = g(K/Y)$, where s is the aggregate saving ratio, g the natural rate of growth (which can include 'labour-saving' technical progress) and K/Y the capital–output ratio. If these three variables are all constant, then it is unlikely that the Harrod–Domar condition can be satisfied. Hence, in order to have a model in which the possibility of steady growth is assured, it is necessary to relax one or another of the assumptions. More precisely, the equality between s and $g(K/Y)$ can be assured by:[1]

(1) the flexibility in K/Y (also referred to as the technology assumption);
(2) the flexibility in s (saving assumption);
(3) the flexibility in g (labour market and/or labour supply assumption).

The above cases can, of course, be combined in various ways as, for

* Helpful comments on earlier drafts of this paper were received from Carlos Casarosa, Walter A. Eltis, John S. Flemming, Hywel G. Jones, James A. Mirrlees, David W. Soskice and numerous seminar participants, none of whom is to be held responsible for the conclusions that I reach. Financial support from the Swiss and Italian National Science Foundations is gratefully acknowledged.

instance, in Samuelson and Modigliani's (1966a) model, where (1) and (2) apply simultaneously.

Solution (1) above was adopted by the neoclassical or 'marginalist' school:

> instead of there being fixed coefficients of production, there may exist a production function offering a continuum of alternative techniques, each involving different capital–labour ratios; ... The consequence is that the capital–output ratio v is adjustable, instead of being fixed, and this provides a way in which s/v and n may be brought into equality. (Hahn and Matthews, 1964, p. 785)

But of course the solution of the Harrod–Domar dilemma was just the beginning; for if, on the one hand, it was necessary to provide a device ensuring equilibrium growth, on the other hand it was necessary to define income distribution in an exhaustive way. Hence, in order to make income distribution determinate, several restrictive assumptions were added, so that in the end the neoclassical economists ended up with a model incorporating a 'well-behaved' constant returns to scale aggregate production function, perfect substitutability between labour and capital, profit-maximizing behaviour, perfect competition in the labour and capital markets, all within a single-commodity framework. In this way, whenever Euler's Theorem applies, both shares are simultaneously determined, and no residual, by definition, can exist. None the less, as the two Cambridges (UK *versus* Massachusetts, USA) controversy on capital theory and on the reswitching of techniques has shown, 'Lower interest rates may bring lower steady-state consumption and lower capital–output ratios, and the transition to such lower interest rate can involve denial of diminishing returns ... (Samuelson, 1966, p. 583). Such a statement from a leading representative of the marginalist school would seem to imply that the whole production function approach is invalidated.

The second answer to the Harrod–Domar dilemma, i.e. the assumption of a flexible aggregate saving ratio, was primarily adopted by the neo-Keynesian or Cambridge school of thought. Of course, there are many ways in which one can give flexibility to s; but the one that has played the major role is the hypothesis of a two-class society (namely, the workers and capitalists), each with a different constant propensity to save. In this way there always exists a distribution of income between the two classes that produces precisely that saving ratio that will equal the value $g(K/Y)$, so satisfying the Harrod–

Domar equilibrium condition. The validity of this approach is reinforced by the fact that the assumption of a unique aggregate saving ratio ignores all possible differences in saving (and consumption) behaviour between, for instance, different classes of income-receivers, or categories of income of even different sectors of the economy. Moreover, the problem of aggregating savings might give rise to particular and unknown difficulties, so that it may be safer to consider it in a disaggregate way, as the neo-Keynesian model does. Third, this assumption also receives empirical support from the observed high rates of saving out of corporate profits and much lower rates out of labour income (cf., for instance, Burmeister and Taubman, 1969; Kaldor, 1966; Moore, 1974; and Murfin, 1980). Considering a full-employment long-run equilibrium growth model with a capitalists' class (whose income is derived entirely from capital) and a workers' class (whose income is derived from wages and accumulated savings), both with a constant propensity to save, the Cambridge economists were in a position to (a) provide a solution to the Harrod–Domar dilemma (by specifying an aggregate saving ratio s which equals $g(K/Y)$, where g and K/Y are both exogenously given); (b) determine the long-run equilibrium value of the rate of profits, the distribution of income between profits and wages, and the distribution of disposable income between the two classes; (c) allow the existence of an income residual, namely the wages, consistent with the assumption of a relationship between the savings of that class of individuals (the capitalists) who are in the position to control the process of production and capital accumulation; and (d) give some insight into the process of accumulation of capital by specifying the equilibrium capital share of the two classes. This impressive range of results is obtained within a relatively simple framework and on the basis of relatively few assumptions, much less 'hybrid, opposite and extreme' than those of the marginalistic model. Although originally adopted by the Cambridge school, the assumption of a flexible savings rate was later taken up by authors working with neoclassical models, primarily Meade (1963, 1966), Samuelson and Modigliani (1966a), Sato (1966) and Stiglitz (1967).

The third answer to the Harrod–Domar dilemma, i.e. that of a flexible rate of growth, has mainly taken the form of considering an endogenously determined technical progress. However, most of these analyses have not been prompted by the desire to provide an answer to the Harrod–Domar dilemma. Clearly, the rate of growth of the labour force could, on classical lines, be considered as an endogenous variable instead of a constant. On the other hand, technical progress (included in g) could be assumed as endogenously determined, as in Eltis (1973, ch. 6), whose approach can be compared to Malthus' theory of population applied to capital accumulation, so that if 'there is too much capital there is not enough demand to feed it. Capital then dies off until it becomes scarce, the rate of profit is driven up, and the birth rate of capital starts rising again' (Kregel, 1974, p. 345). This process, however, is based on the assumption following which the capital–output ratio, assumed to be infinitely flexible, is an inverse monotonic function of the rate of profits, a marginalistic assumption that gives rise to the impasse mentioned at the end of point (1) above.

II SINGLE-SECTOR TWO-CLASS MODELS WITH FIXED SAVING RATIOS: MAIN RESULTS

As pointed out above, the analysis of income distribution and profit determination in a growth model in which the saving propensity of individuals is externally given according to which class they belong was initiated by the Cambridge school. Back in the middle 1950s and early 1960s, Kaldor (1955, 1957) and Pasinetti (1962) investigated the relationship between the steady-state rate of profits, on one hand, and the saving propensities of the social classes and the rate of growth of the economy, on the other hand. Assuming two identifiable classes of individuals who receive different factors payments (i.e. a working class, which receives wages and interest payments, and a capitalist class, which receives only interest payments), Pasinetti (1962) showed that the long-run equilibrium interest rate is equal to the natural rate of growth divided by the propensity to save of the capitalists:

$$P/K = g/s_c \tag{1}$$

i.e. the Kaldor–Pasinetti theorem. This outcome shows that the steady-state rate of interest and the steady-state share of income going to capital ($P/Y = P/K(K/Y)$), where the capital–output ratio is considered as a constant) are both independent of the workers' propensity to save.

Soon afterwards this notable result led to an interchange between Kaldor (1966), Pasinetti (1966; 1974, ch. 6) and Robinson (1966) on one side, and Meade (1963, 1966), Samuelson and Modigliani (1966a, 1966b) and Sato (1966) on the other side. Their reaction was not surprising, since the Cambridge equation (i.e. the Kaldor-Pasinetti theorem) makes the whole well-behaved production function framework irrelevant. With the main preoccupation of defending the theory of marginal productivity of capital, Meade, Samuelson and Modigliani set out to find an escape route for which the Cambridge equation would be prevented from operating. Working within the framework of a neoclassical model (but always retaining the assumption of a constant savings ratio for the two classes), Meade and Samuelson and Modigliani formulated their Dual Theorem, in which not the Kaldor-Pasinetti Theorem, but the traditional (i.e. Solow) result of growth theory, holds. As a matter of fact, the neoclassical economists showed that, when the workers' propensity to save is equal to (or greater than, outside the equilibrium condition) the capitalists' propensity to save weighted by the profit share, the workers' capital stock will grow indefinitely at a faster rate than that of the capitalists, so that the rate of interest can be written as:

$$P/K = (P/Y)\frac{s_w}{n} \tag{2}$$

the Meade and Samuelson-Modigliani Dual Theorem, which is not exogenously determined since it depends on the share of profits in national income and is independent of the capitalists' propensity to save. Of course, in this case the long-run steady state will be of the Harrod-Domar type, since the two-class model would, in the long term, reduce itself to a single-class model. In such an eventual steady state only one category of savers is left, 'and marginal productivity theorists can retreat back' (cf. Pasinetti, 1974, p. 130) to their analysis, which postulates an infinite flexibility of the capital-output ratio as the equilibrating variable of the system.

III MAIN CRITICISMS OF THE ASSUMPTION OF A TWO-CLASS SOCIETY WITH DIFFERENTIATED AND CONSTANT PROPENSITIES TO SAVE

It should come as no surprise that the assumption of a flexible aggregate saving ratio came under attack, especially from the neoclassical quarters. All extreme assumptions had been made by the marginalists in order to make the marginal productivity concept relevant; yet the Kaldor-Pasinetti theorem ('paradox' for the marginalists) makes their assumptions completely useless. But if the capitalists' capital could be eliminated from the system (as in the case of the Meade and Samuelson–Modigliani Dual Theorem), then clearly their propensity to save would not be able to determine the equilibrium value of the rate of profits, and the Cambridge equation would not apply. But what the marginalists did not say or admit is that such a situation (a) is very unlikely to happen in concrete terms, and, more importantly, (b) represents a 'knife-edge' solution, since in equilibrium it applies only when $s_w = s$.

Other more general criticisms of the neo-Keynesian two-class model, which have occupied a prominent place in the literature, seem to concentrate on the following points:

(1) the assumption of the equality, in the long-run, between the rate of profits earned by the capitalists and the rate of interest earned by the workers on their accumulated savings;

(2) the assumption and identification of individuals who retain their class identity for ever, i.e. of classes inter-generationally stable;

(3) the constancy of the propensity to save of the two classes, which is exogenously given and hence independent of such other variables as, for instance, the rate of interest or the rate of population growth;

(4) the lack of explanation relative to the historical relevance of the inter-generational bequest of the two classes (as opposed to their life-cycle savings).

Points (3) and (4) will be the central theme of this paper, as expounded at the end of this section. Points (1) and (2) have already been extensively treated in the literature; summing up, these criticisms turn out to be irrelevant to the validity of most of the results obtained within the framework of the neo-Keynesian model. Let us first consider point (1). In the late 1960s and early 1970s several authors (for a comprehensive list see, for instance, Baranzini, 1976, and Pasinetti, 1974, ch. 6) suggested that, if one were to assume a differentiated rate of return for workers' and capitalists' savings, the Cambridge equation would no longer apply. As a matter of fact, as Pasinetti has formally proved (cf. Pasinetti, 1974, pp. 139–41), this is not true: the hypothesis of a differentiated interest rate in most cases comes to reinforce the Cambridge equation, since 'A rate of interest lower than the rate of profit has the same effect as a higher propensity to save of the capitalists, as it redistributes income in favour of the class that owns the physical capital stock' (Pasinetti, 1974, p. 141).

Point (2) above concerns the assumption of inter-generationally stable classes, which in the framework of a long-run equilibrium growth model seems to be quite a reasonable assumption. Again, one would expect that the relaxation of this assumption should invalidate the relevance of the Kaldor–Pasinetti theorem. But it is not really so, as Bevan (1974) and Vaughan (1979) seem to conclude at the end of their analysis (no other treatment of this particular case has appeared in the literature to our knowledge). Vaughan, for instance, obtains a third solution for the interest rate, which however approaches Pasinetti's solution when *net* transference of individuals between classes is low.

The purpose of this paper is to explore some of the implications of the relaxation of the assumption mentioned under point (3) above and, at the same time, to try to give an answer to point (4). This will be done by introducing the life-cycle hypothesis on saving into the two-class model. There is of course no pretence that all important aspects of the issue will be analysed. Our purpose is simply to extend our knowledge a little further, as well as our intuition concerning some relevant aspects of the topics analysed.

In section IV we discuss the most important aspects of the issue, while in section V we explore the consequences of the introduction of the life-cycle hypothesis into an economic growth model with two classes of savers. More precisely, in the first subsection the basic assumptions of the model are specified, while the second subsection comprises an analysis of the equilibrium properties and of the convergence of the model. In section VI we consider a more general model in which we allow the workers' class to inherit and bequeath assets. In the final section we present the main conclusions that can be drawn from our analysis.

IV   THE FLEXIBILITY OF THE PROPENSITY TO SAVE AND THE LIFE-CYCLE HYPOTHESIS ON SAVING AND CONSUMPTION BEHAVIOUR

The basic contribution of this analysis, namely the introduction of the life-cycle hypothesis into the traditional two-class growth model in order to give more flexibility to the saving assumption and in order to check the validity of the assumption of a fixed propensity to save, was originally suggested to us by Samuelson and Modigliani (1966a), who, concluding their essay on their Dual Theorem, state:

We are much more uneasy with the assumption of 'permanent' classes of pure-profit and mixed-income receivers with given and unchanging saving propensities on which all of our theorems – Pasinetti's as well as ours – depend critically. This assumption completely disregards the life cycle and its effects on saving and working behaviour. In the first place, with a large portion of saving known to occur in some phases of the life cycle in order to finance dissaving in other phases, it is unrealistic to posit values for (s_c, s_w) which are independent of n. This shortcoming is probably not too serious and could be handled without changing our results drastically. (Samuelson and Modigliani, 1966a, p. 297)

Also, other economists do not find the idea of a constant proportion to save appealing: for instance, Bliss (1975, p. 138) asks why the saving propensities of the two classes should not be 'influenced by the growth rate, or the rate of interest, or the price of champagne?' and Atkinson (1975, p. 179): 'The capitalists' class may possibly accumulate without regard to the return, but if working-class saving is interpreted in life-cycle terms, then it is very likely to be influenced by the rate of interest.'

Clearly, the introduction of the life-cycle hypothesis, which makes the saving behaviour of the classes or individuals a function of the parameters of the life cycle and of the interest rate as well, is little compatible with a (neo-) Keynesian framework, where saving decisions ought to be only indirectly dependent on the interest rate. For this reason we shall, in general, consider a neoclassical model; but always with the very neo-Keynesian goal in mind, i.e. to find that distribution of income between the two classes that produces precisely that aggregate saving ratio that satisfies the Harrod–Domar equilibrium condition. With this approach we shall be able to check (and confirm) the validity of the neo-Keynesian assumption of a constant propensity to save for the two classes.

What the life-cycle theory, in this two-class context, can contribute is essentially:

(1) to give more insight into the determination of the distribution of income between factors of production and classes, and to determine the equilibrium variables of the model; moreover, to determine when the equilibrium interest rate is the same for both classes and when there exists the possibility of a multiple equilibrium;

(2) to elucidate the applicability of the Meade–Samuelson–Modigliani condition (following which the capitalists' capital share is equal to zero);
(3) to enable an understanding of the sort of reasons that may lead to a historical class distinction and of the conditions under which the workers' class would start accumulating inter-generational assets;
(4) to appraise the validity of the assumption of a differentiated interest rate (or of the hypothesis of an imperfect capital market), which, as said above, has attracted a good deal of attention in the recent literature on two-class growth models.

Before spelling out the basic assumptions of the model, a word on the bequest motive of the two classes may be worthwhile. If we introduce, at the micro-level, the well-known Ando–Brumberg–Modigliani hypothesis on life-cycle saving into a two-class model, we are faced with the following problem: whether to consider the capital stock of the workers' class simply as life-cycle capital, or as a capital stock which is the sum of life-cycle savings *and* a durable inter-generational asset. In order to give more generality to our approach we shall consider the two cases: first, by analysing a simple model where the workers do not hold inter-generaticnal assets (section V), and a second one in which they do (section VI). For the sake of simplicity the analysis will be carried out within the framework of the familiar two-period model of optimal consumption and investment, since it will allow us to derive, in more simple terms than otherwise, the value of the variables of the model. It may be worth noting that this approach entails no loss of generality, since it has been shown (cf., for instance, Fama, 1968) that, under general conditions, most of the empirically observable implications derived from a multi-period model of saving and consumption are indistinguishable from those implied by a simple two-period model.

V THE RATE OF PROFIT AND INCOME DISTRIBUTION IN A TWO-CLASS LIFE-CYCLE MODEL WITH PURE CAPITALISTS AND PURE WORKERS

The basic assumptions of the model
Let us consider a simple two-period model with just one capitalist and one worker. The basic assumptions are:

(1) *Demographic assumptions:* individuals live two periods (of equal length) and there is no uncertainty about the date of retirement (which concludes the first and 'active' period) and of death (at the end of the second period). At the end of the first period each person has $1 + g$ children, so that population grows at the exogenously given rate g.

(2) *Income:* the worker born at the end of the period $t - 1$ receives during the first period (t) a wage rate equal to W_t; the capitalist on his side will have a disposable income equal to rB_{t-1}, where B_{t-1} is the bequest that he has inherited at the end of period $t - 1$ when he was born. For the sake of simplicity, the retired persons earn no pension.

(3) *Consumption and accumulation plans:* both individuals make their consumption and saving plans in order to maximize the discounted value of their two consumptions $C_t^{c,\,w}$ and $C_{t+1}^{c,\,w}$, to which the capitalist (but not the worker) will add the utility that he will derive from leaving an endowment to his children (of the value B_t). Since, by definition, the worker inherits and leaves no assets, the capital stock of the economy will be made up by the inter-generational bequest of the capitalists' class *and* by the life-cycle savings of both classes.

(4) *Utility functions:* we assume a constant elasticity u-function of the form $U(C_t) = (1/a)(C_t)^a$. Although most of the results are valid for a lower than unity, for the sake of simplicity we focus on the case $a = 0$, i.e. on the widely used logarithmic utility function. The same u-function will be assumed for the bequest motive; this assumption is not new in the literature (cf., for instance, Merton, 1969, 1971; Atkinson, 1974; and Samuelson, 1969) and assumes that the bequest is a final consumption.

Optimal saving and consumption plans

Under these conditions the two individuals will try to maximize the following u-functions (which incorporate a bequest motive for the capitalist):

$$\max \frac{1}{a} \left\{ (C_t^w)^a + \frac{(C_{t+1}^w)^a}{(1 + \phi)} \right\} \tag{3}$$

for the worker,

$$\text{s.t. } W_t = C_t^w + C_{t+1}^w/(1 + r)$$

and

$$\max \frac{1}{a} \left\{ (C_t^c)^a + \frac{(C_{t+1}^c)^a}{(1+\phi)} + B_t^a \frac{1+g}{1+b} \right\} \tag{4}$$

for the capitalist,

$$\text{s.t. } (1+r) B_{t-1} = C_t^c + (C_{t+1}^c)/(1+r) + (1+g) B_t$$

where: a is the (constant) elasticity of the u-function; ϕ is the rate of utility discount for consumption (or pure time-preference); b is the bequest discount rate; r is the rate of interest; B_t is the bequest left by the capitalist at the end of the period t to each of his $1+g$ children.

By writing the two Lagrangeans and solving them with respect to $C_{t+1}^{c,w}$ and B_t, we obtain the optimal values:

$$C_{t+1}^{c,w} = C_t^{c,w} (1+r)^{1/(1-a)} (1+\phi)^{1/(a-1)} \tag{5}$$

$$B^t = C_t^c (1+b)^{1/(a-1)} \tag{6}$$

$$C_{t+1}^c = B_t (1+b)^{1/(1-a)} (1+r)^{1/(1-a)} (1+\phi)^{1/(a-1)}. \tag{7}$$

We are now in a position to rewrite the budget constraints in terms of $C_t^{c,w}$:

$$(1+r) B_{t-1} = C_t^c \{ 1 + (1+r)^{1/(1-a)} (1+\phi)^{1/(a-1)}$$
$$+ (1+g)(1+b)^{1/(a-1)} \} \tag{8}$$

$$W_t = C_t^w \{ 1 + (1+r)^{1/(1-a)} (1+\phi)^{1/(a-1)} \} \tag{9}$$

from which it is easy to obtain the whole consumption and saving plans of the two individuals.

Equilibrium growth and existence of balanced growth paths
Let us now focus on the steady-state behaviour of the model. The question we are interested in is the existence (and eventually the uniqueness) of balanced growth paths. It is easy to see that (at least in this case, where the workers have no inter-generational assets), if there exists a balanced growth path with both classes represented in the system, it is unique. (For a more detailed discussion on this point, cf. Baranzini, 1976, ch. II.) In the absence of technical

progress, when the two classes exist in equilibrium we may write:

$$\dot{k}_c = \dot{k}_w = \dot{k} = 0 \tag{10}$$

and

$$B_{t-1} = B_t = B^* \tag{11}$$

since the capital per capita (life-cycle and inter-generational) of the two classes, in equilibrium, must grow at rate 0 (in the absence of technical progress, at least).

We can now define the equilibrium value of r, the interest rate, which (a) maximizes the utility of the capitalist and, at the same time, (b) assures an equilibrium growth of the capital stock of the two classes. Combining relations (6), (8), (10) and (11), and assuming, for the sake of simplicity, but without much loss of generality, a logarithmic utility function (where $a = 0$), we obtain the following value for the equilibrium interest rate:[2, 3]

$$r^* = g + (1 + b) \frac{2 + \phi}{1 + \phi} \tag{12}$$

which is unique. The partial derivatives $\partial r^*/\partial g = 1$; $\partial r^*/\partial b > 0$; and $\partial r^*/\partial \phi < 0$ show that the equilibrium interest rate is positively associated with the natural rate of growth (g) and with the bequest discount rate (b); it is however negatively associated with the pure time preference (ϕ). From a marginalist point of view the sign of the partial derivative with respect to b may be interpreted in the following way: as the subjective discount rate for the bequest increases, all other things being equal, thriftiness is discouraged and therefore the capital intensity will fall; consequently, the marginal productivity of capital will tend to rise.

At this point the following general remarks are in order:

(1) The optimal equilibrium interest rate r^* does not depend on the form of the production function or on the value of the capital-labour ratio. It depends only on the rate of growth of the economy and on the behavioural parameters of the model. In a certain sense the simplicity of Pasinetti's, and Meade–Samuelson and Modigliani's, solutions is repeated. Additionally, the fact that r^* does not depend on the form of the production function seems to confirm the validity of the Kaldor–Pasinetti theorem.

(2) It is interesting to note that r^*, the equilibrium rate of profit, is greater than the natural rate of growth of the population (g). In our model this outcome is particularly important since it guarantees the existence, in equilibrium, of the capitalists' class, which on one hand has an income equal to rB_t and on the other side leaves to the next generation an amount equal to gB_t. Hence, in order to survive, the capitalists must receive an interest rate higher than the rate of growth of population.

(3) The third point concerns the maximization of consumption per capita. In a state of balanced growth consumption per capita is maximized when the profit rate (r^*) is equal to the rate of growth (g). In our model, consumption per capita can be maximized in the usual way (i.e., $r^* = g$) only when we have $b = -1$ and/or $\phi = -2$, which imply a very strong desire to leave a bequest to the next generation and/or a negative subjective discount rate (the latter being very unlikely to happen in the real world).

(4) It may be noted again that we have postulated for both classes (capitalist and worker) the same identical behavioural parameters. Had we assumed that they are different, then the equilibrium interest rate would not depend on the behavioural parameters of the working class at all.

Convergence analysis
The convergence analysis of this model is clearly more difficult than that of the traditional two-class model, where the saving propensities are constant. A careful investigation of the properties of the model shows, however (cf. Baranzini, 1976, pp. 48–55), that it is, under general conditions, globally stable. The convergence analysis shows also that, when:

$$2 + \phi = r^* \left(1 - \frac{P}{Y}\right) \bigg/ \frac{P}{Y} = \frac{1 - P/Y}{P/Y} \left\{ g + (1 + b) \frac{2 + \phi}{1 + \phi} \right\} \qquad (13)$$

a condition which is very unlikely to be fulfilled in the real world (because it requires a very low value of the pure time preference), the share of capital stock of the capitalists' K_c/K is 0 and the model becomes a one-class model with workers only, for which the equilibrium interest rate r^{**} is:

$$r^{**} = (2 + \phi) \frac{P/Y}{1 - P/Y}. \qquad (14)$$

In this case the steady state is the 'life-cycle' version of the classical Harrod–Domar–Solow type with a single class of savers, namely the workers (or those who receive some income from both work and accumulated savings). Under normal conditions, the chance of this happening is even more remote than that relative to the Dual Theorem of Meade–Samuelson and Modigliani.

VI TOWARDS A MORE GENERAL MODEL: CAPITALISTS AND WORKERS BOTH WITH AN INTERGENERATIONAL CAPITAL STOCK

By making the rather restrictive assumptions that the workers have no bequest motive (i.e. no inter-generational transfer), we have just seen that our two-class life-cycle model has a unique equilibrium rate of interest which is determined solely by the behaviour of the pure capitalists' class and is independent of the form of the production function and of the behaviour of the workers' class. This result, however, rests upon a crucial assumption; namely, the fact that the workers inherit and leave no financial assets. It is thus natural to ask what happens when this assumption is relaxed and we allow the workers to inherit and leave a financial bequest.

If workers are allowed to inherit and leave a bequest B^w, relation (3), which now incorporates a bequest motive, may be rewritten as:

$$\max \frac{1}{a} \left\{ (C_t^w)^a + (C_{t+1}^w)^a/(1 + \phi) + \frac{1 + g}{1 + b_w} (B_t^w)^a \right\} \qquad (15)$$

$$\text{s.t. } W_t + (1 + r) B_{t-1}^w = C_t^w + C_{t+1}^w/(1 + r) + B_t^w (1 + g)$$

where b_w is the bequest discount rate for the workers' class. By using the same procedure expounded in section V above, this time we obtain two equilibrium values of the rate of interest, one for the workers' class (r_w^*) and one for the capitalists' class (r_c^*):

$$r_w^* = \left\{ g(1 + b_w) \frac{2 + \phi}{1 + \phi} \right\} \frac{B^w}{B^w + (1 - X_p)/X_p K} \qquad (16)$$

$$r_c^* = g + (1 + b_c) \frac{2 + \phi}{1 + \phi} \qquad (17)$$

where: B^w is the workers' inter-generational capital stock; X_p is the profit share P/Y; $b_{w,c}$ is the bequest discount rate of the workers' and capitalists' class respectively. We note immediately that the two values r_w^* and r_c^* are not identical. Therefore in this framework the two classes are fitted into the same balanced growth path (assuming that both can exist in equilibrium) when:

(1) the bequest B^w of the workers' class is equal to zero. When $B^w = 0$ we would, essentially, be back to the original model considered in section V above. However, while, there, B^w was assumed, *a priori*, to be 0, here it would be chosen to be 0 according to other elements (like the presence of a high rate of technical progress or a good expectation of the evolution of the wage rate, etc.) for which the workers decide not to have a bequest motive;

(2) we assume a differentiated subjective discount rate of the bequest; i.e. $b_w \gg b_c$, which means that the capitalists' class must be much more willing than the workers' class to leave a bequest to their children;

(3) we assume a differentiated interest rate, higher for the capitalists and lower for the workers. Clearly, in this case the equilibrium interest rate of the model would be a weighted average of the two, so that $r_w^* < r^* < r_c^*$. It is worth noting that this case appears here as an optimality condition, whereas in many other models it is an assumption (cf., for instance, Balestra and Baranzini, 1971; Gupta, 1976; Laing, 1969; Moore, 1974; and Pasinetti, 1974, pp. 139–41).

In this context the possibility of a differentiated discount rate for the bequest seems to be the most interesting case, especially since it allows us to get greater insight into the different patterns of accumulation of capital of the two classes (in equilibrium, at least) and the sort of reasons that may lead to a perpetual class distinction from a historical point of view. The analysis of this particular case (cf. Baranzini, 1976, pp. 61–70) has demonstrated first the conditions under which the capitalists' class can exist in equilibrium, and then the conditions for a workers' positive bequest to exist. It can be shown that, when the capitalists have a much higher propensity to leave a bequest than the workers, the two classes exist in equilibrium and have both a positive share of the total bequest. However, when the capitalists have a low propensity to leave a bequest, the workers will hold all of the equilibrium bequest of the system. The point is that in this model what could not happen for the Pasinetti and Meade–Samuelson and Modigliani model, i.e. that the workers are eliminated from the system, can, in a certain sense, happen here. As a matter of fact, when the propensity to leave assets to the workers' children is low, the workers cannot hold an inter-generational bequest. Of course, the perspective is completely different, since here we are focusing on the inter-generational capital, whereas in the above traditional models the issue concerns the total (life-cycle plus inter-generational) capital stock of each class.

VII CONCLUSIONS

At the end of our exposition we can draw some conclusions concerning the determination of the rate of profits in a two-class growth model. Starting from the Harrod–Domar dilemma, the neo-Keynesian school was able to show that the equilibrium rate of profits is independent of the production function and of the saving propensity of the workers' class. Later, the neoclassical economists discovered (or thought they had) an escape route by eliminating the capitalists from the system and thus preventing the Cambridge equation from operating, so at the same time letting technology become an important variable of the model. But the neoclassical economists went further, and pointed out that the introduction of the life-cycle savings hypothesis would completely invalidate the Cambridge equation.

But this is not the case. Our analysis has proved that the equilibrium profit rate, even in the case of a life-cycle model, is independent of the form of the production function and of the specific behaviour of the workers' class, just as Kaldor and Pasinetti had proved.

NOTES

1 Most of the models that originally stemmed from the Harrod–Domar models are long-run, steady-state, full-employment and single-good models. As Pasinetti (1962, p. 268) points out, 'they consider full employment systems where the possibilities of economic growth are externally given by population increase and technical progress. Therefore the amount of investment – in physical terms – necessary in order to keep full employment through time, is also externally given.'

2 The assumption of a logarithmic utility function has been widely postulated in recent economic literature: cf., for instance, Atkinson (1974), Flemming (1974), Merton (1969) and Samuelson (1969).

3 It is easy to see that, in this case where workers do not have inter-generational assets, if there exists a balanced growth path with both classes represented in the system, it is unique.

REFERENCES

Atkinson, A. B. (1971) 'The Distribution of Wealth and the Individual Life-Cycle', *Oxford Eonomic Papers*, pp. 239-54.

Atkinson, A. B. (1974) 'A Model of Distribution of Wealth', mimeo, University of Essex and MIT.

Atkinson, A. B. (1975) *The Economics of Inequality*, Oxford University Press.

Balestra, P. and Baranzini, M. (1971) 'Some Optimal Aspects in a Two-Class Model with a Differentiated Interest Rate', *Kyklos*, pp. 240-56.

Baranzini, M. (1975) 'The Pasinetti and the Anti-Pasinetti Theorems: A Reconciliation', *Oxford Economic Papers*, pp. 470-3.

Baranzini, M. (1976) 'On the Accumulation of Capital in Two-Class Growth Models', unpublished DPhil thesis, University of Oxford.

Baranzini, M. (1981) 'Taux d'intérêt, distribution du revenu, théorie des cycles vitaux et choix du portefeuille', *Kyklos* (Special issue: 25 years Kaldorian Theory of Distribution), pp. 593-610.

Bevan, D. L. (1974) 'Savings, Inheritance and Economic Growth in the Presence of Earnings Inequality', mimeo, St. John's College, Oxford.

Bliss, C. J. (1975) *Capital Theory and the Distribution of Income*, North Holland, Amsterdam/Oxford.

Britto, R. (1972) 'On Differential Savings Propensies in Two-Class Growth Models', *Review of Economic Studies*, pp. 491-4.

Burmeister, E. and Taubman, T. (1969) 'Labour and Non-Labour Income Saving Propensities', *Canadian Journal of Economics*, pp. 78-89.

Eltis, W. A. (1973) *Growth and Distribution*, Macmillan, London.

Fama, E. F. (1968) 'Multi-Period Consumption Investment Decisions', Report 6830, Center for Mathematical Studies in Business and Economics, Chicago.

Flemming, J. S. (1974) 'Portfolio Choice and Liquidity Preference, A Continuous-Time Treatment', in *Issues in Monetary Economics*, ed. H. G. Johnson and A. R. Nobay, Oxford University Press, pp. 137-50.

Gupta, K. L. (1976) 'Differentiated Interest Rate and Kaldor-Pasinetti Paradoxes', *Kyklos*, pp. 310-14.

Hahn, F. H. and Matthews, R. C. O. (1964) 'The Theory of Economic Growth: A Survey', *Economic Journal*, pp. 779-902.

Kaldor, N. (1955) 'Alternative Theories of Distribution', *Review of Economic Studies*, pp. 83-100.

Kaldor, N. (1957) 'A Model of Economic Growth', *Economic Journal*, pp. 591-624.

Kaldor, N. (1966) 'Marginal Productivity and the Macro-Economic Theories of Distribution', *Review of Economic Studies*, pp. 309-19.

Kregel, J. A. (1974) Review of Eltis' *Growth and Distribution, Economica*, pp. 345-6.

Laing, N. F. (1969) 'Two Notes on Pasinetti's Theorem', *Economic Record*, pp. 373-85.

Meade, J. E. (1963) 'The Rate of Profits in a Growing Economy', *Economic Journal*, pp. 665-74.

Meade, J. E. (1966) 'The Outcome of the Pasinetti Process: a Note', *Economic Journal*, pp. 161-5.

Merton, R. C. (1969) 'Lifetime Portfolio Selection under Uncertainty: the Continuous Case', *Review of Economics and Statistics*, pp. 247-57.

Merton, R. C. (1971) 'Optimal Consumption and Portfolio Rules in a Continuous-Time Model', *Journal of Economic Theory*, pp. 373-413.

Moore, B. J. (1974) 'The Pasinetti Paradox Revisited', *Review of Economic Studies*, pp. 297-9.

Murfin, A. J. (1980) 'Saving Propensities from Wage and Non-Wage Income', *Warwick Economic Research Papers*, no. 174.

Pasinetti, L. L. (1962) 'The Rate of Profit and Income Distribution in Relation to the Rate of Economic Growth', *Review of Economic Studies*, pp. 267-79.

Pasinetti, L. L. (1966) 'New Results in an Old Framework', *Review of Economic Studies*, pp. 303-6.

Pasinetti, L. L. (1974) *Growth and Income Distribution, Essays in Economic Theory*, Cambridge University Press.

Pasinetti, L. L. (1981) *Structural Change and Economic Growth* (A theoretical essay on the dynamics of the wealth of nations), Cambridge University Press.

Robinson, J. (1966) 'Comment on Samuelson and Modigliani', *Review of Economic Studies*, pp. 307-8.

Samuelson, P. A. (1966) 'A Summing Up', *Quarterly Journal of Economics*, pp. 568-83.

Samuelson, P. A. (1969) 'Lifetime Portfolio Selection by Dynamic Stochastic Programming', *Review of Economics and Statistics*, pp. 239-46.

Samuelson, P. A. and Modigliani, F. (1966a) 'The Pasinetti Paradox in Neoclassical and More General Models', *Review of Economic Studies*, pp. 269-302.

Samuelson, P. A. and Modigliani, F. (1966b) 'Reply to Pasinetti and Robinson', *Review of Economic Studies*, pp. 321-30.

Sato, K. (1966) 'The Neoclassical Theorem and Distribution of Income and Wealth', *Review of Economic Studies*, pp. 331-5.

Sheng Cheng, H. (1973) 'On Optimal Capital Accumulation in a Two-Class Model of Economic Growth', *Metroeconomica*, pp. 229-49.

Steindl, J. (1972) 'The Distribution of Wealth after a Model of Wold and Whittle', *Review of Economic Studies*, pp. 263-79.

Stiglitz, J. E. (1967) 'A Two-Sector Two-Class Model of Economic Growth', *Review of Economic Studies*, pp. 227-38.

Tobin, J. (1967) 'Life-Cycle Saving and Balanced Growth', in *Ten Economic Studies in the Tradition of Irving Fisher*, John Wiley & Sons, New York, pp. 231-56; reprinted in J. Tobin (1975), *Essays in Economics*, vol. 2: *Consumption and Econometrics*, North Holland, Amsterdam, pp. 127-53.

Tobin, J. (1972) 'Wealth, Liquidity, and the Propensity to Consume', in *Human Behavior in Economic Affairs (Essays in Honor of George S. Katona)*, ed. B. Strumpel and others, Elsevier, Amsterdam, pp. 36-56; reprinted in J. Tobin (1975), *Essays in Economics*, vol. 2: *Consumption and Econometrics*, North Holland, Amsterdam, pp. 155-74.

Vaughan, R. N. (1979) 'Class Behaviour and the Distribution of Wealth', *Review of Economic Studies*, pp. 447-65.

Yaari, M. E. (1964) 'On the Consumer's Lifetime Allocation Process', *International Economic Review*, pp. 304-17.

16

Dr Wood on Profits and Growth: A Note

I INTRODUCTION

In his *Theory of Profits* Dr Adrian Wood (1975) presents a highly
interesting contribution to the theory of profits and, at the same
time, to the theory of economic growth. His object is to explain the
size of the profit margin of the individual firm and, on the basis of
this, the share of profits in national income. This attempt to infuse
microeconomic life into macroeconomic theories of distribution is
certainly to be welcomed. However, it seems to us that Dr Wood has
not sufficiently stressed the way in which the equilibrium of the firm
is linked to the equilibrium of the economy as a whole. It is, then,
the purpose of this note to discuss briefly the relationship between
the two types of equilibria. It will turn out that the existence and the
stability of an overall (micro- and macro-) equilibrium is closely
linked with the relationship of Dr Wood's model to the neo-Keynesian
theory of distribution and growth as exposed in Kaldor (1955–56).

II THE MODEL SUMMARIZED

Let us first put Dr Wood's model into a nutshell. The aim of each
firm is to grow as fast as possible, subject to two constraints. The
first constraint is the opportunity frontier: given the marginal
capital–output ratio, there exists a trade-off between the profit
margin and the rate of growth of output. The higher the profit
margin, the higher will be the price (or the lower will be the sales

---

* I am greatly indebted to Adrian Wood for having commented extensively on earlier drafts
of this note. Of course, all responsibility remains mine.

promotion expenditure) per unit of output, and thus the lower, given the prices and sales promotion expenditures of other firms, will be the rate of growth of sales (and output), and vice versa. The second constraint is the finance frontier: given the financial asset ratio, the external finance ratio and the gross retention ratio, a particular minimum profit margin is necessary to finance the investment required by any specific rate of growth of output: if a firm aims at achieving a higher rate of growth, then it must put up its profit margin.

Intuitively, it is clear that, given the assumption that each firm tries to achieve the highest possible rate of growth, the profit margin (π) and the rate of growth of output (g) are determined by the intersection of the opportunity frontier and of the finance frontier. (Evidently, given the capital–output ratio, g also determines the level of investment undertaken by a firm.) The solution is unique because the former curve is downward-sloping, the latter upward-sloping.

Macroeconomic equilibrium requires that the additional demand created by additional investment be equal to the increase in output made possible by investment (Wood, 1975, pp. 112–13). Dr Wood's macroeconomic growth relationship is, in fact, a variation of the Harrod–Domar formula from which it differs by the introduction of autonomous expenditures. Thus, once the ratios of saving and of autonomous expenditures to income and the capital–output ratio are given, the *macroeconomic* equilibrium rate of growth is determined.[1] If this rate of growth is introduced into the macro-version of the finance frontier, then the equilibrium share of profits in national income is also determined, since competition ensures that the finance constraint is binding (Wood, 1975, pp. 108–11).

III THE NATURE OF MICRO- AND OF MACROECONOMIC EQUILIBRIA

If, in Dr Wood's model, one wants to establish a link between the equilibria of individual firms and the equilibrium of the economy as a whole, one has to be clear about two points: first, there is, in principle, no difficulty in aggregating the finance frontiers of all firms (Wood, 1975, p. 108). The macroeconomic finance frontier has a straightforward economic meaning: it links the rate of growth of the economy as a whole to the share of profits in national income. Second, the opportunity frontier is essentially a microeconomic concept and has no simple macroeconomic counterpart: 'In the context of the economy as a whole the opportunity frontiers of individual firms serve primarily to determine their growth rates relative to one another – and thus, at any moment of time, their relative sizes' (Wood, 1975, p. 108). Dr Wood goes on to say: 'Thus the form of the individual firm's opportunity frontier, although it depends to some extent on the rate of growth of aggregate demand, is determined mainly by . . . its competitiveness' (p. 109).

There are two issues here. The first is the determination of the growth rates of firms *relative* to each other: if there are two firms, what determines g_1/g_2? The second issue is the determination of the absolute growth rate of each individual firm and, thus, of the economy as a whole. This rate of growth is governed by macroeconomic forces, namely by aggregate demand.

Let us assume for convenience that the growth of aggregate demand, unknown to individual firms, influences the growth rates of all firms in the same way, each firm's growth rate being multiplied by some factor b, which leaves relative positions unchanged, if there are two firms only. Let us further suppose that g_1 and g_2 are the *ex ante* or planned growth rates, while bg_1 and bg_2 are the *ex post* or realized growth rates. If b diverges from unity expectations are not fulfilled, but are unfulfilled to an equal degree for all firms.

Let us thus assume that g_1/g_2, and hence the relative sizes of firms, are already determined, all that remains being the determination of b. This assumption enables us to define a representative firm with the following properties.

(1) The finance frontier (relation (1) below) of this firm is qualitatively the same as the one for the economy as a whole. In fact, this relation is the weighted average of all individual finance frontiers.

(2) The same holds for the opportunity frontier $00'$ of this firm (see figure 16.1 below).

Thus, whenever, in what follows, we speak of a shift of the $00'$ curve of the representative firm, this means that the opportunity frontiers of all firms shift in the same proportion.

Let us now consider Dr Wood's finance frontier (1975, p. 109):

$$\pi = \frac{(1+f-x)}{r} \, kg \tag{1}$$

where π = profit margin or share of profits in national income; r = gross retention ratio; f = financial asset ratio; x = external finance ratio; k = gross incremental capital–output ratio; and g = rate of growth of output); and his macroeconomic equilibrium condition (Wood, 1975, p. 113, equation (3)):

$$l = a + (k - a) g \tag{2}$$

where a = ratio of autonomous demand, other than investment, to output; l = proportional leakage out of income.

If, in addition, one assumes (as Dr Wood does at this point) that l depends upon π in a neo-Keynesian way (Wood, 1975, p. 117, relation (9)), one can write the macroeconomic equilibrium relation (2) as

$$\pi = \frac{a - s_\mathrm{w}}{s_\mathrm{p} - s_\mathrm{w}} + \frac{k - a}{s_\mathrm{p} - s_\mathrm{w}} g. \tag{3}$$

Equations (1) and (3) are two *independent* relationships in π and g. Relation (1) represents the microeconomic equilibrium condition, (3) the macroeconomic one. Both are, in the spirit of Dr Wood's theory, long-run relationships. That is to say, firms carry out adjustments only if there is a sustained tendency of aggregate demand to deviate from aggregate supply. Thus if, in what follows, we speak of disequilibrium, we always mean that disequilibrium has prevailed over several short-run periods so that firms are led to revise their long-run plans.

IV EXISTENCE AND STABILITY OF AN OVERALL (MICRO- AND MACRO-) EQUILIBRIUM

The solution of equations (1) and (3) yields equilibrium values of the share of profits and of the rate of growth. Let us denote these by π^* and g^*. If, then, the representative firm chooses g^* as its growth rate, its expectations will be fulfilled (b will be unity and π will equal π^*): the economy as a whole is in a state of long-run equilibrium. The questions we want to answer now are: (a) in what circumstances does this equilibrium exist in an economically meaningful sense? and (b) in what circumstances does an economy tend towards it?

These questions can be answered quite easily if we map out relations (1) and (3) in a diagram (figure 16.1). The first is represented by line 0π, the second by $\pi_1\pi$.[2] Suppose that, initially, the representative firm believes itself to be faced with the opportunity frontier

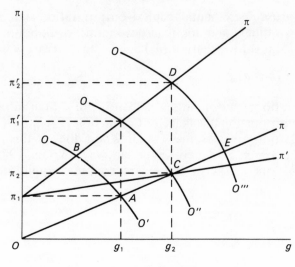

FIGURE 16.1

OO'. Given the finance frontier (cf. relation (1)), *microeconomic* equilibrium is given by (g_1, π_1). However, at a planned growth rate g_1 and prices such that the profit margin is π_1, macroeconomic demand, represented by relation (3), exceeds overall supply; *b* exceeds unity. Given this, let us suppose that firms put up prices to an extent such that, for the economy as a whole, demand equals supply. The realized share of profits will then be π_1^r. If the realized profit share exceeds the planned one for some time (several short-term periods), then firms will revise their long-run plans. They will assume that the opportunity frontier *OO'* has shifted, from *OO'* to *OO''*, for example. Now, according to Dr Wood's model, point *B* on *OO''*, which represents macroeconomic equilibrium, cannot be a microeconomic equilibrium point. Competition will drive firms to point *C*. The new *planned* growth rate and profit share now are g_2 and π_2. But, as is easily seen, point *C* cannot be an equilibrium point either, because the realized share of profits, π_2^r, will exceed the planned one, π_2, in every short-run period. This, again, will lead firms to revise their long-run plans, thus moving to *E*, and so on. The economic system we are considering is, therefore, unstable. Moreover, no economically meaningful point of equilibrium exists, in the sense that the mathematically implied 'equilibrium' occurs at negative values of π and g. At this stage we may remark that, if firms were quantity adjusters instead of price adjusters, the outcome would be exactly the same: if the representative firm is at point A and macroeconomic demand exceeds overall supply, then stocks will be run down and waiting lists will emerge. This situation will persist. Firms will revise their long-run plans and invest more. Prices will be put up in order to satisfy the finance constraint. Thus, there will be a movement from A to C, from C to E and so on.

From relations (1) and (3) and the above figure it immediately follows that, in normal circumstances ($a > s_w$ and $s_p > s_w$), an economically meaningful and stable equilibrium exists only if the slope of equation (1) exceeds that of relation (3) (see lines 0π and $\pi_1\pi'$). The economic meaning of this condition is that, for growth rates on the left of the equilibrium point (g_2, π_2), the share of profits in income required to finance investment *and* autonomous expenditure (line $\pi_1\pi'$) lies above the share that satisfies the finance constraint. Autonomous expenditures include any type of expenditures independent of output: autonomous consumption, government consumption and exports. As a consequence, the leakage as defined by relations (2) on (3) also contains tax and import coefficients. This means that l equals $s + t + i$, where s, t and i represent the fractions of income saved, paid on taxes and imported. Under neo-Keynesian assumptions (relation (3)) the same holds separately for s_p and s_w. Both parameters must thus be reinterpreted to contain savings, tax and import coefficients.

Owing to the fact that, as the growth rate increases, the finance requirements of the economy as a whole (savings, taxes, etc.) grow at a slower pace than the finance provided by all firms to cover part of their investment outlays, the gap between both types of finance is successively reduced. An equilibrium position will be reached because firms will invest more if the realized share of profits (defined by line $\pi_1\pi'$) exceeds the required one as defined by the finance frontier.

An alternative and more conventional way of describing this movement towards equilibrium is to say that to the left of the equilibrium point (π_2, g_2) investment exceeds savings. According to neo-Keynesian theory (relation (3)), the share of profits has to adjust in order to establish a temporary equilibrium. If the share of profits so determined exceeds the share required by firms, investment will increase.

From what has just been said, the economic interpretation of the case where the slope of relation (3) exceeds that of relation (1) is self-evident: here, the finance requirements of the economy as a whole (savings, taxes, etc.) grow faster than the finance provided by firms to cover part of their investment outlays. This may be due, for example, to rapidly increasing autonomous expenditures, above all exports and government consumption.

V AN OBJECTION

An objection can now be raised against the analysis carried out so far. In fact, we have, in the spirit of Dr Wood's model, assumed that relations (1) and (3) are independent of each other. In comparing the two equations doubts as to their independence may arise, however. One may argue that the retention ratio r equals s_p, the fraction of profits saved. Neglecting the financial asset ratio f and the ratio of autonomous expenditures to income, a, the parameter x in relation (1) then represents that fraction of investment expenditures which is financed by savings out of wages.[3] In this case relations (1) and (3) are identical and what we have said above becomes irrelevant.

This would, however, be an unfair way of interpreting Dr Wood's model. In fact, one can safely assume that s_p exceeds r because it is likely that part of the dividends paid to share-holders are saved. In addition, there is no reason to suppose that the external finance requirements of firms are, *a priori*, identical with savings out of wages even if the financial asset ratio, f, equals zero.

But the most important single reason why relations (1) and (3) are not identical is the presence of autonomous expenditures. The leakage as defined by relations (2) and (3) *must* in this case be interpreted to contain savings, tax and import coefficients. Thus, it is the presence of autonomous expenditures and the corresponding interpretation of the leakage that makes relation (1) essentially different from relation (3).[4]

VI COMPARISON WITH THE NEO-KEYNESIAN THEORY OF DISTRIBUTION AND GROWTH

The two cases described in figure 16.1 are of some relevance for the links existing between Dr Wood's model and conventional neo-Keynesian theory of distribution and growth as set forth in Kaldor (1955–56).

Let us first consider the case where the slope of relation (3) exceeds that of relation (1) (no stable and economically meaningful equilibrium exists). Suppose now that, in figure 16.1, g_2 equals the exogenously determined natural rate of growth and that the planned rate of growth is g_1. Firms would be driven to g_2 (the maximum growth rate) because the realized profit margin π^r always exceeds the desired one, π. In macroeconomic equilibrium, the share of profits in national income would, therefore, be given by π'_2.

Distribution is, in this case, governed by conventional neo-Keynesian theory, that is by relation (3). The fact that, at point D, the condition $\pi'_2 > \pi_2$ holds bears some similarity to condition (5) in Kaldor (1955–56), which states that 'the realised share of profit cannot be below the level which yields the minimum rate of profit necessary to induce capitalists to invest their capital, and which we may call the "risk premium rate"...' (p. 375). Thus, Dr Wood's finance function (relation (1)) defines, in the present case, an alternative minimum share of profits below which the realized share cannot fall.

If, on the other hand, a stable and economically meaningful equilibrium exists (the slope of relation (3) is smaller than that of relation (1)), then the distribution of income is governed simultaneously by Dr Wood's and by the neo-Keynesian (Kaldorian) model. But there is, of course, no reason why the equilibrium growth (the 'warranted' rate of growth) should equal the natural rate. In terms of the above figure this means that the lines 0π and $\pi_1\pi'$ may intersect somewhere to the left of g_2, the natural growth rate.

VII CONCLUSIONS

Existence and stability of growth equilibria in Dr Wood's model are closely linked with the relationship of this model with the conventional neo-Keynesian theory of growth and distribution. If one accepts the neo-Keynesian way of linking profits and growth, then this theory must hold because it is nothing else but a macroeconomic equilibrium condition. Dr Wood's theory of profits either comes in to modify the Kaldorian (1955–56) model in the sense that the relevant rate of growth in the latter will equal the 'warranted', not the natural, rate (the second case described above), or it does not affect neo-Keynesian theory. The latter result is obtained if relations (1) and (3) do not yield an economically meaningful equilibrium which, in addition, is unstable (the first case described in the preceding section).[5]

Finally, as we have mentioned already, one has to bear in mind that Dr Wood's theory is fundamentally different from the neo-Keynesian theory only if autonomous expenditures are included in his equations defining the leakage (see relations (2) and (3) above). This leads, of course, to a redefinition of the leakage coefficients s_p and s_w, which now include savings, tax and import coefficients.

NOTES

1 This growth rate corresponds to Harrod's (1939) 'warranted rate of growth'.
2 Notice here that relation (3), as mapped out in figure 16.1, is the same for the representative firm and for the economy as a whole. If, in the macro-relation, we divide on both sides the numerator and the denominator by the number of firms, say m, we get the corresponding micro-relation. As m cancels out, both relations are identical.
3 In fact, putting $r = s_p$, neglecting a and f and combining relations (1) and (3) yields $x = s_w(1 - \pi)/gk$.
4 At some stages of his analysis Dr Wood seems to overlook the implications of this condition for the conclusions he derives. For instance, if in his formula (10) (Wood, 1975, p. 117) one neglects s_w and x (*and* autonomous demand to output, a), then the share of profits is undetermined. (The right-hand side of the equation (10) becomes 0/0, owing to the fact that our relations (1) and (3) above are identical.)
5 A third possible case arises if 0π and $\pi_1\pi'$ intersect to the right of g_2 (see figure 16.1). Distribution is now governed by the Kaldorian mechanism again. It is likely, however, that g_2 will shift to the right as entrepreneurs invest more owing to the fact that realized profits exceed desired ones, making thus the present case identical with the first one described above.

REFERENCES

Harrod, R. F. (1939) 'An Essay in Dynamic Theory', *Economic Journal*, pp. 14-33.
Kaldor, N. (1955-56) 'Alternative Theories of Distribution', *Review of Economic Studies*, pp. 83-100.
Wood, A. (1975) *A Theory of Profits*, Cambridge University Press.

Part Six

Econometrics and Mathematical Economics

17

Dummy Variables in Regression Analysis

PIETRO BALESTRA

I INTRODUCTION

In economics, as well as in other disciplines, qualitative factors often play an important role. For instance, the achievement of a student in school may be determined, among other factors, by his father's profession, which is a qualitative variable having as many attributes as there are professions. In medicine, as another example, the response of a patient to a drug may be influenced by the patient's sex or smoking habits, which may be represented by two qualitative variables. The increasing use of qualitative factors in applied research justifies a systematic look at the problem of specifying and estimating a regression equation whose explanatory variables are both quantitative and qualitative.

In section II we present, for ready reference, the well-known classical regression case with one single qualitative variable. It will be shown that estimation can be performed using a simple transformation which has an interesting interpretation. The extension to multiple qualitative variables is discussed in section III. We shall see there that the simplicity of the solution is lost when multiple qualitative variables are considered. However, there are cases in which an easy solution exists even in the multiple case. Necessary and sufficient conditions for the existence of an easy solution are provided in section IV. Finally, in section V we study the problem in the context of generalized regression and present an application to Zellner's 'seemingly unrelated regression problem'.

II CLASSICAL REGRESSION WITH ONE SINGLE QUALITATIVE
VARIABLE

We consider a classical regression problem in which there are some quantitative explanatory variables and, in addition, one qualitative variable having s mutually exclusive and exhaustive attributes.

If the qualitative variable represents sex, there are two attributes, male and female. In a seasonal model, the qualitative variable representing seasonal effects has four attributes, one for each quarter. Finally, in a regression problem where the professional status plays a role, the qualitative variable has as many attributes as there are professions.

We construct s dummy variables $L_1, L_2, \ldots, L_s$, one for each attribute. If the number of observations is n, each L_j is a n-dimensional column vector having zero elements (for those observations that do not possess the jth attribute) and unit elements (for those observations that do).

The classical regression model with one qualitative variable may be written in the following way:

$$y = L_1\alpha_1 + L_2\alpha_2 + \ldots + L_s\alpha_s + X\beta + \epsilon$$

$$= L\alpha + X\beta + \epsilon \tag{1}$$

where y is a $n \times 1$ vector of observations on the dependent variable, X is a $n \times k$ matrix of observations on k quantitative explanatory variables, L is a $n \times s$ matrix containing the s dummy variables, α is a $s \times 1$ vector of coefficients associated with the dummy variables, β is a $k \times 1$ vector of regression coefficients and ϵ is a $n \times 1$ vector of residuals. We assume that X is fixed and that the matrix $[LX]$ has full column rank $k + s < n$. Note that this implies that X is of full rank k and that it must not contain the constant column. Furthermore, as in classical regression, we assume that $E(\epsilon) = 0$ and $E(\epsilon\epsilon') = \sigma^2 I$.

For each observation, one dummy variable has unit value and all others have zero value. It follows that the vectors L_i are mutually orthogonal and that their sum is equal to the sum-vector of order n, denoted by the letter S_n (a vector of unit elements). We have:

$$L_i'L_j = 0 \qquad i \neq j \tag{2}$$

$$L_1 + L_2 + \ldots + L_s = S_n \Leftrightarrow LS_s = S_n \tag{3}$$

$$L_j'L_j = n_j \Leftrightarrow L'L = \text{diag}(n_1, \ldots, n_s) \tag{4}$$

where n_j is the number of observations having attribute j. Obviously,

$$n_j > 0 \quad \text{and} \quad \sum_{j=1}^{s} n_j = n. \tag{5}$$

Model (1) can be estimated directly by ordinary least squares (OLS). This operation involves the inversion of a $k + s$ matrix. When the number s of attributes is large, it might be interesting and cheaper to transform the model so as to invert a matrix of order k only.

To find the transformation, we use the following known lemma, which can easily be proved by reference to the properties of an inverse of a partitioned matrix.

Lemma 1 For the classical regression model

$$y = X_1\beta_1 + X_2\beta_2 + \epsilon$$

with $[X_1 X_2]$ of full column rank, the OLS estimator of β_2 may be expressed as:

$$\hat{\beta}_2 = (X_2'M_1X_2)^{-1}X_2'M_1y$$

where $M_1 = I - X_1(X_1'X_1)^{-1}X_1'$. The OSL estimator of β_1 is:

$$\hat{\beta}_1 = (X_1'X_1)^{-1}X_1'y - (X_1'X_1)^{-1}X_1'X_2\hat{\beta}_2.$$

Furthermore, the variance–covariance matrices of these two estimators are given, respectively, by:

$$\Omega_{\hat{\beta}_2} = \sigma^2(X_2'M_1X_2)^{-1}$$

$$\Omega_{\hat{\beta}_1} = \sigma^2\{(X_1'X_1)^{-1} + (X_1'X_1)^{-1}X_1'X_2(X_2'M_1X_2)^{-1}X_2'X_1(X_1'X_1)^{-1}\}.$$

Applying these results to model (1), we obtain directly:

$$\hat{\beta} = (X'M_L X)^{-1}X'M_L y \tag{6}$$

where

$$M_L = I - L(L'L)^{-1}L'. \tag{7}$$

The matrix M_L is idempotent of order n and rank $n-s$. It then follows that $\hat{\beta}_2$ can be obtained by applying OLS to the following transformed model

$$\tilde{y} = \tilde{X}\beta + \tilde{\epsilon} \qquad (8)$$

where $\tilde{y} = M_L y$ and $\tilde{X} = M_L X$.

What does this transformation mean? Let us consider a transformed variable, say $\tilde{y}_i, i = 1, \dots, n$. We may write:

$$\tilde{y}_i = (e_i^n)'\tilde{y} \qquad (9)$$

where e_i^n is the ith elementary vector of order n. We get:

$$\tilde{y}_i = (e_i^n)'M_L y = y_i - (e_i^n)'L(L'L)^{-1}L'y.$$

Let us now assume that observation i possesses attribute j. We then have:

$$(e_i^n)'L = (0\ 0\ \dots\ 1\ \dots\ 0) = (e_j^s),$$

$$(e_i^n)'L(L'L)^{-1}L' = (e_j^s)'(L'L)^{-1}L' = \frac{1}{n_j}(e_j^s)'L' = \frac{1}{n_j}L_j'.$$

The final result is:

$$\tilde{y}_i = y_i - \frac{1}{n_j}L_j'y. \qquad (10)$$

The quantity $(1/n_j)(L_j'y)$ represents *the mean of all observations having the same attribute j*, which we shall denote by the symbol $\bar{y}_j$. The same transformation obviously applies to all quantitative explanatory variables. Therefore, we can write:

$$\tilde{y}_i = y_i - \bar{y}_j \qquad \text{observation } i \text{ with attribute } j$$

$$\tilde{x}_{ir} = x_{ir} - \bar{x}_{jr} \qquad \text{observation } i \text{ with attribute } j. \qquad (11)$$

As an example, if the qualitative variable represents sex, for a male we subtract the mean over all males and for a female we subtract the mean over all females.

For the coefficients of the dummy variables, using Lemma 1, we get:

$$\hat{\alpha} = (L'L)^{-1}L'y - (L'L)^{-1}L'X\hat{\beta} \tag{12}$$

and, for each individual coefficient:

$$\hat{\alpha}_j = y_j - \sum_{r=1}^{k} \bar{x}_{jr}\hat{\beta}_r. \tag{13}$$

The variance–covariance matrix of $\hat{\beta}$ is:

$$\Omega_\beta = \sigma^2(X'M_L X)^{-1} = \sigma^2(\tilde{X}'\tilde{X})^{-1} \tag{14}$$

while that of $\hat{\alpha}$ is

$$\Omega_{\hat{\alpha}} = \sigma^2\{(L'L)^{-1} + (L'L)^{-1}L'X(X'M_L X)^{-1}X'L(L'L)^{-1}\}. \tag{15}$$

For each $\hat{\alpha}_j$ we have the following expression:

$$V(\hat{\alpha}_j) = \sigma^2 \left\{ \frac{1}{n_j} + [\bar{x}_{jr}]'(X'X)^{-1}[\bar{x}_{jr}] \right\} \tag{16}$$

where

$$[\bar{x}_{jr}]' = [\bar{x}_{j1}\bar{x}_{j2}\dots\bar{x}_{jk}].$$

Formula (16) can be simplified to yield:

$$V(\hat{\alpha}_j) = \sigma^2 \frac{1}{n_j} + \sum_{r=1}^{k}\sum_{t=1}^{k} x_{jr}x_{jt} \, \text{cov}(\hat{\beta}_r, \hat{\beta}_t). \tag{17}$$

Finally, an unbiased estimator of σ^2 is provided by

$$\sigma^2 = \frac{\widetilde{SS}}{n - (k + s)} \tag{18}$$

where $\widetilde{SS}$ is the sum of squared residuals of the transformed model. Obviously, $\widetilde{SS}$ is equal to SS, the sum of squared residuals of the untransformed model. The vector $\hat{\epsilon}$ of estimated errors, given by

$$\hat{\epsilon} = M_L (y - X\hat{\beta}) \tag{19}$$

has the two following properties: (a) the sum of all estimated errors is automatically 0 $(S_n' \hat{\epsilon} = S_n' M_L (y - X\hat{\beta}) = S_s' L M_L (y - X\hat{\beta}) = 0)$; and (b) the sum of the estimated errors for all observations having the same attribute is also automatically 0 $(L_j' \hat{\epsilon} = L_j' M_L (y - X\hat{\beta}) = 0)$.

An interesting special case is the so-called case of a single event, in which one attribute is possessed by only one observation. Suppose, for instance, that attribute j is possessed only by individual i. For this individual, the transformation yields:

$$\tilde{y}_i = y_i - \bar{y}_j = y_i - y_i = 0$$

and the same result applies to all transformed explanatory variables. Thus the ith observation disappears. It is as if we delete the ith observation and the jth dummy variable. All results remain rigorously unchanged and the number of degrees of freedom stays the same. Yet, the coefficient α_j is estimable. From (13) we get

$$\hat{\alpha}_j = y_i - \sum_{r=1}^{k} x_{ir}\hat{\beta}_r.$$

Since the $\hat{\beta}_r$ are the same as when deleting one observation and one dummy variable, $\hat{\alpha}_j$ is equal to the prediction error obtained when predicting y_i given the values of the other y_i and the values of x_{ir}. This identity justifies the use of a single dummy to test whether or not an additional observation belongs to the same structural model. We simply have to test the significance of α_j.

Some practical remarks will conclude this review of classical results.

Remark 1 The matrix X must not contain the constant column, S_n, since S_n and L are not linearly independent $(LS_s = S_n)$. It is possible to include S_n in X only if one dummy variable is deleted. The results remain unchanged. Only the coefficient α_j must be interpreted as contrast with respect to the omitted effect.

Remark 2 Computationally, it is advisable to use transformed variables with a standard regression program (without constant term). However, the program does not know that s degrees of freedom were lost owing to the transformation. Therefore all variances and covariances must be corrected by the factor $(n - k)/(n - k - s)$.

Remark 3 Estimation can also be performed using transformed variables and a regression program with constant term. The computer will work with the matrix $[S_n \tilde{X}]$ which is of full rank $k + 1$ (S_n and $\tilde{X}$ being orthogonal). The estimation of the constant term should be 0 (apart from rounding errors). Note, however, that in this case the correction factor is $(n - k - 1)/(n - k - s)$.

III EXTENSION TO MULTIPLE QUALITATIVE VARIABLES

We now consider the case of two qualitative variables, having, respectively, s attributes and t attributes. We construct the $s + t$ dummy variables, $L_1, L_2, \ldots, L_s$ and $T_1, T_2, \ldots, T_t$. The properties of the L_j are those defined in the preceding section, equations (2)–(4), while the analogous properties of the T_j are:

$$T_i'T_j = 0 \qquad\qquad i \neq j \tag{20}$$

$$TS_t = S_n, \qquad\qquad T = [T_1 T_2 \ldots T_t] \tag{21}$$

$$T'T = \text{diag}(m_1, \ldots, m_t) \tag{22}$$

where m_j denotes the number of observations having the attribute associated with T_j. We have:

$$0 < m_j \leqslant n \tag{23}$$

$$\sum_{j=1}^{t} m_j = n. \tag{24}$$

Within each qualitative variable, the dummy variables are mutually orthogonal, but not across qualitative variables. Their interactions are:

$$L_i'T_j = v_{ij} \qquad\qquad i = 1, \ldots, s \quad j = 1, \ldots, t \tag{25}$$

$$L'T = [v_{ij}] = V, \qquad\qquad V \text{ being a } s \times t \text{ matrix} \tag{26}$$

$$\sum_{j=1}^{t} v_{ij} = L_i'(T_1 + \ldots + T_t) = L_i'S_n = n_i \tag{27}$$

$$\sum_{i=1}^{s} v_{ij} = (L_i' + \ldots + L_s') T_j = S_n' T_j = m_j. \tag{28}$$

We see immediately that, even if X does not contain the constant column, it is impossible to include all $s + t$ dummy variables in the regression equation, since the matrix $[L \ \ T]$ cannot be of full column rank. In fact, its $s + t$ columns are linearly dependent as shown below:

$$[L \ \ T] \begin{bmatrix} S_s \\ -S_t \end{bmatrix} = S_n - S_n = 0.$$

It is therefore necessary to eliminate one dummy variable. This can be done in an arbitrary way. However, for symmetry reasons, we prefer to omit one dummy variable for each qualitative variable and to include the constant column. The full model may be specified as follows:

$$\begin{aligned} y &= L_1 \alpha_1 + \ldots + L_{s-1} \alpha_{s-1} + T_1 \gamma_1 + \ldots + T_{t-1} \gamma_{t-1} + S_n \alpha_0 \\ &\quad + X\beta + \epsilon \\ &= L^* \alpha^* + T^* \gamma^* + S_n \alpha_0 + X\beta + \epsilon \end{aligned} \tag{29}$$

The coefficients α_i, $i = 1, \ldots, s-1$, and $\gamma_j, j = 1, \ldots, t-1$ must be interpreted as deviations from the omitted effect (α_0).

Model (29) can be estimated directly by OLS, under the usual classical assumptions. We could also, as in the case of a single qualitative variable, use a transformation that eliminates all dummies including the constant term. To this effect, let us define the following matrix Z:

$$Z = [L^* \ \ T^* \ \ S_n]. \tag{30}$$

The transformed model thus becomes:

$$\tilde{y} = \tilde{X}\beta + \tilde{\epsilon}, \ \ \tilde{y} = M_Z y, \ \ \tilde{X} = M_Z X, \ M_Z = I - Z(Z'Z)^{-1}Z' \tag{31}$$

and the estimator of β is given by:

$$\hat{\beta} = (X'M_Z X)^{-1} X'M_Z y. \tag{32}$$

Unfortunately, the transformation M_Z is relatively complicated and its interpretation does not have the nice simplicity encountered in the case of one single qualitative variable. That is the reason why, except in the important cases discussed in the next section, estimation is best performed on the non-transformed model.

An example will clarify this point. It is desired to test the influence of a drug on patients. Let us suppose that we have a sample of n individuals, males and females, smokers and non-smokers. It is believed that sex and smoking habits play an important role. To test this hypothesis, two qualitative variables are introduced in the regression equation, one for sex and one for smoking habits. The four dummy variables are: L_1 for males, L_2 for females, T_1 for smokers and T_2 for non-smokers. (It is the case $s = t = 2$). The characteristics of the individuals, in agreement with our former definitions, are summarized in table 17.1.

TABLE 17.1

	Smokers	Non-smokers	
Males	v_{11}	v_{12}	n_1
Females	v_{21}	v_{22}	n_2
	m_1	m_2	n

Given the data, the transformation may be represented in a number of ways. An interesting representation is the following:

$$\tilde{y}_i = y_i - d^{-1}a_{11}\bar{y}_{L_1} - d^{-1}a_{12}\bar{y}_{T_1} + d^{-1}a_{13}\bar{y} \quad \text{if male and smoker}$$

$$= y_i - d^{-1}a_{21}\bar{y}_{L_1} - d^{-1}a_{22}\bar{y}_{T_2} + d^{-1}a_{23}\bar{y} \quad \text{if male and non-smoker}$$

$$= y_i - d^{-1}a_{31}\bar{y}_{L_2} - d^{-1}a_{32}\bar{y}_{T_1} + d^{-1}a_{33}\bar{y} \quad \text{if female and smoker}$$

$$= y_i - d^{-1}a_{41}\bar{y}_{L_2} - d^{-1}a_{42}\bar{y}_{T_2} + d^{-1}a_{43}\bar{y} \quad \text{if female and non-smoker}$$

where $\bar{y}_{L_1}, \bar{y}_{L_2}, \bar{y}_{T_1}, \bar{y}_{T_2}$ stand for, respectively, the means over males, females, smokers and non-smokers, $\bar{y}$ is the overall mean,

$$d = |Z'Z| = v_{11}v_{21}m_2 + v_{12}v_{22}m_1 = v_{11}v_{22}(v_{12} + v_{21})$$
$$+ v_{12}v_{21}(v_{11} + v_{22})$$

and the coefficients a_{ij} are as in table 17.2.

TABLE 17.2

Coefficients a_{ij}		
$v_{21}m_2n_1$	$v_{12}n_2m_1$	$v_{12}v_{21}n$
$v_{22}m_1n_1$	$v_{11}n_2m_2$	$v_{11}v_{22}n$
$v_{11}m_2n_2$	$v_{22}n_1m_1$	$v_{11}v_{22}n$
$v_{12}m_1n_2$	$v_{21}n_1m_2$	$v_{12}v_{21}n$

It is absolutely clear that, although the transformation has some intuitive appeal, the computation of the coefficients a_{ij} is too laborious to make it operationally interesting. However, there are important situations in which the transformation becomes extremely simple (and therefore operational). Such is the case, for instance, when all quantities v_{ij} are the same (i.e. when $v_{ij} = \frac{1}{4}n$; $m_i = n_j = \frac{1}{2}n$), since $d^{-1}a_{ij} = 1$ for all i and j. In this case, the variables may be transformed simply by *subtracting for each individual the two means for the two attributes he possesses and by adding the overall mean*. The reader may verify that the same result obtains whenever $v_{11}v_{22} = v_{12}v_{21}$.

Are there other situations yielding a simple solution in the general two-qualitative-variables model with an arbitrary number of attributes? This is the question answered in the next section.

IV NECESSARY AND SUFFICIENT CONDITION FOR THE EXISTENCE OF A SIMPLE SOLUTION

We consider again model (29) of the preceding section, in which two qualitative variables appear, with, respectively, s and t attributes. *By simple solution* we mean that the transformed variables are obtained by subtracting from each quantitative variable at the ith observation $(i = 1, \ldots, n)$ the two means over the two attributes possessed by the ith observation and by adding the overall mean. The main result is contained in the following theorem.

Theorem 1 Model (29) has a simple solution if and only if

$$L'T = \frac{1}{n} NM'$$

where

$$N' = [n_1 n_2 \ldots n_s] \quad \text{and} \quad M' = [m_1 m_2 \ldots m_t].$$

The necessary and sufficient condition expressed in the above theorem may also be written $v_{ij} = (1/n)(n_i m_j)$, all i and j. Now, since v_{ij} is a non-negative integer, while n_i, m_j and n are strictly positive integers, two corollaries become evident.

> *Corollary 1*   If (at least) one v_{ij} is zero, there is no simple solution.
> *Corollary 2*   If n is prime, there is no simple solution.

To prove the theorem, let us note that the transformation matrix M_Z is invariant to a non-singular transformation of its columns. We can therefore work with $Z = [L \quad T^*]$. Using the properties of partitioned matrices, we easily can get the following expression:

$$M_Z = M_L - M_L T^* (T^{*'} M_L T^*)^{-1} T^{*'} M_L. \tag{33}$$

On the other hand, the simple transformation is given by the following matrix Q:

$$Q = I - L(L'L)^{-1} L' - T(T'T)^{-1} T' + \frac{1}{n} S_n S_n'$$
$$= M_L - T(T'T)^{-1} T' + \frac{1}{n} S_n S_n'. \tag{34}$$

For the two transformations to be identical, we must have:

$$M_L T^* (T^{*'} M_L T^*)^{-1} T^{*'} M_L = T(T'T)^{-1} T' - \frac{1}{n} S_n S_n'. \tag{35}$$

We are now in a position to prove the theorem.

Necessity Suppose (35) is true. Pre-multiply by L' and post-multiply by T (noting that $L'M_L = 0$). This yields

$$0 = L'T - \frac{1}{n} L'S_n S_n' T.$$

Since $L'S_n = N$ and $S_n' T = M'$, we get $L'T = (1/n)(NM')$.

Sufficiency We now assume that the condition $L'T = (1/n)(NM')$ is true and verify condition (35). Let us call M^* the vector M without its last element. We obviously have $L'T^* = (1/n)(NM^{*\prime})$. We now compute the quantity $T^{*\prime}M_L T^*$:

$$T^{*\prime}M_L T^* = T^{*\prime}T^* - T^{*\prime}L(L'L)^{-1}L'T^*$$

$$= T^{*\prime}T^* - \frac{1}{n^2} M^* N'(L'L)^{-1} NM^{*\prime}$$

$$= T^{*\prime}T^* - \frac{1}{n} M^* M^{*\prime}$$

where we use the fact that $N'(L'L)^{-1}N = S_s'N = n$. The inverse of the above matrix, using results concerning the inverse of a sum of matrices (see, for instance, Balestra, 1978, p. 12), is given by:

$$(T^{*\prime}M_L T^*)^{-1} = (T^{*\prime}T^*)^{-1} + (T^{*\prime}T^*)^{-1}M^*$$

$$\times \left\{ 1 - M^{*\prime}(T^{*\prime}T^*)^{-1}M^* \frac{1}{n} \right\}^{-1} M^{*\prime}(T^{*\prime}T^*)^{-1} \frac{1}{n}$$

$$= (T^{*\prime}T^*)^{-1} + \frac{1}{m_t} S_{t-1} S_{t-1}'$$

owing to the fact that $(T^{*\prime}T^*)^{-1}M^* = S_{t-1}$ and $M^{*\prime}S_{t-1} = n - m_t$.
We next compute the following quantity:

$$T^*(T^{*\prime}M_L T^*)^{-1}T^{*\prime} = T^*(T^{*\prime}T^*)^{-1}T^{*\prime} + \frac{1}{m_t} T^*S_{t-1} S_{t-1}' T^{*\prime}$$

$$= T^*(T^{*\prime}T^*)^{-1}T^{*\prime} + \frac{1}{m_t}(S_n - T_t)(S_n - T_t)'$$

$$= T^*(T^{*\prime}T^*)^{-1}T^{*\prime} + \frac{1}{m_t}T_tT_t' - \frac{1}{m_t}T_sS_n'$$

$$- \frac{1}{m_t}S_nT_t' + \frac{1}{m_t}S_nS_n'$$

$$= T(T'T)^{-1}T' - \frac{1}{m_t}T_tS_n' - \frac{1}{m_t}S_nT_t'$$

$$+ \frac{1}{m_t}S_nS_n'.$$

Since $M_L S_n = 0$, we finally get:

$$M_L T^*(T^{*\prime}M_L T^*)^{-1}T^{*\prime}M_L = M_L T(T'T)^{-1}T'M_L$$

We now only have to show that the right-hand side of the above expression is equal to the right-hand side of (35), when $L'T = (1/n)(NM')$. To do this, let us note first that:

$$M_L T = T - L(L'L)^{-1}L'T = T - \frac{1}{n}L(L'L)^{-1}NM'$$

$$= T - \frac{1}{n}LS_sM' = T - \frac{1}{n}S_nM'.$$

This leads us to the following developments:

$$M_L T(T'T)^{-1}T'M_L = \left(T - \frac{1}{n}S_nM'\right)(T'T)^{-1}\left(T' - \frac{1}{n}MS_n'\right)$$

$$= T(T'T)^{-1}T' - \frac{1}{n}S_nM'(T'T)^{-1}T'$$

$$- \frac{1}{n}T(T'T)^{-1}MS_n' + \frac{1}{n^2}S_nM'(T'T)^{-1}MS_n'$$

$$= T(T'T)^{-1}T' - \frac{1}{n}S_n S_t' T' - \frac{1}{n}TS_t S_n'$$

$$+ \frac{1}{n^2}S_n S_t' MS_n'$$

$$= T(T'T)^{-1}T' - \frac{1}{n}S_n S_n'.$$

Hence, condition (35) is verified and the proof is complete.

Applications We now turn to some applications.

In the 2×2 example given in section III, some easy manipulation gives (replacing n_1 by $v_{11} + v_{21}$, etc.):

$$\frac{1}{n}NM' = \frac{1}{n}\begin{bmatrix} n_1 m_1 & n_1 m_2 \\ n_2 m_1 & n_2 m_2 \end{bmatrix} = \begin{bmatrix} v_{11} & v_{12} \\ v_{21} & v_{22} \end{bmatrix} + \frac{v_{11}v_{22} - v_{12}v_{21}}{n}\begin{bmatrix} -1 & 1 \\ 1 & -1 \end{bmatrix}.$$

For this matrix to be equal to V, it is necessary and sufficient that $v_{11}v_{22} = v_{12}v_{21}$, which is the condition given at the end of section III.

A more interesting application arises in connection with individual/ time effect models. Let us assume that we have observations on s individuals at t periods of time. The total number of observations is $n = st$. Without loss of generality, we shall assume that observations are ordered by taking first the t observations of the first individual, then the t observations of the second individual, and so on. If individual and time effects are thought to be important, we may wish to introduce in the regression equation two sets of dummy variables, one for the individual effect and one for the time effect. The full set of dummy variables may be represented in the following way, using the Kronecker product operator:

Individual dummies: $L = I_s \otimes S_t$

Time dummies: $T = S_s \otimes I_t$

The following quantities may now be computed:

$$L'T = (I_s \otimes S_t')(S_s \otimes I_t) = S_s \otimes S_t' = S_s S_t'$$

$$N = VS_t = L'TS_t = S_s S_t' S_t = tS_s$$

$$M' = S_s'V = S_s'L'T = S_s'S_s S_t' = sS_t'$$

Therefore, the condition of Theorem 1 is satisfied. An easy solution exists for this problem. The simple transformation to be used is:

$$\tilde{y}_{ij} = y_{ij} - \bar{y}_{i.} - \bar{y}_{.j} + \bar{y}_{..}$$

where $\bar{y}_{i.}$ is the mean of the ith individual, $\bar{y}_{.j}$ is the mean of the jth period and $\bar{y}_{..}$ is the overall mean.

V   QUALITATIVE VARIABLES IN GENERALIZED REGRESSION

In section II we saw that in a classical regression problem with one qualitative variable having s attributes, it was possible to apply OLS to a transformed model in which all dummy variables are omitted. Furthermore, the transformation is exceedingly simple.

Does this procedure carry over to the case of generalized regression? In other terms, is it possible, before applying generalized least squares (GLS), to use the simple transformation given in section II? This is the question we seek to answer in the present section.

Formally, we study the following model:

$$y = L\alpha + X\beta + \epsilon \tag{36}$$

where the symbols are the same as in (1). In the present context, however, the residuals are assumed to have the following properties:

$$E(\epsilon) = 0 \qquad E(\epsilon\epsilon') = \Omega_\epsilon \tag{37}$$

Ω_ϵ being a positive definite matrix.

The transformation M_L leads us to the following transformed model:

$$\tilde{y} = \tilde{X}\beta + \tilde{\epsilon} \tag{38}$$

where $\tilde{y} = M_L y$ and $\tilde{X} = M_L X$. (Obviously, as in classical regression, the vector ϵ is also transformed. But one proceeds as if $\tilde{\epsilon}$ has the same properties as ϵ.)

The question raised at the beginning of the section may now be put in the following terms: under what condition is the GLS estimator of β in the transformed model (38) identical to the GLS estimator of β in the true model (36)? The answer is contained in

Theorem 2. We shall call $\hat{\beta}$ the GLS estimator in (36) and β^* the GLS estimator in (38).

Theorem 2 The necessary and sufficient condition for β^* to be identical to $\hat{\beta}$ is

$$\Omega_\epsilon^{-1} L = LA$$

for any arbitrary non-singular matrix A.

The above condition is equivalent to the following one: there exist s orthogonal eigenvectors of Ω_ϵ^{-1} which form a basis for the space spanned by the s columns of L. For reasons of simplicity, we prefer the conditions given in the theorem.

To prove the above theorem, we must compute $\hat{\beta}$ and β^*. Given that Ω_ϵ is positive definite, there exists a non-singular matrix P such that $P\Omega_\epsilon P' = I$, or, equivalently, $P'P = \Omega_\epsilon^{-1}$. Let us now apply the transformation P to model (36). We obtain:

$$Py = PL\alpha + PX\beta + P\epsilon. \tag{39}$$

The transformed vector of residuals, $P\epsilon$, has a scalar variance–covariance matrix and therefore OLS are appropriate. Using Lemma 1 we get directly:

$$\hat{\beta} = (X'P'M_{PL}PX)^{-1}X'P'M_{PL}Py \tag{40}$$

where

$$M_{PL} = I - PL(L'P'PL)^{-1}L'P' = I - PL(L'\Omega_\epsilon^{-1}L)^{-1}L'P'. \tag{41}$$

On the other hand, estimation of model (38) by GLS (using the same variance–covariance matrix Ω_ϵ) yields:

$$\beta^* = (\tilde{X}'\Omega_\epsilon^{-1}\tilde{X})^{-1}\tilde{X}'\Omega_\epsilon^{-1}\tilde{y}$$

$$= (X'M_L\Omega_\epsilon^{-1}M_LX)^{-1}X'M_L\Omega_\epsilon^{-1}M_Ly. \tag{42}$$

For $\hat{\beta}$ to be equal to β^* for any design matrix X, the case must be that

$$P'M_{PL}P = M_L\Omega_\epsilon^{-1}M_L. \tag{43}$$

Now, M_{PL} is idempotent and such that $M_{PL}PL = 0$. Therefore, after some easy computation, we obtain:

$$P'M_{PL}P = M_L(P'M_{PL}P)M_L$$

$$= M_L\{P'P - P'PL(L'\Omega_\epsilon^{-1}L)^{-1}L'P'P\}M_L$$

$$= M_L\{\Omega_\epsilon^{-1} - \Omega_\epsilon^{-1}L(L'\Omega_\epsilon^{-1}L)^{-1}L'\Omega_\epsilon^{-1}\}M_L$$

$$= M_L\Omega_\epsilon^{-1}M_L - M_L\Omega_\epsilon^{-1}L(L'\Omega_\epsilon^{-1}L)^{-1}L'\Omega_\epsilon^{-1}M_L. \tag{44}$$

Condition (43) may now be written:

$$M_L\Omega_\epsilon^{-1}L(L'\Omega_\epsilon^{-1}L)^{-1}L'\Omega_\epsilon^{-1}M_L = 0. \tag{45}$$

Since the matrix $L'\Omega_\epsilon L$ is positive definite, the above equation is satisfied if and only if

$$M_L\Omega_\epsilon^{-1}L = 0. \tag{46}$$

The matrix M_L is idempotent of rank $n-s$. It follows that the homogeneous system $M_L h = 0$ has exactly s linearly independent solutions. Now, since $M_L L = 0$, L being of rank s, the s columns of L represent s linearly independent solutions. Any other solution can be expressed as a linear combination of the columns of L. As a result, condition (46) is verified if and only if the s columns of $\Omega_\epsilon^{-1}L$ are s independent linear combinations of the columns of L; that is, if and only if

$$\Omega_\epsilon^{-1}L = LA \tag{47}$$

for any non-singular matrix A. This completes the proof of Theorem 2.

Whenever condition (47) is satisfied, the variance–covariance matrix of β^* is given directly by

$$\Omega_\beta^* = (\tilde{X}'\Omega_\epsilon^{-1}\tilde{X})^{-1}. \tag{48}$$

For the coefficients of the dummy variables, using again Lemma 1 and noting that $(L'\Omega_\epsilon^{-1}L)^{-1}L'\Omega_\epsilon^{-1} = (L'L)^{-1}L'$, we get

$$\hat{\alpha} = (L'L)^{-1}L'(y - X\beta^*) \tag{49}$$

and, for each individual coefficient, we obtain

$$\hat{\alpha}_j = y_j - \sum_{r=1}^{k} x_{jr}\beta_r^*. \tag{50}$$

The variance–covariance matrix of $\hat{\alpha}$ is given by

$$\Omega_{\hat{\alpha}} = (L'\Omega_\epsilon^{-1}L)^{-1} + (L'\Omega_\epsilon^{-1}L)^{-1}L'\Omega_\epsilon^{-1}X(X'P'M_{PL}PX)^{-1}$$

$$\times X'\Omega_\epsilon^{-1}L(L'\Omega_\epsilon^{-1}L)^{-1}$$

$$= (L'\Omega_\epsilon^{-1}L)^{-1} + (L'L)^{-1}L'X(X'\Omega_\epsilon^{-1}X)^{-1}X'L(L'L)^{-1}$$

$$= A^{-1}(L'L)^{-1} + (L'L)^{-1}L'X\Omega_\beta^*XL(L'L)^{-1}. \tag{51}$$

Again, for each individual coefficient, the variance is equal to

$$V(\hat{\alpha}_j) = \frac{1}{n_j}a^{jj} + \sum_{r=1}^{k}\sum_{r'=1}^{k} x_{jr}x_{jr'}\,\text{cov}(\beta_r^*\beta_r^*) \tag{52}$$

where a^{jj} is the element in position (j, j) of A^{-1}.

An interesting application of the above result is found in connection with Zellner's 'seemingly unrelated regression problem' (cf. Zellner, 1962). In this problem, s regression equations are considered, each having t observations. Assuming that each regression contains the constant term, for the ith regression we write:

$$y_i = S_t\alpha_i + X_i\beta_i + \epsilon_i \tag{53}$$

where S_t is the sum-vector of order t, y_i is the t-dimensional vector of observations on the dependent variable, X_i is a $t \times k_i$ matrix of observations concerning the explicative variables and ϵ_i is a random vector whose properties are specified below.

The full model may be written as

$$\begin{bmatrix} y_1 \\ y_2 \\ \vdots \\ y_s \end{bmatrix} = \begin{bmatrix} S_t & & & \\ & S_t & & \\ & & \ddots & \\ & & & S_t \end{bmatrix}\begin{bmatrix} \alpha_1 \\ \alpha_2 \\ \vdots \\ \alpha_s \end{bmatrix} + \begin{bmatrix} X_1 & & & \\ & X_2 & & \\ & & \ddots & \\ & & & X_s \end{bmatrix}\begin{bmatrix} \beta_1 \\ \beta_2 \\ \vdots \\ \beta_s \end{bmatrix} + \begin{bmatrix} \epsilon_1 \\ \epsilon_2 \\ \vdots \\ \epsilon_s \end{bmatrix} \tag{54}$$

or, in more compact form, as

$$y = L\alpha + X\beta + \epsilon. \tag{55}$$

We observe that $L = I_s \otimes S_t$ represents s dummy variables. The vector α is the vector of coefficients associated with each individual constant term. In this type of problem, the random vector ϵ is characterized by a zero mean, $E(\epsilon) = 0$, and the following variance–covariance matrix:

$$\Omega_\epsilon = \Omega \otimes I_t \tag{56}$$

where $\Omega = [\sigma_{ij}]$ is a positive definite matrix of order s.

Let us compute $\Omega_\epsilon^{-1} L$:

$$\Omega_\epsilon^{-1} L = (\Omega^{-1} \otimes I_t)(I_s \otimes S_t) = (\Omega^{-1} \otimes S_t)$$

$$= (I_s \otimes S_t)(\Omega^{-1} \otimes I) = (I_s \otimes S_t)\Omega^{-1} = L\Omega^{-1}.$$

Hence, the condition of Theorem 2 is satisfied with $A = \Omega^{-1}$. This means that in Zellner's problem, the GLS estimator may be obtained simply by eliminating all individual constant terms and by expressing all other variables as deviations from their respective individual means.

It is interesting to note that, in order to establish Theorem 2, we did not use the particular properties of the matrix L. Hence, the result is true in general for any matrix L, as long as the matrix $[L \ \ X]$ is of full rank $s + k$. This observation allows us to extend the result of Theorem 2 to the case of two qualitative variables, having, respectively s and t attributes.

We consider again model (29), with $E(\epsilon\epsilon') = \Omega_\epsilon$, and ask ourselves the following question: is it possible, before applying GLS, to transform the model using the transformation matrix Q defined in (34)? The answer is given in the following theorem.

Theorem 3 For model (29), with $E(\epsilon\epsilon') = \Omega_\epsilon$, to possess a simple solution by GLS, it is necessary and sufficient that:

$$Q\Omega_\epsilon^{-1} Z = 0.$$

The proof of the above theorem is analogous to that of Theorem 2. It suffices to replace L by Z and M_L by Q. For practical purposes, instead of using the condition given in Theorem 2, it might be more useful to work with the following two equivalent conditions:

$$L'T = \frac{1}{n}NM' \tag{i}$$

and

$$\Omega_\epsilon^{-1}Z = ZB \tag{ii}$$

for B arbitrary but non-singular.

In conclusion, it might be stressed that the results established in the above three theorems lead to very simple computational procedures and therefore extend the bag of tools available to the applied researcher. Most importantly, however, these results shed some new light on the role played by multiple qualitative explanatory variables in regression analysis.

REFERENCES

Balestra, P. (1978) *Determinant and Inverse of a Sum of Matrices with Applications in Economics and Statistics*, IME, Working Document no. 24, University of Dijon.
Zellner, A. (1962) 'An Efficient Method of Estimating Seemingly Unrelated Regressions and Tests for Aggregation Bias', *Journal of the American Statistical Association*, pp. 348–68.

18

Filtering of Time Series by Moving Averages

I MOVING AVERAGES BY LEAST SQUARES

Let u_t be a time series with distribution function F_{u_t} and

$$u_t = \mu + e_t \qquad t = 1, \ldots, T$$

$$E(u_t) = \mu \qquad E(e_t) = 0 \qquad\qquad e_t \sim N(0, \sigma^2). \qquad (1)$$

$$V(u_t) = \sigma^2 I \qquad V(e_t) = \sigma^2$$

We may wish to filter the series by a mathematical expression such as a polynomial; then, instead of dealing with the series as a whole, let us take the first n terms, fit a mathematical function $G_s(a_j)$ to them, and use their middle value as the first term of the filtered series. The operation is then a simple moving average procedure with successive terms of $\hat{u}_t$ each being an average of n terms of u_t; e.g.

$$\hat{u}_t = f(u_{t-m}, \ldots, u_t, \ldots, u_{t+m})$$

$$\hat{u}_{t+1} = f(u_{t+1-m}, \ldots, u_{t+1}, \ldots, u_{t+1+m}).$$

It is convenient to take n to be odd, since u_i and $\hat{u}_t$ will then match along the time axis.

For $n = 2m + 1$ consider any n terms of the original series u_{t+s} for $s = -m, \ldots, m$ and fit the function $G_s(a_j)\, j = 0, \ldots, p$ where $a_0, \ldots, a_p$ are the $q = p + 1$ coefficients to be determined by least

* I would like to thank R. W. Bacon for his comments on an earlier version of the paper. Responsibility for any errors is however my own.

squares (cf. Kendall and Stuart, vol. 3, 1976, pp. 380–3). We then minimize the sum of squares of the residuals

$$S = \sum_{s=-m}^{m} \{u_{t+s} - G_s(a_j)\}^2$$

by differentiating S with respect to $a_0, \ldots, a_p$ and equating to zero:

$$\frac{\partial S}{\partial aj} = -2 \sum_{s=-m}^{m} \{u_{t+s} - G_s(a_j)\} \frac{\partial G_s(a_j)}{\partial a_j} \qquad \begin{array}{l} j = 0, \ldots, p \\ t = m+1, \ldots, T-m \end{array}$$

$$(2)$$

II COMPUTATION OF THE WEIGHTS

Let us consider our filter to be a polynomial; e.g.,

$$G_s(a_p) = a_0 + a_1 s + \ldots + a_p s^p.$$

Then, by equating (2) to 0, we have to solve a set of equations in q unknowns for $j = 0, \ldots, p$:

$$\sum_{s=-m}^{m} (t+s)^j u_{t+s} = a_0 \sum_{s=-m}^{m} (t+s)^j + a_1 \sum_{s=-m}^{m} (t+s)^{j+1}$$

$$+ \ldots + a_p \sum_{s=-m}^{m} (t+s)^{j+p}. \qquad (3)$$

Since in (3) t is a scalar we might as well leave it out without loss of clarity. We can write (3) in matrix form as

$$Du = Qa$$

where

$$D = \atop (q, n) \begin{bmatrix} -m^0 & -(m-1)^0 & \ldots & (m-1)^0 & m^0 \\ -m^1 & -(m-1)^1 & \ldots & (m-1)^1 & m^1 \\ \vdots & \vdots & & \vdots & \vdots \\ -m^p & -(m-1)^p & \ldots & (m-1)^p & m^p \end{bmatrix}$$

$$
\begin{array}{l}
Q = \\
(q,q)
\end{array}
\begin{bmatrix}
\displaystyle\sum_{s=-m}^{m} s^0 & \displaystyle\sum_{s=-m}^{m} s^1 & \cdots & \displaystyle\sum_{s=-m}^{m} s^p \\
\vdots & \vdots & & \vdots \\
\displaystyle\sum_{s=-m}^{m} s^p & \displaystyle\sum_{s=-m}^{m} s^{p+1} & \cdots & \displaystyle\sum_{s=-m}^{m} s^{p+p}
\end{bmatrix}
$$

$$
\begin{array}{l}
u' = (u_{-m}, u_{-(m-1)}, \ldots, u_{m-1}, u_m) \\
(n)
\end{array}
$$

$$
\begin{array}{l}
a' = (a_0, a_1, \ldots, a_p). \\
(q)
\end{array}
$$

Hence

$$
\hat{a} = Q^{-1}Du \quad \text{for} \quad |Q| \neq 0
$$

$$
\hat{a} = Ru \quad \text{where} \quad R = Q^{-1}D. \tag{4}
$$

By substituting $\hat{a}$ back into $G_s(a_j)$ we get a matrix $C(n, n)$ of weights that are independent of the original series u_t. From (4) we have

$$
\begin{bmatrix}
\hat{a}_0 \\
\hat{a}_1 \\
\vdots \\
\hat{a}_p
\end{bmatrix}
=
\begin{bmatrix}
r_{11} & r_{12} & \cdots & r_{1n} \\
r_{21} & r_{22} & \cdots & r_{2n} \\
\vdots & \vdots & \vdots & \vdots \\
r_{p1} & r_{p2} & \cdots & r_{pn}
\end{bmatrix}
\begin{bmatrix}
u_{-m} \\
u_{-(m-1)} \\
\vdots \\
u_m
\end{bmatrix}.
$$

Then, for any p, $n = 2m + 1$ and $G_s(a_j)$,

$$
\begin{aligned}
\hat{u}_s &= \hat{a}_0 s^0 + \hat{a}_1 s^1 + \ldots + \hat{a}_p s^p \\
&= (r_{11}u_{-m} + r_{12}u_{-(m-1)} + \ldots + r_{1n}u_m)\, s^0 \\
&\quad + \ldots + (r_{p1}u_{-m} + r_{p2}u_{-(m-1)} + \ldots + r_{pn}u_m)\, s^p \\
&= c_{s,-m} u_{-m} + c_{s,-(m-1)} u_{-(m-1)} + \ldots + c_{s,m} u_m
\end{aligned}
$$

where

$$c_{s,-m} = r_{11}s^0 + r_{21}s^1 + \ldots + r_{p1}s^p$$

$$c_{s,m} = r_{1n}s^0 + r_{2n}s^1 + \ldots + r_{pn}s^p$$

By varying s from $-m$ to m a complete set of weights are generated which are only dependent on n, the length of the filter and $G_s(a_j)$, the filter itself.

For $s = -m, \ldots, 0, \ldots, m$,

$C_{0,s}$ are the central weights $t = m + 1, \ldots, T - m$

$\left.\begin{array}{c} C_{-m,s} \\ \vdots \\ C_{m,s} \end{array}\right\}$ are the off-central weights

$t = 1, \ldots, m$

$t = T - m + 1, \ldots, T.$

In matrix terms,

$$\begin{matrix} C = \\ (n,n) \end{matrix}$$

$$\begin{bmatrix} C_{-m,-m} & C_{-m,-(m-1)} & \cdots & C_{-m,(m-1)} & C_{-m,m} \\ C_{-(m-1),-m} & C_{-(m-1),-(m-1)} & \cdots & C_{-(m-1),(m-1)} & C_{-(m-1),m} \\ \vdots & \vdots & & \vdots & \vdots \\ C_{0,-m} & C_{0,-(m-1)} & \cdots & C_{0,(m-1)} & C_{0,m} \\ \vdots & \vdots & & \vdots & \vdots \\ C_{m-1,-m} & C_{m-1,-(m-1)} & \cdots & C_{m-1,m-1} & C_{m-1,m} \\ C_{m,-m} & C_{m,-(m-1)} & \cdots & C_{m,m-1} & C_{m,m} \end{bmatrix}$$

$$(5)$$

Then $\hat{u}_t = Cu_t$, or

$$
\begin{bmatrix} \hat{u}_1 \\ \vdots \\ \hat{u}_m \\ \hline \hat{u}_{m+1} \\ \vdots \\ \hat{u}_{T-m} \\ \hline \hat{u}_{T-m+1} \\ \vdots \\ \hat{u}_T \end{bmatrix}
\begin{matrix} = \\ \\ \\ = \\ \\ \\ = \\ \\ \end{matrix}
\begin{bmatrix} C_{-m,-m} & \cdots & C_{-m,m} \\ \vdots & & \vdots \\ C_{-1,-m} & \cdots & C_{-1,m} \\ \hline C_{0,-m} & \cdots & C_{0,m} \\ \vdots & & \vdots \\ C_{0,-m} & \cdots & C_{0,m} \\ \hline C_{1,-m} & \cdots & C_{1,m} \\ \vdots & & \vdots \\ C_{m,-m} & \cdots & C_{m,m} \end{bmatrix}
\begin{bmatrix} u_1 \\ \vdots \\ u_m \\ \hline u_{m+1} \\ \vdots \\ u_{T-m} \\ \hline u_{T-m+1} \\ \vdots \\ u_T \end{bmatrix}
$$

The smoothed series $\hat{u}_t$ has the same sequence of expected values as u_t but with a smaller variance.

$$
\hat{u}_t = \sum_{s=-m}^{m} \mu c_s + \sum_{s=-m}^{m} e_{t+s} c_s
$$

$$
E(\hat{u}_t) = \mu; \quad \text{hence} \quad \sum_{s=-m}^{m} c_s = 1 \tag{6}
$$

$$
V(\hat{u}_t) = E\{\hat{u}_t - E(\hat{u}_t)\}^2 = \sigma^2 \sum_{s=-m}^{m} c_s^2.
$$

However successive terms of $\hat{u}_t$ are correlated,

$$
E(\hat{u}_t \hat{u}_{t+h}') = \sum_{s=-m}^{m} \sum_{r=-m}^{m} c_s c_r E(u_{t+s} u_{t+h+r})
$$

$$
= \sigma^2 \sum_{s=-m+h}^{m} c_s c_{s-h} \qquad h = 0, \ldots, n
$$

$$
= 0 \qquad h = n+1, \ldots, T
$$

$V(T, T) = E(\hat{u}_t \hat{u}'_{t+h})$ is a positive–definite matrix partitioned into four sub-matrices, $V_1(n, n)$, $V_2(T - n, T - n)$, $V_{1,2}(n, T - n)$, and $V_{2,1}(T - n, n)$, as follows:

$$
\begin{bmatrix}
\sum_{s=1}^{n} c_s^2 \sum_{s=1}^{n-1} c_s c_{s+1} & \cdots & \sum_{s=1}^{1} c_s c_{s+n-1} & & 0 \\[2ex]
\sum_{s=1}^{n-1} c_s c_{s+1} \sum_{s=1}^{n} c_s^2 & \cdots & \sum_{s=1}^{2} c_s c_{s+n-2} & & \\[2ex]
\vdots & & \vdots & & \\[2ex]
\sum_{s=1}^{1} c_s c_{s+n-1} & \cdots & \sum_{s=1}^{1} c_s^2 & & \\[2ex]
\hline
& & & \sum_{s=1}^{n} c_s^2 & 0 \\[2ex]
& 0 & & & \\[2ex]
& & & 0 & \sum_{s=1}^{n} c_s^2
\end{bmatrix}
$$

III MINIMUM VARIANCE FILTER

For a given set of weights c's we look for an optimum length, if it exists, with some desirable properties. The obvious choice for our investigation is the Toeplitz matrix V. It is convenient, for later comparison, to consider the standardized covariance matrix P:

$$
P = V/\sigma^2 = \begin{bmatrix} P_n & 0 \\ \hline 0 & I_{T-n} \end{bmatrix}.
$$

Let us first notice that

$$
V(\hat{u}_t) = \sigma^2 \sum_{s=-m}^{m} c_s^2 \tag{7a}
$$

$$
\det P = |P| \tag{7b}
$$

Euclidean norm of $P \parallel P \parallel = \left(\sum_i \sum_j p_{ij}^2 \right)^{1/2}$ (7c)

are all decreasing monotonically, since by definition the variance (7a) decreases monotonically as the length n increases and (7b) and (7c) are both functions of (7a).

Next, we consider whether P contains all the 'information' needed for our purpose. For an arbitrary vector c and a symmetric matrix P^{-1} such that $c'u = 1$ where u is the unitary vector, we can write c as follows:

$$c' = qu'P^{-1} + d'$$ (8)

where $q = (u'P^{-1}u)^{-1}$ and

$$d'u = 0$$ (9)

since $c'u = qu'P^{-1}u + d'u = 1$. Then let us consider the quadratic form $c'Pc$. From (8),

$$c'Pc = (qu'P^{-1} + d')P(d + P^{-1}uq')$$

$$= qu'd + qu'P^{-1}uq' + d'Pd + d'uq'$$

$$= q' + d'Pd$$

from (9). Hence,

$$c'Pc = (u'P^{-1}u) + d'Pd$$

which shows the relationship between c, P and d; furthermore,

$$u'P^{-1}u = (c'Pc - d'Pd)^{-1}.$$

If $c = $ weights, then only the matrix P is needed for further analysis.

IV TEST FOR MINIMUM VARIANCE

Let us consider the quadratic forms

$$x'Px = x' \left[\begin{array}{c|c} P_n & 0 \\ \hline 0 & P_{T-n} \end{array} \right] x$$

$$x'Ix = x' \left[\begin{array}{c|c} I_n & 0 \\ \hline 0 & I_{T-n} \end{array} \right]$$

or

$$x'Px = x'P_n x + x'I_{T-n}x \qquad \text{since } P_{T-n} = I_{T-n}$$

$$x'Ix = x'I_n x + x'I_{T-n}x.$$

Then $g = x'P_n x / x'I_n x$ is our test for minimum variance. If x' denotes the radius vector, running coordinates $(x_1, \ldots, x_n)$, and if a matrix P^{-1} is positive-definite, then

$$x'Px = 1$$

is the equation of an ellipsoid with centre $0'$ and semi-axes equal to the square roots of the characteristic roots of P^{-1}. Since the equation of the ellipsoid is

$$x_1^2/a_1^2 + x_2^2/a_2^2 + x_3^2/a_3^2 = 1 \tag{10}$$

and the given quadratic form is $x'Px$, let us make an orthogonal transformation $x = Qy$ where Q is made up of an orthonormal set of eigenvectors for P; then

$$y'Q'PQy = y'Dy = \sum_{j=1}^{n} (\lambda_j y_j^2).$$

Conversely,

$$y'D^{-1}y = \sum_{j=1}^{n} (y_j^2/\lambda_j)$$

which implies that the semi-axes are $a_j = (\lambda_j)^{1/2}$ from (10). For $n > 3$ we have an hyper-ellipsoid whose volume is ($n =$ odd) (cf. Courant and John, 1976, vol. 2, pp. 454, 455).

$$V_n = 2a_n V_{n-1} \int_0^{\Pi/2} (\cos^n x) \, dx$$

$$= (a_1 a_2 \ldots a_n \Pi^{n/2})/\Gamma(n + 2/2).$$

But

$$\Gamma(n + 2/2) = \Gamma(2m + 1 + 2/2) = \Gamma(m + 1/2)$$

$$= 1.3.5 \ldots (2m - 1)/2^m \, \Gamma(1/2)$$

and

$$\Gamma(1/2) = \Pi^{1/2}.$$

From (7) we already know that in order to get some results we have to look at a subset of P: the obvious choice is P_n. After deriving the normalized eigenvalues of P^{-1} we rank them in ascending order (eigenvalues of I are all 1's) and calculate the ratio

$$g = \frac{\text{volume (of hyper-ellipsoid) of } P_n}{\text{volume (of hyper-ellipsoid) of } I_n} \quad n = \text{length of filter.}$$

We might conclude with the following practical example. For

$$G_s(a_3) = a_0 + a_1 s + a_2 s^2 + a_3 s^3$$

we obtain table 18.1. These numerical results show that, by using a cubic as a filter, a length of 21 gives the 'best' relative minimum variance.

TABLE 18.1

Volume (P)	Volume (I)	g	n
0.00139268	0.14098111	0.00987853	17
0.00033081	0.04662160	0.00709569	19
0.00007345	0.01394915	0.00526600	21
0.00015321	0.00381065	0.04020622	23
0.15449329	0.00095772	161.31322390	25

REFERENCES

Courant, R. and John, F. (1976) *Introduction to Calculus and Analysis*, vol. 2, John Wiley, New York.

Kendall, M. and Stuart, A. (1976) *The Advanced Theory of Statistics*, vol. 3, Charles Griffin, London.

19

A Comment on the Economics of Natural Resources

AUGUSTO SCHIANCHI*

I INTRODUCTION

Economic analysis of natural resources has been a major topic in the 1970s. The major conclusions are now fully developed in a compact exposition in several textbooks including that of Dasgupta and Heal (1979).

Nevertheless, despite their growing importance, some aspects of the theory have been receiving only limited attention. We are referring to *exploration activity* in particular, which is generally held to remain a key element in increasing the supply of resources.

In this regard, we can quote only a few exceptions, particularly those contributions by Arrow and Chang (1978) and Pindyck (1978). In this short paper we would like to try and construct a simplified framework that will contain a few basic issues of exploration activity.

II THE DETERMINISTIC CASE

Let us visualize the problem by considering, say, a monopolistic oil producing company. Let us assume that its rate of sales at time t, $S(t)$, depends on the known stock of already discovered reserves, $R(t)$, the price per barrel, $p(t)$, and on other exogenous variables (for instance, world demand conditions for oil), $W(t)$; i.e.,

$$S = S(p, R, W).$$

* I would like to thank the Cassa di Risparmio di Parma (Italy) for a financial contribution.

$c(S)$ is the rate of total extraction costs; therefore the total net profit, P, of extraction costs is

$$P(p, R, W) = pS(p, R, W) - c(S).$$

The level of presently available reserves of oil, $R(t)$, includes the effects of current and past investments in exploration activity. In fact, we can assume that $R(t)$ is 'measured' in exploration expenditure: that implies that the value of one unit of reserves is equal to one unit of exploration expenditure. The stock of known reserves increases because of exploration activity and shrinks over time because of extraction activity, which engenders correspondent sales. Let us assume that extraction proceeds at a constant proportional rate δ; therefore

$$\dot{R} = E - \delta R, \quad R(0) = R_0 \tag{1}$$

where $(\cdot)$ denotes conventional time derivative and $E = E(t)$, the current exploration effort (in financial terms).

Relation (1) simply says that level of reserves varies according to the difference between exploration and extraction activities. The net revenue of exploration expenditure is then

$$P(p, R, W) - E.$$

Let us assume that the oil-producing company wants to maximize the present value of net revenue flows discounted at a fixed interest rate, r; i.e.,

$$\max J = \int_0^\infty \exp(-rt) \{P(p, R, W) - E\} \, dt \quad (E \geqslant 0) \, (p \geqslant 0) \tag{2}$$

subject to (1). First, we can maximize J by maximizing P in respect to price p, holding R fixed, and then we can maximize the result in regards to E. Thus,

$$\frac{\partial P(p, R, W)}{\partial p} = S + p \frac{\partial S}{\partial p} - c' \frac{\partial S}{\partial p} = 0$$

where the prime sign denotes differentiation in respect to the argument. The foregoing condition implicitly gives the optimum price

$p^+(t) = p(R, W)$; and, defining $e^p = -(p/s)\,\partial S/\partial p$ as the elasticity of demand with respect to price, we get:

$$p^+ = e^p c'/(e^p - 1) \tag{3}$$

which is the conventional formula for the monopolist. The objective function (1) can be written as:

$$\max J = \int_0^\infty \exp(-rt)\,\{P(R, W \mid p^+) - E\}\,dt \quad (E \geqslant 0) \tag{4}$$

where (|) denotes 'given'.

We can form the current-value Hamiltonian

$$H = P(R, W \mid p^+) - E + i(E - \delta R) \tag{5}$$

with the adjoining variable i satisfying the differential equation

$$\dot{i} = ri - \frac{\partial H}{\partial R} = (r + \delta)\,i - \frac{\partial P(R, W \mid p^+)}{\partial R} \tag{6}$$

and the condition that

$$\lim_{t \to \infty} \exp(-rt)\,i(t) = 0.$$

The adjoining variable $i(t)$ is the shadow price associated with the stock of reserves at time t. Thus, the Hamiltonian can be read as the instantaneous profit rate which includes the value iR of the new reserves $\dot{R}$ which originated in the exploration activity E.

Expression (6) corresponds to the familiar equilibrium relation for investment in capital goods (cf. Arrow and Kurz, 1970). The marginal opportunity cost $i(r + \delta)$ of investment in exploration activity should be equal to the sum of the marginal profits from increased reserves and the capital gain $\dot{i}$.

Now, defining $e^R = (R/S)\,\partial S/\partial R$ as the elasticity of demand with respect to reserves, after some manipulation, we obtain

$$R^+ = \frac{e^R p S}{e^p \{(r + \delta)\,i - \dot{i}\}}. \tag{7}$$

At the optimum point, the ratio of reserves to sales revenue is directly proportional to reserves elasticity and inversely proportional to the elasticity of price and to the sum of the marginal opportunity cost $i(r + \delta)$ of investment and the rate at which the potential contribution of a unit of reserves to profits becomes its past contribution $(-i)$ (see Sethi, 1978). In order to obtain the optimum long-run stationary equilibrium $\bar{R}$ we must use $i = 0$ and the value for i such that $\partial H/\partial E = 0$; in our case it is equal to 1. We get

$$\bar{R} = \frac{e^R pS}{e^P(r + \delta)}. \tag{8}$$

If $R_0 < \bar{R}$, it is best to jump to $\bar{R}$ by applying an appropriate impulse at $t = 0$ and then $E^+(t) = \bar{E} = \delta\bar{R}$ for $t > 0$; if $R_0 > \bar{R}$, the optimum control is $E^+(t) = 0$ until the level of reserves shrinks to the level $\bar{R}$, at which time the control switches to $R^+(t) = \delta\bar{R}$ and stays at this level to sustain the level of reserves in stock at $\bar{R}$.

Note that, when demand is linear in logarithms,

$$S(p, R, W) = ap^{-e^P}R^{e^R}W^{e^W}$$

$-a$ being the parameter – and the total cost is linear, $c(S) = cS$; the optimum stationary solution implies a constant ratio of reserves to sales.

One unappealing aspect of the foregoing model is the fact that the solution is represented, in control theory terms, by a 'bang–bang' policy. To overcome this problem, we may try a nonlinear extension of the model.

We may utilize a suggestion by Gould (1970), by assuming that the cost of exploration activity is a nonlinear function of the exploration effort – more precisely, by assuming increasing marginal costs of exploration, which implies, very realistically, increasing costs in converting exploration efforts into actual oil reserves. In such a case optimum behaviour is not a 'bang–bang' solution. For $R_0 < \bar{R}$, the optimal policy is to invest in exploration activity most heavily in the initial periods and gradually to decrease to the level $\bar{E} = \delta\bar{R}$ as R approaches the equilibrium value $\bar{R}$.

III THE STOCHASTIC CASE

A second aspect of the model that is worth overcoming concerns its 'too deterministic' internal structure.

Suppose that both coefficients for the conversion of exploration effort into actual reserves and for the conversion of available reserves into sales are probabilistic ones. Let us consider a line taking the values $R = 0, 1, 2, \ldots, R^M$, and let us denote by $\pi(R, t)$ the probability of reserves being R units at time t. At time $t + \Delta t$, the probability of reserves R is given (following a birth–death process) – b being the parameter – by

$$\pi(R, t + \Delta t) = \pi(R + 1, t)\, \delta(R + 1)\, \Delta t + \pi(R, t)\{1 - \delta(R)\, \Delta t\}$$
$$\cdot \, [1 - b\{R, E(t), R^M\}\, \Delta t]$$
$$+ \pi(R - 1, t)\, b\{R - 1, E(t), R^M\}\, \Delta t$$

where $\delta(R)\, \Delta t$ is the probability that a unit of reserves is consumed and $b\{R, E(t), R^M\}\, \Delta t$ is the probability that a unit of reserves is discovered by an exploration expenditure $E(t)$ in the period Δt. In the limit, when Δt is small, we have the well-known Kolmogorov forward equations:

$$\dot{\pi}(R, t) = \delta(R + 1)\, \pi(R + 1, t) - [\delta(R) + b\{R, E(t), R^M\}]$$
$$\times \, \pi(R, t) + b\{R, E(t), R^M\}\, \pi(R - 1, t)$$

$$\dot{\pi}(0, t) = \delta(1)\, \pi(1, t) - b\{0, E(t), R^M\}\, \pi(0, t)$$

$$\dot{\pi}(R^M, t) = - [\delta(R^M) + b\{R^M, E(t), R^M\}]\, \pi(R^M, t)$$
$$+ b\{R^M - 1, E(t), R^M\}\, \pi(R^M - 1, t). \qquad (9)$$

A solution with the restriction

$$\sum_{R_0}^{R^M} \pi(R, t) = 1$$

for whatever t is considered will yield the probability of oil reserves being R units at time t as a function of $E(t)$, once the functional forms of δ and b are specified.

Supposing $\delta(R) = \delta R$ and $b(R, E, R^M) = E$ with R^M assumed infinite, we obtain the corresponding partial differential equation for the probability generating function $F(z, t)$:

$$\frac{\partial F}{\partial t} = (z - 1) \left(EF - \delta\, \frac{\partial F}{\partial z} \right), \qquad F(z, 0) = z^{R_0}.$$

Taking partial derivates, we obtain the mean-variance evolution for reserves as:

$$\dot{R} = E - \delta R, \qquad\qquad R(0) = R_0$$

$$\dot{V} = E - \delta R - 2\delta V, \qquad V(0) = 0 \qquad\qquad (10)$$

where $R = \epsilon(R)$, $V = \epsilon(R^2) - \epsilon =$ expectation operator. Thus, the model may be reformulated by assuming that the company's utility function depends on the mean and on the variance of the stock of reserves as follows:

$$\max J = \int_0^\infty \exp(-rt)\{P(R, V \mid p^+) - g(E)\}\, dt \quad (E \geqslant 0) \quad (11)$$

where $g(E)$ is Gould's production function for producing R. The optimum solution converges monotonically, sinusoidally, or does not converge at all to a stationary optimum equilibrium, depending on parameters of the problem and the initial conditions. However, it should be noted that the utility function depends on the mean and the variance rather than on expected utility function; the foregoing problem, which is stochastic in origin, collapses in a deterministic control problem, with a relevant loss of interest.

One alternative (Arnold, 1974) may be the introduction of a diffusion approximation of the Kolmogorov equations by replacing $\pi(R + 1, t)$ and $\pi(R - 1, t)$ by the first three terms of their Taylor series expansions about $\pi(R, t)$. The resultant equation is:

$$dR = (E - \delta R)\, dt + s(E, R)\, d\xi \qquad\qquad (12)$$

where $d\xi(t)$ is a standard Wiener process and s is the standard deviation.

The stochastic optimum control problem becomes:

$$\max J = \epsilon \int_0^\infty \exp(-rt)\{P(R \mid p^+) - g(E)\}\, dt \quad (E \geqslant 0) \quad (13)$$

subject to (12). An immediate solution to this problem may be that of stochastic dynamic programming, but since the resulting Hamilton–Jacobi–Bellman equation is nonlinear, the solution may become very difficult to reach.

An alternative solution based on the stochastic maximum principle (Bismuth, 1975) looks more promising. The current-value Hamiltonian becomes:

$$H = P(R \mid p^+) - g(E) + i(E - \delta R) + vs(E, R) \tag{14}$$

with i satisfying the stochastic differential equation

$$di = (ri - \partial H/\partial R)\, dt + vd\xi + dI$$

$$= \{(r + \delta)\, i - \partial P/\partial R - v\, \partial s/\partial R\}\, dt + vd\xi + dI \tag{15}$$

where $i(t)$ is the current-value shadow price of reserves at time t and $v(t)$ represents the instantaneous uncertain consequences of exploration activity. Thus $-v(t)$ is the unknown current-value cost of risk-taking at time t.

The Hamiltonian can be read as the profit rate which includes the expected increment in reserves evaluated at its marginal expected value less the risk associated with this expenditure in exploration activity evaluated at the cost of taking risks.

Equation (15) means (cf. Bismuth, 1975) that, in current-value terms, the conditional expected rate of consumption (owing to sales) of one marginal unit of reserves $(ri - i)$ is equal to the sum of its contribution to the instantaneous profits $(\partial P/\partial R)$ plus its contribution to increasing the expected rate of the increment in reserves $(i \cdot \partial (E - \delta R)/\partial R = -di)$, minus its contribution to increasing the conditional standard deviation of the increment in reserves evaluated at the cost of risk $(-v\, \partial s/\partial R)$.

To sum up: knowing the instantaneous attitude toward risk (v), which is positive if the firm is 'risk-taking' and negative if the firm is 'risk-averting', the company is able to weight present assured profits and future uncertain profits, and to compute the expected rate at which reserves will be consumed. As for the remaining terms in the expression, $v\, d\xi$ is a correction term in the evolution of i, and reflects the difference between δR and $\epsilon(\delta R)$; the term I integrates the necessary information not contained in the past value of ξ, for instance because of the introduction of new fuel technology in the market. When this happens, the company has to re-evaluate its prediction in order to take this new information into account. This information may either increase the marginal value of reserves or lower it. The necessary condition for an interior optimum is given by:

$$\partial H/\partial E = - \partial g/\partial E + i + v\, \partial s/\partial E = 0 \tag{16}$$

which implies

$$g'(E) = i + v/2s.$$

That is, an optimum exploration policy implies that the marginal cost of exploration activity equals the marginal profit (from exploration activity) plus a marginal return owing to uncertainty. Since $s(E, R) > 0$, risk aversion ($v < 0$) means that the marginal cost of exploration will have to be set on a lower level, on account of the assumptions on $g(E)$, which implies a lower level of exploration. For the risk-taker, the opposite will hold true.

IV CONCLUDING REMARKS

In this paper we have tried to solve a basic problem in the economic analysis of exploiting natural resources: the optimum policy for exploration activity. We have analysed the issue both in the deterministic case and in the stochastic one. We have reached a solution by applying engineering control theory techniques. We have assumed a profit-maximizing company that sells 'oil'; moreover, we have supposed that it owns a certain amount of reserves, which shrink because of sales, but which may be increased by exploration activity.

In the deterministic case, i.e. where exploration continues successfully, conventional marginal results are confirmed. In the stochastic case, i.e. where sales are stochastic and exploration does not necessarily lead to new reserves, deterministic results must be adjusted in order to incorporate an uncertainty parameter; moreover, different 'risk attitudes' of the firm may lead to an alternative optimum exploration policy.

REFERENCES

Arnold, L. (1974) *Stochastic Differential Equations: Theory and Applications*, John Wiley, New York.

Arrow, J. K. and Chang, S. (1978) *Optimal Pricing, Use and Exploration of Uncertain Natural Resource Stocks*, Technical Report no. 31, Harvard University Press, Cambridge, Mass.

Arrow, J. K. and Kurz, M. (1970) *Public Investment, the Rate of Return and Optimal Fiscal Policy*, Johns Hopkins Press, Baltimore.

Bismuth, J. M. (1975) 'Growth and Optimal Intertemporal Allocation of Risks', *Journal of Economic Theory*, pp. 239-57.

Dasgupta, P. S. and Heal, G. M. (1979) *Economic Theory and Exhaustible Resources*, Cambridge University Press/James Nisbet, Welwyn Garden City.

Gould, J. P. (1970) 'Diffusion Processes and Optimal Advertising Policy', in *Microeconomic Foundation of Employment and Inflation Theory*, ed. E. S. Phelps *et al.*, W. W. Norton, New York, pp. 338-68.

Pindyck, R. S. (1978) 'Optimal Exploration and Production of a Nonrenewable Resource', *Journal of Political Economy*, pp. 841-62.

Sethi, S. P. (1978) 'A Survey of Management Science Applications of the Deterministic Maximum Principle', in *Applied Optimal Control*, ed. A. Bensoussan, P. A. Kleidorfer and C. S. Tapiero, North-Holland, Amsterdam, vol. 9, pp. 33ff.

Index of Names

Index of Subjects